D0408615

A SHEARWATER BOOK

Kinship to Mastery

Now that there is a perspective of time . . . something else is emerging from the pages which equally arrests my attention. It is the meditative perception of the relation of "Nature" (and I include the whole cosmic picture in this term) to the human spirit. . . . Nature is a part of our humanity, and without some awareness and experience of that divine mystery man ceases to be man. When the Pleiades and the wind in the grass are no longer a part of the human spirit, a part of very flesh and bone, man becomes, as it were, a kind of cosmic outlaw, having neither the completeness and integrity of the animal nor the birthright of a true humanity.

HENRY BESTON

The Outermost House:
A Year of Life on the Great Beach of Cape Cod

Kinship to Mastery

Biophilia in Human Evolution and Development

Stephen R. Kellert

ISLAND PRESS / Shearwater Books
Washington, D.C. • Covelo, California

A Shearwater Book
published by Island Press

The author is grateful for permission to reprint the following previously copyrighted work:

"I Heard a Fly Buzz—When I Died" is reprinted by permission of the publishers and the Trustees of Amherst College from *The Poems of Emily Dickinson,* Thomas H. Johnson, ed., Cambridge, Mass.: The Belknap Press of Harvard University Press, Copyright © 1951, 1955, 1979, 1983 by the President and Fellows of Harvard College.

"Anecdote of the Jar" is reprinted from *Collected Poems* by Wallace Stevens. Copyright © 1923 and renewed 1951 by Wallace Stevens. Reprinted by permission of Alfred A. Knopf, Inc.

LIBRARY OF CONGRESS CATALOGING-IN-PUBLICATION DATA

Kellert, Stephen R.
Kinship to mastery : biophilia in human evolution and development / Stephen R. Kellert.
p. cm.
Includes bibliographical references and index.
ISBN 1-55963-372-7 (cloth)
1. Environmental degradation. 2. Human evolution. 3. Human ecology. 4. Biological diversity conservation. I. Title.
GE140.K47 1997
304.2′8—dc21 96-29893
CIP

Printed on recycled, acid-free paper

Manufactured in the United States of America

10 9 8 7 6 5 4 3 2 1

To the memory of Paul Shepard
for his many insights into
the bonds between humans
and the natural world

Contents

Acknowledgments *xi*

Prologue *xiii*

CHAPTER ONE: The Notion of Biophilia *1*

CHAPTER TWO: The Material Basis *11*

CHAPTER THREE: The Aesthetic Appeal *33*

CHAPTER FOUR: The Measure of Empirical Knowledge *51*

CHAPTER FIVE: Nature As Metaphor *69*

CHAPTER SIX: The Quest for Exploration and Discovery *85*

CHAPTER SEVEN: Yearning for Kinship and Affection *105*

CHAPTER EIGHT: The Urge to Master *121*

CHAPTER NINE: Seeking Meaning and Transcendence *133*

CHAPTER TEN: Of Fear and Loathing *147*

CHAPTER ELEVEN: Diminishing Nature, Self, and Society *163*

CHAPTER TWELVE: The Pursuit of Self-Interest *191*

Notes *219*

Index *249*

Acknowledgments

I wish to express my considerable thanks to Barbara Dean, editor extraordinaire, whose labors on behalf of this book have been both prodigious and extremely helpful. I also appreciate the helpful comments of my agent Katinka Matson and the encouragement of her colleague and husband, John Brockman, who initially urged me to tackle this project and made it possible. I am deeply indebted to many inspiring and helpful students over the years, of late Tori Derr who assisted me with aspects of the manuscript. I wish to thank Don Yoder for his exceptional good judgment and understanding of the written word. I am especially grateful for the saintly patience, good advice, and unwavering support of my wife, Cilla. Finally, I want to thank my daughter Emily for her helpful and insightful comments, and my daughter Libby for her interest and good cheer.

Prologue

A flicker of movement catches the corner of my eye as I tap electronic letters onto the computer screen. I sit before the desk, facing the large window looking east, on the third floor of the tall house. It always feels a little like being in a tree house, perched high among the tall oaks that march in a line from my neighbor's house on the left through mine to the neighbor's on the right. The first tree lords over the others—four hundred years old, twenty feet around, branches resembling entire trees. The pistils hang like tassels in the brisk morning air, leaves barely emergent—in May I am still able to see between the tangle of branches stretching out to the horizon. In the distance looms the large vertical traprock. Along its base the meandering river winds a path to the nearby ocean.

I struggle to keep my mind on the shimmering light of the monitor's artificial glow. Deadlines and commitments draw me into the screen's vicarious reality. A second flicker passes through the branches, distracting me again. Glints of animation on the move, dancing within and between the flowering tassels. I cannot resist the temptation to look. Rushing for my binoculars, I remember the time of year. Warblers on the move. Reproductive fever urging these tiny birds northward in great waves, irresistibly seeking their ancestral breeding grounds.

Returning to the desk, I scan the canopy, frustrated now by the absence of movement. Then, remembering their diminutive size, far smaller than the symbol of spring they occupy in the niche of my mind's eye, I slow down.

Again I am caught by a flicker. Ballet dancers skipping along nascent leaves and branches of the treetops. Closing in, I find and then capture my visual prey. A chestnut-sided warbler! Then another. Then a third. A magnolia warbler and a blackburnian! Restless spirits of arresting color and exuberant life on the move. Absent yesterday, they take possession of the oaks today as if the forest could hardly exist without them.

I stare at the colors and glorious patterns. A motif of rich sienna arches along the white body of the chestnut-sided, a bright yellow caps the head. The blackburnian blazes in brilliant orange, edged by an emphasizing black; the magnolia is in bright yellow, black striping, calling for attention.

But these warblers signal much more than beauty to me. The motion, the eruption of energy, the ghostly specter—all suggest the restless and expansive character of spring, the time of fresh creation. I welcome, too, their practical role in the cycling of nutrients, their complicated contribution to the continuity of associated plants, their place in a stream of ecological functions and processes on which all life, including my own, ultimately depends. From a more immediate perspective, I am reassured by their role in protecting valuable trees of the northern forest, sources of timber and paper, from excessive insect damage and disease.

These migrating wonders allow me to be young again. Seeking them out indulges my passion for discovery, stimulates my curiosity, feeds my hunger for adventure. Today I pursue the feathered storm from the window, but tomorrow I will be in the forest and along the river. Their quick beauty represents a powerful aspect of their appeal, but they also engender an inquisitive impulse and competitive urge to find, locate, and identify the birds.

I thrill at their reappearance, but an underlying lament lingers over the possibility of a future lacking this spirited reminder of the returning spring. Great gaps of cleared and converted forest already have fragmented vast swaths of their wintering, migratory, and nesting grounds. Annual counts suggest population declines of various species.[1] Ecological adages from the past echo inside my head: adages from Rachel Carson's *Silent Spring* and Aldo Leopold's "Thinking Like a Mountain."[2] A world lacking warblers would seem mute and barren without their richness of sound, color, vivacity, the promise of another spring of hope and rebirth. Their exuberant passage reaffirms connections with the wonder of tenuous life. With their diminution the world of organized and purposeful matter would contract; without them the edge of a more universal deadness and dissolution would advance.

The red cliff, the winding river, the spreading floodplain, lacking warblers and other life, would offer little more than a stony silence. For the warblers transform the dynamic of rock, soil, and water into a flowing fountain of energy and matter. Through them I sense a living essence in the forest, mountain, and river. Through them I recognize a vibrant core transforming the heap of inanimate stuff into an ecological superorganism, not exactly alive, but nonetheless animate and organized.

The warblers represent one thread among the many cords of relationship binding the human experience to the great tapestry of life and nonlife. Standing at the pinnacle of existence, we recognize that the apex of a pyramid is only as strong as its base. A modern ecological understanding underlies the ancient wisdom of a nursery rhyme:

> Surely, wisdom is given
> To all living things,
> And the tiniest of creatures
> Are the teachers of kings.[3]

As I shut the computer down for the day, my eye catches another flicker of movement. A black and white warbler, not so colorful as the others, but nonetheless striking contrasts powerfully seductive. I am drawn in. Along with the bird my eye skips from tassel to branch to flower. Among the branches, carried along by the wind, my eye takes wing. My backyard becomes a place of enchantment. My bounded universe becomes a microcosm of the world. Along with the warbler's spirit, my mind soars in the treetops. Like the warbler I bathe in the warmth of the early spring. Blazing a trail to the north woods, dissipating remnants from the winter's weariness, reigniting hope for yet another year, the warblers lift and inspirit me.

Chapter One

The Notion of Biophilia

Buried within the human species lies a deep and enduring urge to connect with living diversity. Nature offers an essential medium for our development, both individual and collective, a link that is as vital today as it was in the past. We evolved in the company of other creatures and in a matrix of conditions making this varied existence possible. And we continue to rely—physically, emotionally, intellectually—on the quality and richness of our affiliations with natural diversity. Our identity remains rooted in our connections with the natural world. This human need to affiliate with nature, and its influence on our physical and psychological development, are the focus of this book.

The Harvard biologist Edward O. Wilson coined the term "biophilia" to describe this inherent human affinity for life and lifelike process, and his concept will be central to our exploration.[1] Wilson suggests that as humans evolved with the rest of creation, they developed a biologically based attraction for nature and life. As Wilson reflects, the human mind generated many of its assumptions of normality from its myriad associations with natural diversity:

> The brain is prone to weave the mind from the evidences of life, not merely the minimal contact required to exist, but a luxuriance and excess spilling into virtually everything we do. People can grow up with the outward appearance of normality in an environment largely stripped of plants and animals. . . . Yet something vitally important would be missing, not merely the knowledge and pleasure that can be imagined and might have been, but a wide array of experiences that the human brain is peculiarly equipped to receive.[2]

Some years before, the psychologist Erich Fromm had independently invoked the term "biophilia." Fromm defined biophilia as a "passionate love of life and of all that is alive; it is the wish to further growth, whether in a person, a plant, an idea, or a social group."[3] He used the term to underscore the need for cultivating the capacity for love as a basis for our mental health and emotional well-being.

Although Fromm's notion of biophilia relates to the concept advanced in this book, it also differs in important respects. Fromm emphasized a "passionate love of life," whereas the stress here is on a broad affinity for natural diversity. This distinction may seem minor, but it is in fact critical. The notion of biophilia advanced here emphasizes our physical, emotional, and intellectual inclinations for nature and life. A "passionate love of life" represents a critical aspect of this inclination, but it is just one among many emotional and intellectual expressions of this tendency. People connect with nature in other ways as well: through curiosity, kinship, dominance, exploitation, fear, and other affinities described in the pages to come. These diverse inclinations range from "passionate" to more moderate and limited expressions. Although Fromm describes biophilia as a love of life, "whether in a person [or] a plant,"[4] his work focuses almost exclusively on human interactions. The emphasis of this book is on people's need to connect with the whole realm of living diversity.

Wilson introduced the biophilia notion in a 1984 book focusing on his intellectual development and a general human propensity for bonding with other forms of life. In 1993, Wilson and I edited another book, *The Biophilia Hypothesis,* whose various authors engaged in a scholarly examination of the concept from many angles. That volume explored the evidence for and against biophilia, how this tendency developed over the course of evolution, and why its continuing realization remains essential even in modern times. The current book continues the exploration of the human need for connecting with nature and living diversity. We will examine various expressions of the human affinity for life, as well as the habitats, landscapes, and ecosystems that, while not technically alive, make life possible and thus are often imbued with life-like qualities.

Biophilia reflects the human tendency to impute worth and importance to the natural world.[5] This tendency is no trivial matter. Indeed, the satisfactory realization of diverse expressions of biophilia is an essential condition for the effective unfolding of our individual and collective humanity. Over the millennia, humanity's affiliation with life and natural process conferred distinctive advantages in the human struggle to persist, adapt, and thrive as a species. During the long course of human evolution, we valued nature and living diversity because of the adaptive benefits it offered us physically, emotionally, and intellectually. And people continue to need rich and textured relationships with natural diversity in order to achieve lives replete with meaning and value. My argument, therefore, is essentially simple: our inclination for affiliating with life functions today as it has in the past as a basis for healthy human maturation and development.

The chapters that follow examine many different expressions of biophilia. They describe the natural world as a source of material utilization and exploitation, physical beauty and appeal, empirical knowledge and understanding, communication and thought, exploration and discovery, bonding and companionship, mastery and control, moral and spiritual connection, and fear and repression. We will explore the physical, emotional, and intellectual benefits people derive from these diverse expressions of the need to affiliate with nature and life. We will examine, too, how human personality and society depend on the effective realization of these affinities—and the consequent risks associated with the widespread biological depletion and environmental degradation occurring today.

We need to qualify, however, the notion of an inherent inclination to affiliate with nature and life. The various expressions of biophilia hardly constitute "hard-wired" instincts like breathing or eating. In fact, the human affinity for nature represents a collection of relatively *weak* biological tendencies. All the various strains of biophilia depend on adequate learning and experience—on a sufficient diet, that is, of individual opportunity and social support. Without repeated experience, the various strands of biophilia lie dormant and frustrated. Thus the different aspects of biophilia are best viewed as products of "biocultural" evolution—inborn tendencies shaped by the mediating influence of learning, culture, and experience.[6]

This emphasis on socialization and social support suggests that thwarting the human opportunity for meaningful connection with natural diversity inevitably impedes the realization of the different expressions of biophilia. Such an impoverished experience contributes to a compromised material and mental existence. But various forces in modern life have indeed impoverished the human experience of nature and life—most significantly through unprecedented levels of biological destruction and environmental contamination.[7]

This tide of blight and devastation must be reversed if only for selfish reasons. The notion of biophilia emphasizes that healthy and diverse natural systems represent less a luxury than the potential for helping us realize lives of satisfaction and meaning. Celebrating our connections with nature inevitably renders our existence richer and more rewarding. Natural splendor is still the crucible in which our physical and mental well-being is forged.

We must recognize that biophilia represents neither a simple nor a singular tendency. A biologically based inclination for affiliating with nature embraces a complex of feelings, thoughts, and behavior—a range of human values and expressions, each reflecting a particular patterning of beliefs and dispositions to act toward the natural world. These tendencies express themselves in many ways, sometimes obvious, sometimes subtle, occasionally direct, but often indirect, insinuating themselves into our lives like an intricate tapestry of implicit and explicit understanding and experience.

Our wide-ranging expressions of biophilia are reflected in a mosaic of perceptions, attitudes, and behavior toward different species and landscapes. Reactions to spiders and snakes, for example, sometimes reveal an intuitive recognition of the potential danger of these predators. Sometimes we realize our existence depends on a panoply of connections with other life forms—often barely apparent organisms. Occasionally we appreciate the involuntary character of many of our responses to nature—the instant appeal of young creatures with round faces and large eyes, the immediate allure of brightly colored flowers and birds, the irresistible charm of open landscapes traversed by ponds and streams. These and a myriad of other encounters with the natural world reflect our fundamental affinities for nature and life. These obvious, occasionally subtle, and sometimes barely apparent human responses and interactions reflect our diverse material, emotional, and psychological ties to the natural world.

This book explores aspects of the extraordinary variability and intricacy of the human response to natural diversity. Most people encounter only a small fraction of the estimated 10 million species on earth. Yet we have evolved and developed, whether we recognize it or not, in the company of thousands of distinctive life forms and associated landscapes and natural features. Moreover, any species can function as a "magic well" of human emotional and intellectual experience: the more we confront its mysteries, the more we encounter an endless frontier of exploration and discovery.[8] All these encounters with natural diversity pass through the interpretive filter of our inclination to attach meaning and value to the world.

The diverse expressions of biophilia serve a multiplicity of human needs. The tendency to affiliate with natural diversity emerged because of its importance in human development. This significance encompasses more than material benefit. The human struggle for sustenance and security embraces a wide range of physical, emotional, intellectual, and spiritual dimensions. Our affinity for nature certainly facilitates material progress—we reap rewards of food, clothing, medicine, and various ecological services from various aspects of natural diversity. Yet our inclination to connect with nature also addresses other needs: intellectual capacity, emotional bonding, aesthetic attraction, creativity and imagination, even the recognition of a just and purposeful existence. Each of these engagements with natural diversity enhances our potential for attaining lives of satisfaction and security.

The key point here at the outset is that our species evolved these values of nature because they enhanced our capacity to survive and prosper physically, emotionally, and intellectually. Yet, as noted, these relatively weak dispositions tend to wither without learning, experience, and social support. The influence of society has a great effect on the content, intensity, and direction of these tendencies to affiliate with nature. The emergence of our varying expressions of biophilia reflects on how we are creatures of our biological heritage, yet capable of exercising choice and free will in seeking adequate opportunities for nurturing our basic inclinations to affiliate with the natural world. The various forms of biophilia may be rooted in our biology, but once they take shape as a consequence of individual experience and cultural influence, they take on a life of their own and are not simply reducible to our inborn tendencies.

The most significant time in the learning and development of these tendencies is, not surprisingly, childhood and adolescence. Children engage nature in a multiplicity of subtle and complex ways—building sand castles and looking for shells along beaches, constructing miniature worlds within bushes and brambles, erecting real and fantastic structures along streams and banks. These and countless other enchantments reflect the many ways children organize and develop their feelings, thoughts, and beliefs about the natural world. Yet the variety and complexity of the human experience render any age relevant in the unfolding of our many connections with the natural world. Although childhood represents the most critical developmental period, we remain open to the nurturing attraction of nature throughout life.

A recurrent theme in this book is how often we focus our experience of nature on other life forms, particularly creatures that remind us of ourselves. Certain aspects of nature can elicit powerful emotional and intellectual responses. Yet it is the diversity of life that constitutes the most salient and provocative element of nature. Bears, wolves, elephants, whales, dolphins—these and many other creatures strike us as possessing an analogous experience. We seem incapable of resisting the attraction to other forms of life: often we are drawn to these creatures like moths to light. Young children especially revel in their affinity for life at a time when nature seems synonymous with the shape and form of species that appear to resemble us.

As our inquiry develops, it will become clear that the healthy and satisfying experience of natural diversity is not incompatible with modern life. Meaningful encounters with natural diversity are not restricted to pristine and bucolic settings where nature remains, presumably, less contaminated by contact with industrial existence. Yellowstone National Park holds a world of splendor, but many urban and suburban areas contain a wealth of healthy and diverse natural complexity. Abundant and accessible nature represents an essential condition for the full realization of our humanity. But the quality and intimacy of these connections can occur in nearly any location. A depleted and impoverished natural environment may be more common in urban areas, but most cities still offer countless opportunities for meaningfully experiencing natural diversity.

A degraded environment can never erase the human desire for affiliating with nature and life. But it can diminish our appreciation of the role of natural diversity in healthy human development. Without adequate learning and experience, the various impulses to connect with nature can become frustrated and atrophy. Individuals and societies can thwart the human capacity for engaging natural diversity with meaning and satisfaction. Disconnection from nature often characterizes modern life. Contemporary society frequently fails to recognize the significance of maintaining rich and healthy ties with natural diversity. The illusion emerges that humans can live apart from nature, somehow transcending the need for experiencing natural diversity with access, intimacy, and care. Thus a vicious cycle develops: denying the importance of natural process and connection encourages apathy and destructive excess, further estranging people from their fundamental physical and mental dependence on a healthy living environment.

The following chapters explore how the quality of human existence continues to rely on the richness of its connections with natural diversity. Each aspect of biophilia—and we will examine many—underscores how we remain physically, materially, intellectually, emotionally, and spiritually dependent on the quality of our relationships with the natural world. We will consider how nature persists in meeting our various material needs. We will investigate how natural diversity enhances our emotional capacity for kinship, affection, awe, nurturance, and beauty. We will examine how nature engenders physical and intellectual development and promotes a capacity for problem solving, creativity, discovery, and control. We will consider the social and biological conditions necessary for the healthy realization of the varying aspects of biophilia. We will examine various trends in modern society that have compromised nature's ability to sustain our personal and social well-being. And, finally, we will consider ways to restore the biological, social, and ethical foundations for connecting with natural diversity.

If this book proves successful, it will be as meaningful for the lay person as it is for the scientist and professional resource manager. Considerable evidence will be marshalled from various studies to make the case for biophilia and its role in human maturation and well-being. But this book does not brim with data, tables, and hypothetical qualifications (although the notes at the end offer many references for those who wish to pursue the scientific study of this subject). Not only has the book been written in a largely nonscientific manner, but fictional vignettes appear at various points to illustrate the role of natural diversity in human development. These vignettes will bring the complexities of the human/nature connection to life, I hope, in a vivid and compelling fashion.

It should be apparent by now that this is not a work of detachment and neutrality. A healthy and diverse natural environment is viewed as an essential condition for human lives of satisfaction and fulfillment. The current wave of biological destruction is regarded as a fundamental threat to our material, emotional, intellectual, and spiritual well-being. If our journey proves successful, the reader will become convinced that preserving natural diversity represents less an act of kindness or compassion than a profound expression of self-interest. Our nourishing experience of nature is, ultimately, a celebration of our humanity.

Chapter Two

The Material Basis

Most of us have little difficulty recognizing how the natural world has long served humanity as an indispensable means for rendering life more physically and materially secure and how this function may have played a critical role in human evolution and development. Today the diversity of life still serves as the source for a remarkable number of practical and tangible benefits. Moreover, we continue to cultivate our intellectual development through encounters with utilizing wild nature.

In some respects, this aspect of biophilia is both the easiest to comprehend and the most difficult to recognize as still exercising a critical relevance in modern society. Most of us appreciate how our ancient ancestors and a small number of "backward" peoples today depend on wild nature to satisfy most of their needs for food, medicine, clothing, and other products. From one point of view, a distinguishing characteristic of modern society is having been "freed" from this ancient dependence on wild nature. We may recognize nature's bounty in the cotton in our shirt, the wool in our sweater, the silk in our tie, the hide in our shoes, the flesh in our meat, perhaps even in the mold in our penicillin. But most of us view the controlled production of these resources as among the great achievements of modern civilization. We often view contemporary life as having "transcended" nature by converting the formerly wild into the creation of human invention, manipulation, and large-scale production.

This perspective regards an extensive reliance on products from the wild as the characteristic of "primitive" peoples and "backward" societies. Among the countries that exploit natural diversity for much of their food and medicine are Bangladesh, Ghana, Liberia, Congo, the Philippines, Zaire—the poorest of the poor.[1] "Undeveloped" nations remain subject to the vagaries of nature. By contrast, modern nations seemingly rise above wild nature and achieve independence from it.

Before considering the validity of this assumption, suppose we explore its cultural roots. In many respects, this point of view derives from a long tradition in Western society regarding the character of progress and civilization.[2] Greco-Roman and Judeo-Christian beliefs often connected economic and social advancement with the notion of people's independence from wild nature. These views encouraged the assumption that humans are both unalterably different from—and fundamentally superior to—the rest of creation. Only humanity has the potential to transcend the limits of the physical world, both materially and spiritually.

The cultural historian Lynn White, in his classic essay "The Historic Roots of Our Ecologic Crisis," discusses the particularly Western assumption that people alone enjoy the capacities for reason, morality, and, most of all, the possibility for release from natural and physical constraints.[3] According to this view, a fundamental duality distinguishes humans from nature. People alone rise above their material roots, achieving spiritual salvation by pursuing a "good and righteous" life. Only humans are conceived in the image of a single and all-powerful God. Only humans possess ethical standing and intrinsic value.

Wild nature, by contrast, consists of mere raw material lacking consciousness, the capacity for self-improvement, or moral worth. Nature can thus be exploited and transformed by people without consideration of its possible feelings or rights. Lacking selfhood and sentience, nature is used in "a mood of indifference. . . . A tree consists of no more than a physical fact."[4] Since nature exists mainly to serve humanity, its subjugation can be pursued without guilt or inhibition. As the English historian Keith Thomas has suggested, this perspective reflects "a breathtakingly anthropocentric view. . . . Man's authority over the world is virtually unlimited. Animals [and nature] have no rights."[5]

According to this view, the only constraints on human behavior toward nature stem from the limits of our technology and the ethical obligation to respect how our exploitation may affect other people. Science and technical innovation flourished in this intellectual and cultural climate. Armed with moral right, material incentive, and spiritual motivation, Western society sought mastery over nature and the capacity to free itself from natural and physical limitations. As Thomas comments: "Civilization and science [became] synonymous with the conquest of nature."[6] Progress emerged as the measure of one's distance from—and control over—the natural world. In time, the superiority of Western values seemed apparent in its material affluence, scientific knowledge, and technological control.

The virtues of domesticating nature and transforming natural landscapes were presumably proved by our victories over hunger, disease, and scarcity. Western civilization prided itself on food surpluses and material affluence achieved through the mass production of cultivated crops and the elimination of wild competitors. Modern medicine achieved its ends by controlling and eradicating other organisms; industrial production and urbanization by subduing and transforming natural habitats; contemporary agriculture and forestry by creating enormous monocultures through homogenizing and simplifying natural landscapes. These "triumphs" of modern life required conquering wild nature and confirmed a view of progress and civilization as synonymous with controlling and transforming natural diversity.

Despite the many successes of modern science and technology, the belief in our having achieved material independence from wild nature is nothing more than an illusion. People have always relied on the natural world for physical sustenance and security. And our practical need for wild nature may be as great today as ever. Despite the material gains of modern technology and urbanization, current human population numbers and advances in scientific knowledge have created a considerable dependence on wild living diversity to maintain our current—and especially future—standard of living. Moreover, our intellectual development still depends on the stimulating experience of some degree of personal exploitation of nature, no matter how peripheral this utilization may be. This chapter describes our continuing material dependence on wild living diversity by highlighting three aspects of this reliance: utilizing wild resources for various products; using wild species to improve domestic production and future product development; and materially benefiting from healthy ecological functions and services.

Utilizing Wild Resources

The direct use of nature and wildlife can be linked to food production, medicine, clothing, building materials, decorative products, and a variety of other uses.[7] Many countries today rely to a considerable degree on wild nature for much of their sustenance. The Philippines, Zaire, Ghana, and Bangladesh, for example, derive a large proportion of their protein from nature. Many rapidly developing nations such as Indonesia, South Korea, and Thailand also secure a major share of their food from the natural world. Even in such highly industrialized countries as Japan and Russia, a surprisingly substantial fraction of the caloric intake originates in the wild, particularly fish from the sea. Fishing represents the last great harvest of wild free-roaming animals. According to the World Conservation Monitoring Centre: "global fish production exceeds that of cattle, sheep, poultry or eggs, and is the largest source of either wild or domestic animal protein for the world's expanding human populations."[8] An estimated 95 million tons of seafood worth approximately $82 billion is harvested worldwide each year—5.5 million tons or $2.5 billion worth in the United States alone.[9] Wood and paper obtained from natural forests represent another critical harvest from the wild. The worldwide value of pulp and timber products is currently estimated at $84 billion annually—$8 billion in the United

States.[10] Moreover, a large proportion of this trade originates in such modern nations as the United States, Canada, Finland, and Russia.

Societies differ substantially in their reliance on natural diversity. Many Asian nations, for example, retain a strong cultural affinity for consuming wild foods and using various species for decorative and medicinal purposes.[11] Most Western countries, by contrast, obtain a larger proportion of their food and medicines from domesticated or mass-produced organisms. Japan continues to harvest many wild creatures, particularly from the marine environment, often at considerable variance with the traditions of Western nations. These differences in cultural bias are often at the root of controversies regarding the exploitation of whales, crocodiles, sea turtles, bluefin tuna, and other marine species.[12] Continuing interest among many Asian nations in utilizing various species for medical and decorative purposes has also resulted in major conflicts over harvesting elephants, musk deer, rhinoceroses, tigers, bears, and other creatures.

Wild terrestrial species continue to play an important role in human food production—not only many kinds of mammals, birds, and reptiles, but even a considerable number of invertebrates. Indeed, many cultures consume various species of beetles, termites, ants, and other insects. Honey from bees probably represents the most significant food obtained from an invertebrate.[13] At least 800,000 tons of honey is annually produced today, most extensively in Russia, China, the United States, Mexico, and India. "Shellfish"—clams, mussels, shrimp, oysters, lobsters, and others—represent another widely consumed group of invertebrate animals.[14] In the United States, the total dollar catch of finfish only slightly exceeds that of shellfish. Many kinds of plants are also harvested extensively from the wild, including various kinds of berries, mushrooms, maple syrup, nuts, and seaweed. The entomologist David Pimentel of Cornell University and his colleagues estimate that the total worldwide economic value of wild foods is $180 billion annually.[15]

Many people continue to covet the opportunity for harvesting food from the wild even when such exploitation is no longer necessary. The majority of American hunters, for example, indicate that obtaining the meat represents their primary reason for participating in the activity. (This harvest yields some 150,000 tons of game meat annually worth an estimated half-billion dollars.)[16] Although few hunters depend on this activity for sustenance or survival, many continue to be motivated by cherished traditions of independence and self-reliance, as well as an important dietary supplement. Similar motivations apply to recreational fishing, wild berry collecting, mushroom hunting, and other plant and animal harvesting. The economic importance of these recreational pursuits is substantial: American anglers and hunters spend some $41 billion annually.[17]

The enthusiastic pursuit of such activities, often in the absence of necessity, reflects our species' long evolutionary history of material dependence on nature. We remain biologically inclined to respond to the living world with an abiding interest in discovering and exploiting its practical utility. Collective statistics obscure how often we respond to wild species and landscapes with an eye toward deriving some material benefit from them. When we select a piece of land for purchase, choose a place to camp, take a walk in the woods, or engage in many other outdoor activities, we frequently scan and assess these areas with an interest in discovering their utility. Given the opportunity to exploit nature directly—whether picking berries, gathering mushrooms, harvesting firewood, digging clams, fishing, or hunting—we often acquire these skills quickly and with great satisfaction, even when we lack prior experience and training.

We continue to participate in exploiting nature, even when its practical value is limited, because these pursuits reflect a passion for extracting at least a portion of our sustenance from the land and its creatures. Beyond the obvious material gains, we harvest physical, emotional, and intellectual benefits, including a deep connection with vast natural processes. Consuming a life from the wild reminds us of our continuing reliance on other forms of life and our role in the cycle of energy and nutrients through the biosphere. This utilitarian experience also enhances our physical fitness and sense of self-reliance. Despite the technological marvels and complexity of the modern world, we affirm our capacities to persevere with skill and craft. We hone our competence and build self-confidence along with the material rewards. No matter how removed we become from wild nature, we demonstrate our cunning and dexterity.

Such satisfactions are illustrated in the following two vignettes. The two stories take us beyond the abstract exercise of cataloging diverse utilitarian benefits to a world in which people derive profound personal rewards from experiencing nature's enduring practical significance.

With a doctorate in mathematics and engineering from Cal Tech, Tom worked for a moderate-sized computer company. He lived with his wife and two daughters in a Silicon Valley suburb. An accomplished tennis player and hiker, he had fished only twice in his life before being invited by three of his colleagues to participate in a canoe trip in a Canadian wilderness area. Although Tom gladly accepted, he was anxious about his lack of experience and worried a little that he might embarrass himself.

After fourteen hours of flying and driving, they finally arrived at their destination, the Quetico–Superior National Park in southern Ontario. They spent the next week paddling and portaging a complex of lakes and rivers. Tom was especially struck by the beauty and wildness of the area—a mosaic of waterways, each possessing its resident loons and eagles, banks crowded with pines, coves flush with ducks and wading birds. Even the occasional portages added to the feeling of remoteness and an uneasy sense of pushing ever deeper into the wilderness.

Initially nervous, Tom soon relaxed in the knowledge of how quickly he learned the rudiments of fishing even though he lacked the finesse of his friends. His newfound satisfaction more than compensated for any awkwardness at the beginning. He reveled in learning to best the fish. And the more he honed his skills and craftiness, the more the air and water came to assume a sharp and more detailed character. He felt an almost childlike joy in catching the fish, each day consuming a portion for lunch and dinner, sometimes even for breakfast. The pungent freshness of the creatures seemed alive with flavor and energy.

Tom delighted in learning how to skin and bone the animals, and in watching the gulls and eagles feed on the remainder. He especially treasured the feeling of deep connection with the world around him. An intense sense of relationship flowed from locating, catching, and consuming the creatures. He felt bound by an intimate movement of energy from one level of existence to another and finally into himself.

Not long after returning home, Tom read a magazine article that seemed to capture his experience. A professor, Paul Shepard of Pitzer College, was quoted as saying that harvesting a life from the wild confirms the feeling of "continuity with the dynamic life of animal populations and [one's] role in the complicated cycle of elements . . . and in the patterns of the flow of energy. . . . [It offers] a reenactment of past conditions when contact with the natural environment and the virtues of this contact were less obscured by the conditions of modern life."[18]

Sally had a deep bias against eating wild mushrooms, believing most of them were poisonous. But residing in central Michigan she encountered quite a few, particularly during moist summers such as the current one. She especially feared that one day her four-year-old, during his many ventures crawling along the ground, might find one and eat it. Her worst nightmare became a reality when she received a frantic call from her next-door neighbor that her boy had been rushed with the babysitter to a nearby hospital after having consumed a wild mushroom.

She practically sped the entire way to the emergency room. Rushing through the doors, she spied her boy and could hardly believe her eyes. He was playing a card game with the babysitter, and a pleasant-looking nurse was monitoring his progress closely. The nurse, it turned out, was an amateur mushroom collector who spent many a weekend searching for edible varieties. She informed Sally the mushroom had been harmless.

After considerable reassurance and Sally's happy reunion with her son, the nurse suggested Sally might join her for a mushroom hunt the following weekend. Perhaps, the nurse suggested, she could teach Sally to identify the truly dangerous varieties and thereby dispel some of her prejudice against the fungi. After some hesitation, Sally decided to accompany this pleasant woman and a number of her friends on the mushroom-hunting foray.

It turned out to be a far more satisfying experience than she would have ever imagined—a little like a treasure hunt in the wild. As they searched for mushrooms among the fields and forests, she quickly learned to identify the poisonous kinds and was delighted to discover that in fact there were very few dangerous varieties. Distinguishing mushrooms, she learned, is no more difficult than telling one flower or bird from another. She soon became familiar with many of their distinctive colors, shapes, smells, and locations.

Perhaps the high point occurred after returning home, when she and her friend concocted a delicious and fragrant hors d'oeuvre, and then a stew, from the mushrooms. Sally loved her newly acquired knowledge and the feeling of security and self-sufficiency she derived from being able to distinguish one mushroom from another. She now looked forward to future hunts, and joining in this previously unknown side of life, in practically her own backyard.

MEDICAL AND INDUSTRIAL BENEFITS

Wild plants and animals provide people with important medical benefits. Throughout the world, many people rely extensively on various wild species for treating assorted illnesses and diseases. The World Conservation Monitoring Centre, for example, reports that "80% of people in developing countries [principally] rely on traditional medicines."[19]

Reflecting the cultural bias often associated with this use, some Asian nations, such as China, Korea, and Japan, widely employ wild plants and animals in a medical tradition dating back more than four thousand years.[20] Some of these purported benefits have been questioned and others have generated controversy—particularly when they have led to overharvesting and even endangering of species such as the rhinoceros and tiger. Still, these therapeutic effects can sometimes be demonstrated, and a growing natural health movement reflects increasing interest in the healing effects of various wild species. Although overexploiting wildlife for medicinal purposes should certainly be discouraged, this problem may be viewed as more an issue of developing effective management procedures than any intrinsic wrong associated with harvesting species from the wild.

Despite the advances of modern science and pharmaceutical manufacturing, it is surprising how much contemporary medicine continues to rely on wild plants and animals for treating various illnesses, as well as in carrying out research activities.[21] Wild species often provide the raw material and associated knowledge leading to the mass production of various medicines. Indeed, an estimated one-quarter to one-half of all pharmaceuticals today owe their origin to a wild plant or animal, including 24 percent from plants, 13 percent from bacteria, and 3 percent from animal species.[22] Some 70,000 plants have been utilized for medicinal purposes. Annually some $84 billion globally, and $20 billion in the United States, can be linked to the use of wild living species for medical purposes.[23]

Wild plants and animals are also utilized in various industrial products—including the manufacture of paints, pesticides, plastics, oils, latexes, cosmetics, and various decorative items.[24] Latex or natural rubber offers a good example of a diverse collection of tropical plants used in producing tires, belts, clothing, and other products. Natural latex still accounts for one-third of the world's rubber production due to its considerable versatility. Moreover, synthetic rubber would never have been developed without the knowledge derived from wild species.

The manufacture of oils, lubricants, and waxes also relies on many plant and animal species. Sperm whale oil, for example, is among the finest lubricants known, although its use has been severely curtailed due to changing attitudes and past overexploitation of whales. Wild plant and animal species are used in soaps, tanning solutions, inks, perfumes, and flavorings. Resin from trees remains an important ingredient in products designed to protect wood.

People continue to benefit materially, in one form or another, from some 100,000 different wild species.[25] This extraordinary range of products suggests how much we still depend on wild nature to satisfy diverse needs for sustenance and security. Moreover, the range of medical, food, and industrial products derived from wild living diversity is likely to expand in the future, spurred by a number of factors. First, more and more new species are being identified as a consequence of expanding exploration in largely unknown areas of the world, such as the tropical rain forests and deep oceans, along with the related development of innovative collection and biological prospecting techniques. We need to remember that only an estimated 15 percent of the earth's species have been scientifically identified thus far.[26] Second, governments, pharmaceutical companies, and nongovernmental organizations have, in recent years, committed considerable resources to the task of identifying potentially beneficial wild species. Third, rapidly expanding knowledge in molecular biology, genetics, and bioengineering will greatly expand our ability to exploit the biochemical properties of various wild species.

COMPLEXITIES OF THE WILDLIFE TRADE

The case of the sperm whale, cited earlier, indicates the need for exercising restraint and respect in pursuing the utilization of wild species. A creature's material value is no excuse for unbridled exploitation. Unfortunately, the history of harvesting wildlife does not offer much assurance that we will behave with restraint and respect if a species generates large profits and becomes associated with presumed medical or restorative powers. Many species have been eliminated or driven to the brink of extinction under these circumstances. Even today, one-third of endangered vertebrates owe their plight to the impact of overexploitation.[27]

Although it may seem irrational to eliminate a species that provides a source of livelihood, people often disregard the future—particularly when extreme poverty suggests few options, or, conversely, huge profits offer the opportunity to reinvest the income in other areas of economic return. Many people assume they have no choice or that human ingenuity will somehow compensate for a creature's commercial or biological extinction. The idea of sustainable use suggests strong incentives for maintaining a continuous supply of a species by limiting its exploitation to the creature's capacity to replace itself. But overexploitation is often spurred by a view of species as inexhaustible, easily replaced by other creatures, or irrelevant because of presumed future inventions and new technology.

Human greed, ignorance, and ineffectual regulatory and management practices often exacerbate these problems. The sad history of the large whales—the blue, bowhead, fin, gray, humpback, right, sei, and sperm whales—provides an instructive illustration.[28] The marine biologist Kenneth Norris once observed: "No other group of large animals has had so many of its members driven to the brink of extinction."[29] Five hundred years of commercial whaling nearly drove all the large whales to oblivion. The killing peaked during the 1930s at more than 60,000 animals, but in overall weight harvested the height of this exploitation occurred as recently as 1960 when 4 billion tons or 15 percent of the world's "fish" catch consisted of whale meat.[30] Ironically, few other species of wildlife have received more regulatory attention than whales: international whaling conventions initially developed in the 1920s and then revised following World War II. Until a moratorium on commercial whaling was declared in the mid-1980s, the populations of most large whales increased only during World Wars I and II—when people were busier killing one another than harvesting whales.

Still, any wild species can, theoretically at least, be harvested in perpetuity. The African elephant offers a particularly controversial example today of the pros and cons of exploiting wild species commercially. This debate demonstrates the complexity of wildlife utilization in a global economy—especially in cases involving highly popular, biologically complex species whose use primarily serves a nonessential purpose. Like the whale, the elephant has had a long history of human exploitation spanning thousands of years.[31] Elephants have been used in a remarkable number of products including jewelry, medicines, food, clothing, art, and musical instruments. Because of its durability and relative rarity, raw ivory has sometimes been used like gold as a form of wealth, particularly during times of political instability.

The decade of the 1980s was unrivaled for its degree of destructive, cruel, and excessive elephant exploitation. The combined effects of war, corruption, international transport, new markets (particularly among the emerging affluent nations of Asia), and widely available weaponry resulted in some 50,000 to 90,000 elephants killed each year. From an estimated 1.2 million in 1980, the African elephant population plummeted to approximately 600,000 by 1990. The wildlife biologist Dr. Ian Douglas-Hamilton somberly remarked: "The elimination of the elephant over much of its range represents one of the most wasteful tragedies of our century."[32]

The wholesale killing provoked widespread protest. The United States passed an Elephant Protection Bill, and the Convention on International Trade in Endangered Species of Flora and Fauna (an agreement involving more than 120 nations) initiated a moratorium on the commercial trade in ivory. Various southern African nations protested, claiming they possessed abundant elephant populations, effective management practices, widespread conflicts between elephants and people, and cultural traditions and economic needs that justified a controlled elephant harvest. The current controversy provides a useful example of the larger issue of commercially exploiting wildlife.[33]

Those opposed to elephant exploitation, and many other forms of wildlife trade, argue that large profits, in a world of international commerce and highly lethal weaponry, almost always leads to the decline and endangerment of a slow-breeding animal like the elephant. They also charge that the emphasis on profit encourages unethical and cruel harvesting practices, extensive poaching, and government corruption—especially among poor African nations with limited scientific and regulatory abilities. Moreover, opponents express grave doubts regarding the purported economic benefits of elephant exploitation and other forms of wildlife trade. They argue that indigenous peoples rarely receive the monetary rewards; instead, most of the profits accrue to a small group of commercial operators, government elites, and foreigners. Indeed, these elites often exclude local people from areas where the commercial species exists—creating the impression that wildlife are more important than indigenous people, especially when the products mainly serve the luxury needs of a wealthy and foreign clientele. Finally, many object morally to harvesting species, like elephants and whales, that are viewed as highly intelligent animals possessing complex social lives and an especially developed capacity for experiencing pain and suffering.

But the advocates of elephant exploitation and, more generally, wildlife utilization cite the animal's practical benefits and characterize their opponents as naive, ignorant, ideologically biased, and elitist. These proponents believe that wildlife can be harvested sustainably and ethically and argue this trade represents an economic necessity for nations burdened by poverty and dependence on natural resources for most of their foreign exchange. The sustainable harvest of 15,000 elephants annually could yield, it has been suggested, some $100 million annually while employing many thousands and protecting crops and people from harm. Advocates further argue that the greatest long-term threat to African wildlife is not exploitation but the spread of agriculture and other forms of modern development. Widely roaming species like elephants will presumably be saved only by economically outcompeting other land uses. Profits derived from the ivory trade and sport hunting, proponents claim, could provide this economic incentive. Trade proponents also suggest that elephant utilization represents a more compatible cultural tradition than wildlife preservation—an "alien value system" imposed by a largely Western elite. Finally, they argue that problems of sustainable utilization can be resolved through better management, improved science, and more effective enforcement.

This debate illustrates the complexities of wildlife harvesting and trade. Commercially exploiting wild plants or animals is neither ethically wrong nor theoretically an unsustainable activity. Still, the material uses of wild creatures must proceed with caution—and these benefits should never compromise equally compelling aesthetic, ecological, scientific, moral, recreational, symbolic, and other values of nature. Sustainable wildlife use means ensuring a steady stream of all human dependencies on nature and living diversity.[34] Harvesting nature's bounty is a privilege, not an unlimited right, and with this privilege come associated moral duties and ethical responsibilities.

Using Wild Species to Improve Domestic Production

Wild species also help to maintain and even enhance the productivity, health, and vigor of many domesticated plants and animals. The yield, durability, and disease resistance of various cultivated species can be improved by infusing these species with the genetic characteristics of related wild species.[35] When properties from the wild are crossed with domesticated species, the results can be striking: significant increases in production, improved capacities to withstand pests and disease, and sometimes the creation of new breeds better adapted to new, harsh, or previously unexploited environments.

The importance of this activity is reflected in the fact that an estimated one-fifth to two-fifths of the world's increase in agricultural yields during the past half century have been brought about by improvements resulting from genetic breeding with or introductions of wild plants.[36] The recent creation of an important hybrid rice, for example, increased this crop's value by $1 billion in just two years. The economic and material significance of this practice is suggested by the 6,000 plants that have been introduced in recent years into the United States for various food, forage, and ornamental purposes, although this activity can sometimes pose considerable ecological problems. Analogous benefits can be cited with respect to livestock production. David Pimentel and his colleagues estimate that $139 billion worldwide, including $32 billion in the United States, flows annually from the use of wild living diversity for agricultural breeding purposes.[37]

The current large-scale loss of global biological diversity has resulted in the elimination of many wild species of potential importance to agriculture and related activities. In this regard, the World Conservation

Monitoring Centre recently noted: "At a time when more genetic diversity is needed in crop breeding programmes to increase food production this diversity is rapidly disappearing or has already been lost."[38]

Wild species can also be used to increase the ability of domesticated plants and animals to adapt to new environmental conditions. This potential is especially important as humans disseminate into regions historically considered inaccessible or uninhabitable—a process that expands the need for hardy domesticated crops that can survive harsh conditions and compete with local species. The ability of cultivated species to survive these new circumstances often depends on cross-breeding with wild relatives that have demonstrated a capacity for withstanding severe or novel situations.

The disease resistance of domesticated crops and animals can also be improved by infusing them with the chemical and physical properties of wild species. A single type of tree, for example, may contain a thousand chemicals, many associated with repelling or withstanding threatening and competing organisms.[39] Cross-breeding and genetic engineering can, theoretically at least, capture these resistance characteristics. A wild strain of corn, for example, which nearly became extinct in Mexico due to deforestation, was successfully bred with domesticated corn to increase the latter's ability to withstand a damaging blight. As indicated the global importance of breeding and domestication of wild species for this purpose is suggested by an estimated $139 billion derived each year from this activity.[40]

The agricultural, medical, and commercial importance of wild living species will likely increase in the future as a consequence of expanding scientific knowledge and technological capacity. While some of these gains will be sought and expected, many will be unanticipated. Indeed, the great majority of new material benefits obtained from wild species during the past hundred years could not have been predicted one hundred years ago. Unexpected discoveries occur all the time as a consequence of accident, luck, and new technology. This process of unanticipated gains is likely to accelerate as our information processing and application abilities expand. Rapid increases in our knowledge of biology, chemistry, and the physics of life will inevitably result in an ever increasing ability to generate new and unforeseen discoveries.

Humans derive a vast array of material benefits in the search for new knowledge and understanding of the natural world. The capacity to exploit wild living diversity owes much to this yearning for exploration and discovery. For material reasons alone, we need to maintain the conditions that encourage this inquisitive drive. In so doing, we will increase our capacity to exploit in the future, to a degree unimaginable today, the earth's immense and incalculable storehouse of potential genetic wealth.

We must preserve, as well, our ability to respond to the unexpected in nature. All species represent millions of years of evolutionary trial and error as they adapted to the intense pressures of survival within the community of life. Each species reflects countless variations on a theme—a chemical resistant to another creature's predatory advances, a physical property that withstands a particular stress, a body part that enhances mobility or concealment. These countless adaptations, hammered into a creature's genes under the unyielding pressures of time and natural selection, almost always hint at some conceivable benefit to human beings. Like some ancient hieroglyphic, this potential depends on our ingenuity, our knowledge, and our luck in deciphering its code. Without the raw material, however, this potential means nothing. Natural diversity remains the template upon which human knowledge develops and depends. Living species constitute the ultimate raw material—an extraordinary repository of largely untapped wealth. To exterminate species before their utility has been demonstrated is to pass a burden of debt on to future generations. To lose a species is to liquidate irreplaceable wealth before its benefit has been realized.

The future importance of wild species may be illustrated by today's search for new ways to treat the growing incidence of cancer. The National Cancer Institute has identified, for example, more than a thousand tropical plants possessing some degree of cancer-fighting property.[41] Another analysis suggests 3,000 wild plants and 1,500 wild animals contain some cancer-inhibiting quality.[42] A recent study reports that the world's flowering plants could potentially yield $147 billion by providing an estimated 328 disease-fighting drugs.[43]

Many of these irreplaceable species are being lost, however, before their utility has been established. Some one-half of the world's 350,000 flowering plants, for example, occur in the tropical rain forests—a biome experiencing 1 to 2 percent deforestation each year. The cases of the rosy periwinkle in Madagascar and the Pacific yew in the northwestern United States illustrate the harm that can result from eliminating species before their value has been demonstrated.[44] Chemicals associated with these two plants have proved useful in treating certain types of cancer, yet both species have been threatened by deforestation. These are just two of many examples of species whose future material importance might be foolishly eradicated before their utility has been fully revealed.

Benefiting from Ecological Processes

People derive an extraordinary range of material benefits from the healthy ecological functioning of diverse plants, animals, and associated habitats. These ecosystem processes assist in agricultural production, waste decomposition, the control of pollutants, soil formation and retention, air and water production, and other life-support functions and benefits.[45]

Agriculture especially depends on the ecological services of many wild creatures including bees, wasps, butterflies, and other invertebrate species. Some 130 agricultural crops in the United States depend on the pollinating activities of wild species.[46] Bees, for example, play a vital role in the production of apples, alfalfa, almonds, avocados, blueberries, cherries, cranberries, cucumbers, melons, plums, pears, and other crops. Many other agricultural products rely on wild free-roaming species to assist in seed dispersal and pollination. An estimated one-third of the world's food production depends on the reproductive assistance of wild species—assistance that generates some $200 billion in economic benefits each year.[47]

Many agricultural plants rely on the protective role of insects and other organisms to control harmful pests. Anne and Paul Ehrlich have estimated that natural predators control more than 90 percent of agricultural pest damage as well as insect-borne disease.[48] Insects, frogs, snakes, songbirds, bats, and other species provide invaluable assistance in controlling pest populations. One songbird, for example, can consume 100,000 to 250,000 insects annually.[49] The economic value of birds alone to American forests is an estimated half-billion dollars in prevented insect damage each year. This statistic suggests how much artificial—and potentially harmful—pesticide would be required if drastic reductions occurred to the populations of songbirds, insects, bats, and other pest-eating creatures.

Decomposition of human wastes represents another critical material benefit we derive from normal ecological functioning. Microbial organisms and invertebrate species break down and recycle most of our organically produced waste. Americans generate some 130 million tons of organic waste each year, while our livestock produce another 12 billion tons of manure.[50] Microbes and invertebrates decompose some 99 percent of this material.

Pollutants associated with petroleum by-products, pesticides, heavy metals, and the estimated 70,000 chemicals used in various industrial processes can be mitigated and sometimes controlled by the ecological activities of various wild organisms. In fact, David Pimentel estimates that natural biological processes degrade 75 percent of these potentially harmful impacts.[51] Bioremediation has become, as a consequence, one of the fastest-growing pollution control technologies today. Noise and dust pollution can also be greatly diminished and filtered by healthy ecological communities, particularly forests and wetlands.

Various organisms, particularly worms and ants, help maintain and generate fertile soils, especially critical in agricultural and forestry production. These creatures disintegrate fibrous tissues, recycle nutrients, mix organic materials, and increase soil porosity and drainage.[52] The depletion and destruction of these organisms can precipitate significant declines in soil fertility and subsequent reductions in food and fodder.

Indeed, the disappearance of entire civilizations has been hypothetically associated with extensive soil loss.[53]

The abundance of commercially beneficial species often depends on the existence of healthy ecological communities. Economically important marine and tropical species often rely on highly specialized and intricate ecological relationships. One-third of all fish species, for example, depend on coral reefs for at least part of their life cycle.[54] This ecosystem, in turn, relies on the health and abundance of a small number of coral species—if these species are harmed, inevitably a cascading effect harms other organisms associated with this ecological community. Tidal wetlands perform an analogous role in the United States: a majority of this country's commercial fish species depend on these areas as nursery grounds for breeding and early development.[55]

Various biological and chemical cycles associated with healthy ecosystem functioning provide humans with basic life-support benefits such as water and oxygen production. The vegetative cover of forested ecosystems, for example, performs vital roles in water retention and recharge. Large-scale deforestation, therefore, can lead to significant reductions in water quantity and quality. Healthy wetlands offer a host of material benefits including groundwater recharge, flood control, sediment retention, bank and seashore stabilization, waste decomposition, soil production, pollution control, and habitat for commercially important species. Despite these benefits, more than half of the freshwater and saltwater wetlands of the United States have been lost or significantly degraded during the past three hundred years.[56]

The collective benefits associated with normal ecosystem functioning can sometimes obscure the personal satisfaction people obtain from materially depending on healthy ecological communities. Here is another story to try to bring this situation to life.

Jim and Denise had little intention, let alone the skills, to cut firewood. They simply desired more light around their new home on their fifteen-acre woodlot twenty miles outside Knoxville. Cutting the trees had pro-

duced the desired effect, as well as the added pleasure of seeing the distant hills and the contrasting line of field against forest. Their problem now consisted of the six-foot logs that were left. Since their new home contained two fireplaces, they decided to cut the logs for firewood.

They bought a chain saw and splitting maul and learned to use them. They had not expected to enjoy the process quite so much. Beyond the obvious value of clearing the debris and cutting the wood, the warmth of the logs and the beauty of the fire's ever changing light and colors provided many pleasures. But they especially enjoyed learning about the trees—their varying grains and hardness, the particular contours of the barks, their shapes and growth patterns, even the past and present uses of the different woods beyond simply burning them. They became fascinated by the realization that they could harvest their woodlot without diminishing its overall age, distribution, composition, and number of trees. They used the firewood as their excuse for creating an overall plan for their property—one that sought to nest the practical value of the trees within the broad objective of maintaining the beauty, health, and harmony of the land.

They sometimes tried describing these various pleasures to friends and family but, given their natural reticence, rarely burdened themselves or others with such complicated explanations. One day, though, Jim stumbled upon a passage from a book by the ecologist Aldo Leopold that eloquently captured some of their many satisfactions. "Denise" he called, "listen to what this man said":

> *There are two spiritual dangers in not owning [land]. One is the danger of supposing that breakfast comes from the grocery, and the other that heat comes from the furnace. To avoid the first danger, one should plant a garden. . . . To avoid the second, he should lay a split of good oak on the andirons . . . and let it warm his shins while a February blizzard tosses the trees outside. If one has cut, split, hauled, and piled his own good oak, and let his mind work the while, he will remember much about where the heat comes from, and with a wealth of detail denied to those who spend the week-end in town astride a radiator.57*

The Bottom Line

This chapter has described some of the social and personal benefits we derive from materially exploiting nature. Our continuing reliance on wild species and natural processes is reflected in a finding by the biologists Christine and Robert Prescott-Allen: in 1980 some 4.5 percent of the U.S. economy derived from the contributions of wild living diversity.[58] Based on a 1995 U.S. gross national product of some $6 trillion, this percentage converts to almost $300 billion. David Pimentel recently calculated a slightly higher figure of $318 billion. For the world as a whole, he estimates that $3 trillion, or 15 percent of the global economy of $21 trillion, is obtained from the wild.[59] These figures include both direct and indirect expenditures, as well as realized and potential benefits. Collectively, they dramatically demonstrate our continuing reliance on wild nature and living diversity for our material well-being.

Chapter Three

The Aesthetic Appeal

Few experiences in life exert as much effect on people as the physical attraction of nature.[1] Fascination and delight often characterize our reactions to the colors and delicate form of a flowering orchid, the grandeur and shape of a white-capped mountain, the harmony of a flock of waterfowl—and these compose but a small fraction of the multiplicity of experiences of nature likely to elicit a strong aesthetic response. These reactions also occur under widely varying cultural, historical, and geographic circumstances. Whether in Central Africa or Central Park, the fifth century or the modern age, in prison or on 5th Avenue, people react with combinations of wonder and admiration at the sight of a glorious sunset, a stretch of pristine beach, a colorful bird, or a wide variety of other creatures and landscapes.

There is a consistency in the human aesthetic response to nature that unites us all despite our enormous variations in upbringing and experience. This unanimity of aesthetic response suggests a biologically based tendency. The strength of the aesthetic link to nature intimates a pivotal rather than a trivial element in the human experience. Certain species and landscapes evoke especially powerful feelings—and in a multiplicity of social and physical contexts.

The consistency of the aesthetic response to nature is suggested by our proclivity to prefer natural over artificial scenes and situations. This inclination has been revealed, not only across cultures, but even when comparing the views of urban and rural dwellers. Professor Roger Ulrich of Texas A&M University, after an extensive review of the research literature, concluded: "One of the most clear-cut findings . . . is the consistent tendency to prefer natural scenes over built views, especially when the latter lack vegetation or water features. . . . Even unspectacular or subpar natural views elicit higher aesthetic preferences . . . than . . . all but a very small percentage of artificial views."[2] Studies in the far different nation of Nigeria reached similar conclusions: "All groups of respondents, whether poor, rich, educated or uneducated . . . urban or rural . . . exhibited a strong preference for natural landscapes. . . . Urban scenes without nature were particularly viewed by urbanites as 'ugly' and 'disgusting.'"[3]

People do vary, of course, in their aesthetic preferences in response to taste, fashion, sophistication, and culture, and these differences occasionally produce conflicts of opinion regarding the appeal of nature. Yet underlying these variations, an extraordinary consensus of aesthetic judgment persists—whether toward the grandeur of a tiger, the grace of a gazelle, the allure of an iris, or the awesome sight of a towering redwood.

Although the aesthetic response to nature seems deeply rooted in the human psyche, people frequently undervalue its significance. Why might this occur? Perhaps we view the aesthetic aspects of nature as merely picturesque, a dispensable but rarely necessary or vital pleasure. Perhaps we tend to view art as a cultivated capacity that transcends the natural world. In many minds, an aesthetic "eye" must be nurtured and developed, becoming attuned to refinements of form, balance, color, and meaning. Aesthetic judgment suggests personal preference and taste, as if each person or culture could be distinguished by its particular artistic sensibility and sophistication. Variations in judgment, however, do not annul the human tendency to respond in consistent ways to certain elements of the natural world. The consisteny of our aesthetic reactions to nature suggests regularity rather than randomness, a universal disposition rather than a dispensable one. The malleability of aesthetic judgment does not mean that we can deny the underlying biological thrust of our unavoidable attraction to nature.

Later in this chapter, we will discuss variations in aesthetic judgment among Japanese and Americans, as well as dramatic shifts in the historic appeal of certain creatures like wolves and whales or desert landscapes like the Colorado Plateau. Yet underlying these variations we find a consistency in the attraction and repulsion of certain natural elements—and, more important, we find that despite variation and change the underlying emotional pull of these species and landscapes remains constant. Aesthetic reactions to wolves and whales may have shifted, but these creatures continue to evoke powerful aesthetic responses. Perceptions of the Colorado Plateau may have shifted from hellish visions to vistas of great sculpted beauty, but the intensity of the aesthetic response to this landscape has persisted throughout. Some may love and others may hate large predators, snakes, and high mountains, but these creatures and landscapes continue to arouse strong aesthetic reactions under widely varying cultural and geographical circumstances.

Five Adaptive Benefits

What adaptive benefits might have produced this consistency and intensity of the human aesthetic response to nature? The development of an aesthetic sensitivity can be linked to five areas of potential evolutionary advantage: a view of harmony and striving after an ideal; perceptions of order and organization; a sense of sustenance and security; feelings of mystery and discovery; and physical healing and mental restoration. Yet the aesthetic response, like all expressions of biophilia, remains subject to learning and experience—as we will discover when we later explore how aesthetic judgments toward certain species and landscapes have changed over the years. But first let us examine the possible evolutionary and developmental advantages of an aesthetic attraction to nature.

A VIEW OF HARMONY AND STRIVING AFTER AN IDEAL

Perceiving beauty in nature can engender feelings of harmony, balance, and symmetry, no matter how fleeting or even illusory these feelings may be. Certain elements of the natural world offer a model of perfection in form. We discern unity and symmetry in the brilliance of a colorful butterfly or crane, the flowering of a desert cactus or rose, the funneling of breaking waves, the grandeur of snow-capped mountains, the breaching of humpback whales, the bugling of elk at the height of their breeding impulse. Each suggests a glimpse of perfection in a world where frailty, shortcoming, and chaos often seem normative. These encounters may be infrequent, but they occur with sufficient regularity to suggest an ideal of perfection in nature and life.

These images inspire and instruct—and, as objects of admiration, sometimes they prompt the desire to mimic or emulate. Often we seek to incorporate these expressions of symmetry and balance into our lives. We feel better for having witnessed them, and occasionally more proficient when able to adapt some of their attributes into our existence. Symbolically the jaguar's strength, speed, and grace suggest a motorized excellence; while, more directly, we model the dolphin's shape and motion to facilitate our movement through water.

Natural beauty hints at perfection when we witness a species or landscape in its idealized form. These qualities of harmony and perfection intimate, as the environmental philosopher Holmes Rolston suggests, "an ideal toward which a wild life is striving."[4] In glimpsing the prototype, we perceive the potential for excellence, refinement, and elegance in the human experience as well. As we transcend mere pleasure, we encounter clues to a more exemplary and worthwhile existence.

The aesthetics of nature can function as a kind of monumental design model. These environmental attributes suggest proven pathways of success in a multiplicity of shapes and forms. By discerning beauty and harmony in the natural world, we advance the belief and sometimes the understanding of how certain configurations of line, space, texture, light, contrast, movement, prospect, and color may be employed to produce analogous results in the human experience. This ideal provides a template for action—a methodology, through mimicry and ingenuity, for achieving a more rewarding existence.

PERCEPTIONS OF ORDER AND ORGANIZATION

Perceiving order and organization represents a related aspect of the aesthetic experience of nature. A sense of coherence and pattern in a landscape or living element can be not only satisfying but beneficial. By discerning a unifying structure in the natural world, we invest life with meaning and integrity rather than randomness and chaos. The aesthetic experience of nature fosters the perception of order and organization in place of what might otherwise appear to be confusing and meaningless.

Consider the common reaction to an unfamiliar landscape such as a forest crowded with trees, shrubs, and thickets. Viewed initially, from a distance or close up, the forest appears confusing, a slovenly and undifferentiated collection of details and elements.[5] We strive to impose order and organization on the landscape by using certain features or landmarks, establishing boundaries, imposing shape and meaning. Prominent signposts are typically laden with striking aesthetic qualities—a large tree, a high point, a body of water, an eagle's nest, the place where deer gather. Without these pivots, feelings of imbalance, confusion, and chaos often prevail.

Sometimes the commonplace can offer this sense of organization and structure, as Wallace Stevens suggests in his poem, "Anecdote of the Jar":

> I placed a jar in Tennessee
> And round it was, upon a hill.
> It made a slovenly wilderness
> Surround that hill.
>
> The wilderness rose up to it,
> And sprawled around, no longer wild.
> The jar was round upon the ground
> And tall and of a port in air.
>
> It took dominion everywhere.
> The jar was gray and bare.
> It did not give of bird or bush,
> Like nothing else in Tennessee.[6]

A simple jar may suffice, but rarely does it represent our preferred means for achieving structure and organization. For one thing, it lacks the aesthetic power of a natural element. Striking environmental features—a towering tree, a rocky prominence, a charismatic species—arrest our attention in ways that few artificial creations can rival. Given the option, people almost always select a beautiful and compelling natural feature for structuring their experience and locating themselves—whether the choice be a high vertical cliff instead of a radio tower, a lake instead of a building, a stately tree in preference to a mailbox, a bird rather than a jar.

Aesthetically conspicuous wildlife—deer, cranes, swans, eagles, bears, whales, and so on—can transform an undifferentiated landscape into one filled with emotional significance and focus. Think of a group of people on a boat on a calm flat ocean. For hours the boaters confront an endless and boring expanse of unbroken sea. Suddenly, they become alerted to a tiny speck at the edge of the horizon. Against the vastness of the sea it appears minuscule—but recognized as a whale it produces an explosion of delight. The humpback whale breaches as the boat approaches, and at once the monotonous ocean becomes replete with structure, appeal, and significance.

Even the image of a species never actually seen can confer emotional meaning and intellectual organization upon a landscape. Very few people visiting Yellowstone or Glacier national parks, for instance, are likely to encounter a grizzly bear or wolf. But the mere knowledge of these animals' presence energizes the human experience and attracts many to these areas despite the extremely low probability of ever seeing these creatures. Commenting on the aesthetic role performed by such species, Aldo Leopold noted how the ruffed grouse and the wolf affected him (although this aesthetic niche could no doubt be filled by different creatures):

> The autumn landscape in the north woods is the land, plus a red maple, plus a ruffed grouse. In terms of conventional physics, the grouse represents a millionth of either the mass or energy of an acre. Yet subtract the grouse and the whole thing is dead. An enormous amount of some kind of motive power has been lost. . . . My own conviction on this score dates from the day I saw a wolf die. . . . We reached the old wolf in time to watch a fierce green fire dying in her eyes. I realized then, and have

> known ever since, that there was something new to me in those eyes—something known only to her and to the mountain.[7]

Leopold's experience of the grouse and the wolf lent aesthetic meaning, order, and worth to the landscape. He recognized how a single creature could provide structure and appeal, causing us to "think like a mountain." The "green fire" dying in the eyes of the last wolf marked the extirpation of an aesthetic as much as a biological reality. The ecologist George Schaller experienced a similar phenomenon when the elimination of the Himalayan Mountains' most distinguishing fauna, their wild goats and sheep, prompted him to refer to this area as "stones of silence."[8] The aesthetically pivotal creature conferred structure as well as beauty; their absence signified a mute and disturbing silence.

Every person—rich or poor, educated or uneducated, city or country dweller—possesses this aesthetic connection to nature. We encounter countless examples: potted plants adorning apartment windows, posters of nature hanging in the simplest abodes, the importance of the stately neighborhood tree, the attraction of nearby lakes and watercourses. These expressions of nature's beauty help us create pattern, order, and design in our lives. Removing, spoiling, or destroying these elements produces a feeling of dis-ease and deterioration, a sense of having rendered familiar places less assuring, less attractive, less habitable.

These elements of the aesthetic experience of nature help elucidate why we so often prefer naturalistic over abstract art.[9] In contrast to the sense of order often associated with beautiful species and landscapes, abstract art frequently elicits feelings of chaos and confusion. Commenting on waning German interest in abstract art, Heinz-Otto Peitgen remarked: "Everything was very geometric straight-line approaches. The work of [one artist], for example, trying to discover the relation of colors . . . essentially just squares of different colors put onto each other. . . . People don't like it."[10] Abstract art frequently fails to convey a sense of order amidst its enigmatic complexity. Nature, by contrast, typically provides organized patterns, a harmony of connection and relationship, despite its immensity of details and features. Alluding to this difference between the natural and artificial, the physicist Gert

Eilenberger asks: "Why is it that the silhouette of a storm-bent leafless tree against an evening sky in winter is perceived as beautiful, but the corresponding silhouette of any multi-purpose . . . building is not, in spite of the efforts of the architect? The answer seems to me, even if somewhat speculative . . . [that] our feelings for beauty are inspired by the harmonious arrangement of order and disorder as it occurs in natural objects—in clouds, trees, mountain ranges, or snow crystals. The shapes of all these are dynamical processes jelled into physical forms, and particular combinations of order and disorder are typical of them."[11]

We do not so much dislike abstract art or the artificial as the frequent failure of these designs to nest complexity within recognizable patterns and structures. A similar effect occurs when viewing a landscape or patch of nature divorced from its normal context. Take, for example, a tangle of brush seen apart from a surrounding forest, or a section of leaf magnified many thousands of times, or a stretch of coastline viewed from an enormous distance. Seen in this way, all these familiar and often attractive features become irregular, fragmented, even incomprehensible. They have been separated from their organizing circumstances; a central focal point is lost; wholeness has been replaced by chaos. Put these same fragments back into a textured, patterned, and familiar framework, however, and again they become meaningful, orderly, and attractive. Complexity and mystery—whether in nature or in abstract art—do not repel so much as the lack of an integrated and structured dynamic. The aesthetic appeal of nature often originates in its power to convey a sense of organization despite the disorder so often encountered in life.

INCREASED SUSTENANCE AND SECURITY

People's aesthetic preference for certain landscapes and species has also been related to the increased likelihood of encountering safety, sustenance, and security.[12] People favor, for example, natural settings with long vistas and prospects. Generally we prefer viewing a clear directional path, observing long distances, looking down from a high vantage point. We reveal these tendencies in our outdoor recreational choices, our landscape designs, our painting and photographic choices, even in the way we select hotel rooms, homes, and apartments. When we can afford it, most of us opt for "a room with a view," the choice reflecting as much a basic inclination as any cultivated taste.[13] A myriad of locations and vantage points confronts us, but aesthetically we tend to choose those with clearly demarcated courses of action and an enhanced likelihood of encountering safety, achieving sustenance, and avoiding danger.

Even our preference for bright colors in nature reflects this association of environment and security. Bright hues frequently connote the greater likelihood of encountering food—often signified by ripe fruits, animal life, or an aggregation of feeders. Some gardens and flower arrangements emphasize shape over color, but most people gravitate to horticultural compositions marked by brilliant reds, oranges, purples, yellows, and blues, or shrubs and trees distinguished by an unusual abundance of vivid and prominent colors. Few landscapes provoke as much aesthetic pleasure as the blossoming of spring flowers or an autumn of radiant leafage. Asked to depict an ideal landscape, people envision "tropical paradises" of cascading waterfalls, fruits, and flowers or parklike settings of bright colors, nearby water, and the absence of predators. Even the typical Japanese garden emphasizing trees and shrubs over flowers appears dominated by prominent bushes, the bright foliage of Japanese maples, and the distinctive branching and canopy shape of trees found on the open savanna.[14] Our "instinctive" aesthetic appears to be tied to the increased likelihood of encountering sustenance and security during the long course of human evolution.

This hypothesized association of environmental aesthetics and adaptive problem solving in human evolution has been insightfully explored by Professors Gordon Orians and Judith Heerwagen of the University of Washington.[15] They provide diverse evidence to support the proposition that people's attraction to nature can indeed increase their potential for achieving shelter, safety, and security. In a series of ingenious studies, they report that most people prefer paintings, photographs, tree shapes, park designs, and ornamental plants that seem to offer physical sustenance and protection. They note a decided preference for landscapes with water, landscapes offering enhanced sight and mobility, and landscapes affording the likelihood of spotting danger and locating security. When they examined reactions to forty-six sunset and sunrise paintings by prominent artists, as well as nine prior sketches and subsequent landscape paintings by the nineteenth-century English painter John Constable, they found most respondents preferred depictions that offer shelter and refuge, prospects, open vistas, and orientation.

The significance of water was especially notable in this and other research. Indeed, various studies report a tendency for most people to choose scenes with some element of water. The highly popular English park tradition, for example, favors landscapes that feature a lake, meandering stream, or flowing brook nestled among rolling hills, open fields, and stately trees. We frequently encounter bodies of water in the American landscape painting tradition as well. Most of us, when we can, opt for homes with water views, whether next to a lake, river, or ocean, and these areas often command the highest property values.

By contrast, landscapes lacking water, shelter, escape opportunities, and a diversity of plants and animals frequently strike us as unattractive and even repulsive. Change these landscape elements (or the perception of them), however, and a radical shift in aesthetic perception can often be achieved. The Biologist Colleen Rush observed this change in a study of historic reactions to the Colorado Plateau over the past two centuries.[16] Early explorers and artists largely depicted this area of deep canyons, searing deserts, and undrinkable rivers as harsh, uninhabitable, and horrid. For many, it constituted a vision of hell: "Perceptions of the canyonlands of the Colorado Plateau described an impassable region of hidden threats, devoid of life, and mostly without water, and the region was considered to be both worthless and fearsome. Written descriptions of the earliest white explorers of this region were infused with strong negative emotion and a prevailing sense of dread."[17]

Over the years, a radical transformation in aesthetic attitude toward the plateau occurred: today the area is widely regarded as a place of great sculpted beauty and attractive colors. This aesthetic change developed along with a dramatic alteration in our feelings of safety, sustenance, and security in relation to this landscape. New knowledge and technology turned a lifeless environment into one of abundant water, energy, and prolific wildlife. Wild and undrinkable rivers were impounded and purified; ample food was imported; transport was secured; a previously unsuspected life was abundantly revealed underground and at night. This landscape, in effect, was transformed from alien to picturesque—from a hellish vision to a place where the problem of too many admirers is its foremost challenge. While attitudes toward this desert landscape shifted dramatically, the strength of our reactions did not. Like all deserts, the plateau exerted a consistent and powerful pull on our aesthetic emotions and imagination.

I can recall an analogous experience during a recent trip to Cape Cod. I had been visiting an area known as Pilgrim Spring, a place where Cape Cod makes its final oversized hook far out into the North Atlantic. The spot was close to where the Pilgrims first landed in the "new world." After three long November days, the Pilgrims finally found on the site "sweet" drinkable water. The historian Kate Caffrey envisions the moment: "They were parched with thirst, and the woods were full of dense thorny thickets that tore their clothes and wrenched at their armor. . . . At last they found water, at the spot called today Pilgrim Spring, the first New England water they had tasted. Bradford wryly commented that this was 'now in great thirst as pleasant unto them as wine or beer have been in foretimes.'"[18] The Pilgrims not only struggled to find food and water, but shortly after landing they experienced "strong winds, snow settling six inches deep, and piercingly cold nights."[19] After a month's struggle, they abandoned the desertlike conditions of the outer cape—an area of giant sand dunes, porous and infertile soil, meager game, and little drinkable water. On December 11, they departed and landed at Plymouth, the site traditionally celebrated as the beginning of the great English experiment in North America.

Cape Cod represented for the Pilgrims a fearsome, horrific, and aesthetically repelling wilderness. To me, nearly four centuries later, it seemed extraordinarily attractive and appealing. I especially benefited from the path constructed by the National Park Service through once nearly impenetrable thickets, eventually leading to a high promontory. From this spot I gazed across a wide panorama of colorful fall vegetation: brilliant oranges, reds, and yellows. A creek traversed the center of my vision, ducks gliding along the surface. At the edge of the horizon, the ocean spread beyond the giant dunes, great rolling waves breaking onto the white sandy beach. In the glory of the early fall morning a wave of migrating warblers was moving from one low-lying tree and bush to another. A movement in the nearby marsh revealed a large deer, a bright tawny coat, a crown of pointed antlers.

The Pilgrims' aesthetic differed radically from my own in our assumptions of sustenance and protection. They experienced cold, thirst, and hunger. I had been sustained by imported energy, a nearby bed and breakfast, and easy access to the high and picturesque promontory. The deer and the warblers stirred in me feelings of living abundance and diversity; the Pilgrims confronted a largely lifeless, unseasonably cold, and parched wilderness. Our aesthetic sensibilities, in effect, followed along different paths of presumed safety and security.

FEELINGS OF MYSTERY AND DISCOVERY

Aesthetic appreciation can also provoke a sense of wonder and mystery—and, in so doing, enhance our interest and penchant for exploration, creativity, and discovery. Part of nature's aesthetic appeal derives from its extraordinary diversity: it is the most "information-rich" environment we will likely ever encounter.[20] This aesthetic variety offers endless opportunities for exercising our imagination, for encountering new and challenging situations, for pushing the edge of our creativity. Natural diversity provokes in us feelings of fascination, wonder, adventure, and discovery.

Our aesthetic response to nature developed in part because it fostered our capacities for learning and discovery. We rejoice in the presence of ancient forests, river corridors, enormous trees, and other aspects of the natural world because they promise a wealth of exploratory opportunities within a context of spontaneity, meaning, and organization. Unappealing nature, by contrast, offers little chance for exercising our imagination. Instead we encounter boredom, sameness, monotony. Too much detail can provoke confusion, but too little can invite feelings of sterility and ennui. We will return to this issue—the capacity of living diversity to promote human learning and discovery—in subsequent chapters.

PHYSICAL HEALING AND MENTAL RESTORATION

The aesthetic response to nature can exert a pronounced healing effect, particularly in times of acute stress and disorder. Nature's therapeutic potential has long been celebrated in anecdote and legend. When confronted with illness, grief, and distress, we often seek the restorative powers of beautiful gardens, seashores, mountains, hot springs, and other environments perceived as aesthetically pleasing.

Recent studies offer scientific evidence to document this assertion.[21] Roger Ulrich and his colleagues have reported significant reductions in physiological signs of disorder, improved and faster recovery rates from illness, and lower stress among patients exposed to attractive natural settings, especially when compared with persons lacking such contact with nature. They compared, for example, the postoperative recovery rates of patients exposed to natural scenes (both real and depicted) with those who had not experienced this contact. They found: "Patients with the natural view had shorter postoperative stays, far fewer negative comments in nurses' notes . . . and tended to have lower scores for minor postsurgical complications such as persistent headache or nausea requiring medication. The wall-view patients required more injection of potent painkillers, whereas the tree-view patients more frequently received weak oral analgesics."[22]

Other studies have similarly revealed the therapeutic impact of natural settings—especially attractive and physically appealing environments. In addition to its capacity to inspire, instruct, and sustain, natural beauty appears to comfort and restore, especially during moments of stress and dysfunction. This obviously adaptive benefit provides yet another reason why the aesthetic inclination toward nature could have become biologically encoded during the long course of human evolution.

We will return to the healing and restorative effects of nature in Chapter 7, particularly the therapeutic benefits associated with the companionship of other creatures.

Variation and Change

All expressions of biophilia are viewed as deeply rooted biological tendencies. The aesthetic response to nature has been depicted as a characteristic of all societies, reflective of the various benefits described in this chapter. Still, like all expressions of biophilia, the aesthetic impulse is a weak biological tendency, mediated and shaped by experience, learning, and culture.

The aesthetic response often varies from person to person and culture to culture. Although certain creatures and landscapes exercise a strong aesthetic hold on the human imagination, our response to these natural features may change. Their capacity to act as aesthetic magnets of human intellect and emotion, however, seems invariable. Indeed, various features of the natural world—snakes, wolves, spiders, deserts, mountains, oceans, rivers, forests—have played a critical role in human evolution. Perceptions of these environmental elements may shift, but not their power to serve as significant conduits of human emotion and aesthetic projection.

Take snakes, for instance. Many people fear snakes and avoid them.[23] A smaller number view this creature with awe, fascination, and sometimes affection. A strong inclination to respond emotionally to snakes may well have become ingrained in the human species because of the considerable threat this creature posed to a terrestrial animal like ourselves traversing the open forests and savannas. The snake has long figured in human story, myth, dream, and tale. A villain and violator most of the time, at others it has been an object of veneration. What has remained constant is the power of this animal to evoke strong feelings in most of us.

The wolf is another creature tending to elicit strong aesthetic and emotional responses.[24] Although both the wolf and the mountain lion are native to North America, the wolf occurs ten times more often in Native American legends.[25] Among the European settlers of this continent, the wolf was largely viewed as a repulsive creature and became the focus of an extermination campaign well into the twentieth century. As Stanley Young recounts: "There was a sort of unwritten law of the range that no cow man would knowingly pass by a carcass of any kind without inserting in it a goodly dose of strychnine sulfate, in the hope of killing one more wolf."[26] Eliminating the wolf became an expression of moral duty and community obligation. Regarded as ugly, slovenly, foul, bloodthirsty, ruthless, devilish, the wolf was primarily perceived as a threat to civilizing settlement, livestock, and children.

As the wolf became rare and new knowledge revealed this animal's intelligence, sociability, and minimal human threat, these antagonistic sentiments began to give way to more positive perceptions during the second half of the twentieth century. For many the wolf became a potent symbol of nature's beauty and a tragic comment on the despoliation of America's wilderness. Still, this creature remains a lightning rod for highly charged aesthetic and emotional projections. The wolf continues to mirror our changing perceptions of the natural world. As a result of its great size, predatory nature, intelligence, phylogenetic similarity to humans, and potential for domestication, the wolf's image has been fired into our brain. It remains a sensitive barometer of our aesthetic attitudes toward the natural world.

The whale in the ocean, like the wolf on land, occupies a similar aesthetic niche.[27] Once viewed as a monstrous creature, a denizen of inhospitable places, the whale challenged our presumptions of dominance over nature. As a valuable source of commodities, the whale became an object of unbridled exploitation and many species were driven to the brink of extinction, though the motivation for the slaughter more often reflected greed than dislike. Like the wolf, the whale's increasing rarity, new scientific knowledge, and traditional symbolic importance helped to make this creature a rallying cry for an emerging ethic of wildlife and nature protection during the latter half of the twentieth century. The whale became aesthetically transformed from a monstrous "fish" to a mammal of great intelligence, beauty, and similarity to humans. We now celebrate the "singing" of humpback whales, the "talking" of dolphins, the "kindness" of killer whales. This new aesthetic serves as an important basis for a whalewatching industry that generates one-half billion dollars annually and attracts 3 million participants.[28] What has remained constant throughout this change has been the whale's capacity to exercise a powerful hold on our aesthetic imagination.

How universal is this aesthetic impulse? The Japanese aesthetic of nature illustrates the relative as well as universal character of this expression of biophilia. A Japanese affinity for nature's beauty has long been associated with prominent cultural traditions in painting, poetry, gardening, flower arranging, calligraphy, religion, and architecture.[29] These activities reflect an especially refined appreciation of a select set of environmental attributes, often admired in a transformed and embellished state. Typically this aesthetic emphasizes favored aspects of the natural world according to an idealized conception. The Japanese rock garden, bonsai plant, or haiku poem share a common interest in capturing and refining a presumed perfection in nature. The natural world in a raw and wild state is generally regarded as uninteresting and unattractive. The aesthetic goal is to achieve beauty through manipulation and alteration. In Japan, a proper aesthetic requires the artistic skill of humans to heighten certain features of nature in order to express their centrally valued characteristic. Mastering nature and transforming it unveils its hidden beauty.

One Japanese scholar has described this environmental aesthetic as "going to the edge of the forest, viewing nature from across the river, seeing natural beauty from a mountain top, but rarely entering into or immersing oneself in wildness or the ecological understanding of natural settings."[30] This appreciation tends to stand outside wild nature. Instead it focuses on the artistic rendering of an original and primitive state. One scholar has described this view as "freezing and putting walls around nature . . . stealing aspects of nature and creating an art form around it."[31]

The writer Alan Graphard similarly observes: "What has been

termed the Japanese love of nature is actually the Japanese love of cultural transformations . . . of a world [that], if left alone, simply decays."[32] This aesthetic seeks to transcend the impurities of an imperfect world through creative and cultural refinement. This highly refined aesthetic can encourage indifference toward wild nature and ecological process by emphasizing the manipulation of the natural environment. As the philosopher Yuriko Saito suggests: "Nature is not lived or respected for its own sake but because it allows one to escape."[33] A bonsai tree may be beautiful, but it reflects a stunted transformation of the natural world. The Japanese aesthetic of nature suggests once again the shaping influence of learning and culture.

The Benefits of Beauty

Without experience and social support, a person's aesthetic inclination for nature can become frustrated and atrophied. Someone incarcerated in a dark and dismal prison, for example, would probably reveal a stunted capacity for appreciating natural beauty. Yet, given this basic biological disposition, this inmate would likely respond with appreciation and wonder, even if fitfully manifest, when suddenly exposed to a beautiful sunset, lovely flower, or magnificent creature. The Japanese aesthetic for nature may reflect the other extreme: how such a tendency can become exaggerated and, perhaps to some extent, dysfunctional.

Our aesthetic reponse to nature developed because it addresses a variety of fundamental human needs and desires. But the benefits we derive from this relationship to the natural world rely on a diet of learning and social support. The full, functional, and healthy realization of any expression of human biophilia, including the aesthetic, depends on the shaping influence of society as much as on our personal response to basic biological urges.

Chapter Four

The Measure of Empirical Knowledge

Our pursuit of a scientific understanding of the natural world often relies on our capacity for conceptualization and abstract thought—a quest that strikes many of us as the product of a modern and largely Western point of view. As a way of suggesting the universal and timeless character of this aspect of biophilia, let us begin with a story.

Jamie Hines sat nervously as the business part of the meeting of the "Friends of Holbrooke Library" concluded. He was anxiously awaiting Mr. Howard's introduction—the very Mr. Howard whose lawn, it seemed like just yesterday, he had mowed for a mere two dollars an hour. As he looked out at the audience, he could see it included many old friends, neighbors, and family. No doubt they expected a heroic presentation of triumphant explorations in the Brazilian rain forests. He supposed he might disappoint some—or at least counter their deeply held assumptions about the superiority of Western science and civilization. He still could abandon his planned remarks and retreat back to the old familiar slide show—what he called "eco-porn"—of beautiful and exotic creatures and the "great white scientist" pushing the boundaries of human knowledge, endeavoring to "save the world." He knew, however, such a telling would provide a distorted picture, and perhaps the least interesting aspect of his explorations in the tropics. Besides, as a black man who had penetrated the largely white world of modern conservation biology, he had little reason to perpetuate the myth of the "great white scientist."

Out of the corner of his fretting mind, he heard the president of the Friends of Holbrooke Library completing his financial report, reiterating the schedule of remaining speakers for the year, and calling for nominees to the board. Then his ears burned in a forced déjà vu return to his adolescence. The president had begun his introduction:

"I can't tell you how pleased I am to introduce our honored speaker for this evening. It seems like only a few short years ago when I caught a teenaged Jamie Hines and his friends breaking into our boathouse, believing we still languished in Florida. I recall the sweet odor of 'Turkish' cigarettes lingering behind as they fled the scene of their 'crime.' Little did I imagine that one day he would stand before us, a highly respected and accomplished scientist, and a credit to his race, although I might have suspected as much given Jamie's considerable intelligence and fine upbringing. It is my very great pleasure to welcome back our local hero, and for all of us to learn from his tales of discovery in the dark jungles of South America."

Jamie rose to the podium, avoiding as best he could all those familiar faces, particularly the laughing eyes of his first girlfriend, Connie Williams, one of the participants in the great boathouse fiasco.

"I am very proud and, I might add, a little terrified to speak with you tonight. Without doubt, it would be much easier to make a presentation to a group of scientists than to confront so many faces familiar to my childhood. I feel a little like a school kid pretending to be an adult for the evening. Still, I hope you will enjoy hearing about some of my wonderful and sometimes enlightening experiences in the Amazonian tropics."

Jamie paused, gathering his wits, before proceeding to tell the story he had not imagined at the outset of his journey some eighteen months before.

"As many of you know, during the past year and a half I participated in a project located at the headwaters of a small tributary of the Amazon River, whose approximate position is circled in red on the map. I had the incredible good fortune of being part of a major research project intending to learn as much as possible, as quickly as possible, about the various plants, animals, and habitats of this area. The research was inspired by two major concerns and an associated sense of urgency. First, we know surprisingly little about the overall distribution of life on earth, despite our considerable contemporary scientific knowledge. Our understanding is especially limited in little-explored areas like the tropical rain forests that possess a remarkably large proportion of the life on earth. Let me share some statistics with you regarding this point. Current estimates are that 10 to 100 million species of plants and animals inhabit the planet. Fewer than 2 million species have been scientifically identified and described.[1] *The tropical rain forests contain perhaps 50 to 90 percent of these species, because of conditions of high humidity, constant temperatures, a long history of stability, and other factors. A square mile of rain forest, for example, may contain 300 butterfly species compared to 10 to 15 in our town of Holbrooke. Most of this tropical life has yet to be 'discovered' or described by modern science. The first objective of our project was to identify as many new species as possible in the shortest period of time."*

Having repeated the now familiar mantra, Jamie gathered poise and confidence before continuing.

"The second objective was to ascertain, to the greatest extent feasible, the practical benefits that might be derived from these newly discovered species. Our study site had two distinctive characteristics in this regard. First, the area possesses an extraordinary abundance and diversity of species—some claim the several thousand square miles surrounding the tributary harbor more kinds of plants and animals than all but a handful of other places on the planet. Second, large-scale deforestation

tragically threatens the survival of many of these species. Gold has been discovered in the area and thousands of desperately poor Brazilians have recently colonized the region, established mining operations, built roads, and set the forest ablaze to create farms and settlements. These activities have already destroyed hundreds of thousands of acres. There are laws prohibiting this destruction, but many government officials welcome the presumed economic progress, as well as its help in defusing political unrest by providing opportunities for landless peasants in a country with one of the world's most inequitable distributions of land and income."[2]

Jamie now sensed his audience's interest, and he rushed on knowing that at this rate he would never finish what Mr. Howard insisted should be a presentation of no more than twenty minutes followed by ten minutes of questions.

"By scientifically identifying and assessing the practical importance of as many species as possible, as quickly as possible, we hoped we could make a convincing case to the Brazilian government, as well as to the international community, about why this area should be protected. The first step was to gather information about the unique creatures of the region, their survival needs, and their potential contribution to human economic and social well-being. I might note, to illustrate this point, that an estimated one-quarter to one-half of all modern medicines have their origin in one or another wild plant and animal, many from the tropics."

Jamie took pleasure in his audience's apparent sympathy and support, but suspected his next remarks might erode the valiant image he had erected for the project and himself.

"During the next eighteen months, we learned a great deal about thousands of plants and animals, many never previously known to science. We also identified many species of great potential medical, agricultural, and industrial importance. Rather than take any more of my rapidly disappearing time describing these fascinating creatures and their possible uses, I would like to tell you the surprising way we ob-

tained much of this new knowledge, especially during the project's early months."

Jamie took a deep breath and plunged into this far riskier and, he supposed, less satisfying part of his presentation.

"We achieved many of our goals, but frankly this seemed very much in doubt at first. During the initial six months, our results were extremely meager and disappointing. I was very discouraged and seriously considered abandoning the project and returning to the States, believing we could never accomplish our objectives without far more resources, knowledge, and personnel. I concluded that, given our ignorance and the conditions we faced, we had been quite naive about the information that could be obtained in the time allotted.

"Let me briefly describe the status of the project at this point. The first few months mainly focused on setting up camp, becoming familiar with the area and local peoples, and hiring a few native assistants. I was literally a babe in the woods, and it took me several months before I possessed even a rudimentary knowledge or the confidence to venture beyond a restricted security zone of modern gadgets, imported food, and artificially generated power."

Jamie paused, sipping some water, before revealing what saved the project.

"What rescued our rapidly failing undertaking was the accumulated knowledge and wisdom of the local peoples—those seemingly primitive natives who resided in this presumably inhospitable jungle they called home. Our first inkling of what they had to offer occurred about the fifth month. I had become exceedingly frustrated by then about how little we had accomplished. My daily ritual, largely unproductive, consisted of spending each morning in an elevated and concealed blind observing the forest birds—a fauna I especially emphasized because of my ornithological training and, unlike most other animals, their tendency to be active during the day. To assist me I had some very powerful optical and acoustical equipment. But despite my training, equipment, and capture nets, the great majority of birds remained unidentified.

Most of the species stayed in the high forest canopy, alluding my ability to locate them visually with my powerful spotting scope or capturing them in my nets."

Jamie shuffled his notes, trying to calm himself, aware that his allotted time was rapidly disappearing.

"Fortunately, at the height of my frustration and increasing inclination to call it quits, the local tribesmen came to my rescue. By then I had hired a few local assistants. A very shy and reserved people, they rarely interfered or offered advice to the Western scientist who had traveled so far and possessed such extraordinary technology. On one particularly futile day, however, perhaps recognizing my exasperation and despair, an especially bold young man, named Imudi, grabbed me by the shoulder and forcefully gestured toward some high branches in an enormous two-hundred-foot-high tree. Using my powerful spotting scope, I followed the direction of his pointing, but I couldn't see anything out of the ordinary. I offered Imudi the use of my equipment, but he refused. To my shock, he pulled me away from the scope, gesturing excitedly at the tree's high branches. Finally, after considerable effort, I discerned a flicker of movement. I continued to follow the creature with only my bare eye, sensing after a while that this was, in fact, a species I had very much wanted to see. Only then did I get the scope, locate the creature, and confirm it as the species I had supposed.

"Many similar experiences occurred during the following days, weeks, and months. This marked the beginning of a period of extraordinary discovery, distinguished by the collaborative help of my native assistants who helped me locate and identify many unique plants, birds, mammals, reptiles, fish, insects, and other forest creatures. I came to see the landscape, in many ways, as they did, learning to recognize the world through my own eyes before a manyfold magnification. In the process, my vision became more attuned to the tiniest anomaly, the slightest movement, the smallest aberration in the overall landscape that alerted and directed me to the distinctive features and signs of forest life. Once I had developed this capacity for seeing and sensing, the many individual parts of the overall whole became more apparent. Only then

did I use my wonderful, complex, but ultimately limited technology to refine my initial perceptions and judgments."[3]

Jamie sensed the impatience in Mr. Howard's restless movements. No doubt the tone and the length of his speech were taking their toll. He took comfort in the flicker of empathy in his former girlfriend's eyes.

"Over the many succeeding months, we derived a tremendous amount of information and understanding from these illiterate, Stone Age people. While they lacked a strictly scientific approach, I came to appreciate their surprising degree of empirical knowledge of the natural world, and how much it rivaled, in many ways, our own. I discovered they knew the identity and behavior of many rain-forest species. With their help, we identified almost nine hundred bird species and cataloged some previously unknown to science. (Keep in mind that fewer than eight hundred bird species occur in all of the United States.) To my amazement, the local people often possessed specific names for each of these species. In their own scientific fashion, they had classified almost every forest bird. They further possessed detailed knowledge of the behavior and ecology of many of these species. They could, for example, distinguish highly similar creatures by their behavior, their presence in certain habitats, and their association with other species. Frequently these included creatures I had trouble identifying from physical features alone. At first I assumed this reflected more on my own deficient knowledge than on their remarkable scientific understanding. But after returning to the States, I read a similar account by one of the world's foremost biologists, Dr. Jared Diamond. Let me read a brief excerpt from a similar experience he had in Papua New Guinea. Diamond reports:

> *I found that the Foré people apply 110 different Foré names to the 120 different bird species occurring regularly in the Foré area. Of these 110 names, 93 correspond one-to-one to individual bird species recognized by Western taxonomists. . . . Along with this detailed naming system come detailed knowledge of habits and acute abilities of field identification. For example, one of the banes of ornithologists in New Guinea is the warbler genus* Sericornis, *consisting of two dozen drab, very similar populations about whose relationships and grouping into species*

> *taxonomists have been arguing for a century. In the area occupied by the Foré people of New Guinea's eastern highlands occur two of these warblers . . . which differ slightly in size and in depth of olive and orange wash on the face. When I first arrived in the Foré area and began catching these species in mist nets, I could not distinguish them as I held them alive in the hand. It took me several weeks of work in the reference collection of the American Museum of Natural History, comparing and measuring my stuffed study skins, before I was able to separate most specimens. . . . It was therefore humbling to discover that the Foré themselves had separate names for the two* Sericornis *species in their area. . . . To make matters more embarrassing, the Foré distinguished [them] in the field without binoculars. . . . I eventually realized that they did so not by relying on the minute differences in plumage, which Western observers waste their time trying to distinguish with binoculars, but on differences in behavior and song.*[4]

Jamie paused, allowing the implications of Diamond's experiences as well as his own to become apparent, before offering a more pointed conclusion.

"Many other scientists have commented on the unexpected knowledge of seemingly primitive peoples and attempted to explain its origins. Some attribute it to various practical, aesthetic, and spiritual reasons, and certainly this accounts for much of their knowledge. Yet I found, as others have found, that much aboriginal understanding cannot be explained by these factors alone. Many species have been studied and learned by these peoples because the creatures strike them as intrinsically interesting. They take pleasure and pride, in other words, in understanding and knowing their world with authority. An outstanding anthropologist, Dr. Richard Nelson, drew a similar conclusion after he had lived with the native peoples of the Arctic. As he describes:

> *Several times, when an Inupiaq hunting companion did something particularly clever, he pointed to his head and declared: "You see . . . Eskimo scientist!" At first I took it as hyperbole, but as time went by I realized he was telling the truth. Scientists had often visited his community and he recognized a familiar commitment to the empirical method.*

> *. . . Traditional Inupiaq hunters spend a lifetime acquiring knowledge—from other members of their community and from their own experience and observation. . . . When I first went to live with Eskimo people, I often doubted things they told me or had difficulty taking them seriously. Somehow I had learned that Western knowledge, embedded in our scientific tradition, carried a more substantial weight of truth than what was often termed "folk knowledge." But the longer I stayed, the more I trusted their assertions, because experience so frequently showed them right.*[5]

Jamie gazed about the audience. He had already exceeded his allotted time and sensed not only their interest but also some confusion and perhaps disappointment. Most believed in the heroic accomplishments of Western science and its commitment to "saving the world." By praising the wisdom of primitive peoples, he may have deflated or at least tarnished his own and, by implication, society's image. He concluded on what he hoped might be a more reassuring note.

"I certainly do not wish to denigrate contemporary science and technology or its record of accomplishments. Modern ecology has made many important discoveries in understanding and protecting the world's rapidly disappearing species and natural heritage. Our expanding knowledge of the earth's creatures is, without question, historically unprecedented. We have just begun to penetrate the mysteries of life, and this understanding will produce enormous discoveries and benefits in the future. Yet, as I personally found in the jungles of South America, we must also acknowledge the scientific and ecological urge in indigenous and primitive peoples. We must recognize, too, that this scientific tradition is not unique to our civilization. The desire to comprehend the world, empirically and systematically, is probably an inherent characteristic of all people and part of what it means to be human. A famous biologist, Professor Edward O. Wilson of Harvard, alluded to this possibility when he suggested: 'The more we know of other forms of life, the more we enjoy and respect ourselves. Humanity is exalted not because we are so far above other living creatures, but because knowing them well elevates the very concept of life.'[6] *Perhaps this constitutes as*

important a reason as any for resisting the current destruction of so much of life on earth. This knowledge provides the source of our understanding of the miraculous creation and, ultimately, ourselves."

The Scientific/Ecological Outlook

The scientific/ecological outlook on the natural world appears to represent a characteristic of all people. Certainly nature and living diversity provide a vast repository of human empirical knowledge. The yearning to comprehend life may sometimes seem like the brilliant afterglow of modern science, but it probably represents an ancient disposition buried deep within human genetics. As a species, we have a need to know and understand our world. This chapter describes several features of this scientific/ecological relationship to nature. The functions of empirical and objective knowledge, the desire to create categories and classificatory schemes, and the interest in conceiving conceptual frameworks for explaining nature and life are particularly emphasized.

The scientific/ecological tendency confers a variety of benefits that have been instrumental in our evolution and development. This expression of biophilia fosters intellectual and cognitive growth. It also encourages the pursuit of empirical knowledge, which, over time and by chance, inevitably yields some degree of practical benefit. Finally, the ecological/scientific outlook promotes an attitude of respect for nature and life, ultimately dissuading us from heedlessly destroying elements of our world. All of these functions have proved advantageous during the long course of human development—resulting in a biological tendency to respond to the natural world with a desire to know and understand. Given adequate nourishment and support, the scientific/ecological perspective emerges as an invaluable facet of our individuality and society.

The scientific/ecological perspective emphasizes, above all else, empirical and objective knowledge of the natural world.[7] This pursuit encourages patient, careful, and impartial inquiry. It implies systematic study and may even suggest modern science. Yet this outlook represents a likely characteristic of all peoples and cultures, though it may be especially developed in certain individuals and societies in certain times and places. Empirical investigation relies heavily on the senses of sight, smell, hearing, touch, and taste to form judgments about the natural and living world. It suggests a willingness to substantiate impressions through cautious and repeated observation. It means developing standards of evidence and, in its most refined expression, seeking comparative and sometimes quantifiable proof.

Often we encounter a behavioral progression in the scientific/ecological approach to inquiring about nature. Initially this perspective focuses on identifying and classifying objects of the natural world. Following careful and repeated examination, this approach produces an impression of regularities, which become the basis for rendering predictions under varying circumstances. After long and careful assessment, general concepts, principles, and even laws can emerge about the natural and living world. Throughout this progression, there is a primary commitment to deriving conclusions based on empirical observation and systematic inquiry of nature and life. These features of the scientific/ecological perspective emphasize its largely intellectual rather than emotional approach to life. Feelings are generally repressed in favor of a detached posture of observation and analysis of the natural world. Emotions are not exactly denied; rather, they are subordinated to a higher priority of cognitive and rational thinking.

A more scientific focus emphasizes the underlying properties of nature and therefore inclines to be reductionistic. The primary units of interest often occur below the level of species, ecosystems, and landscapes. With regard to living creatures, the emphasis is usually on the physical and mechanical functioning of organisms, bodily parts, and, more recently, cells and genes. Anatomy, morphology, physiology, taxonomy, and, today, cellular and molecular biology represent major intellectual focuses. A more ecological focus, by contrast, stresses an understanding of species, their relationship with other creatures, and associated properties of nature. Here the connections and interdependencies among organisms and environments constitute major concerns. Understanding life necessitates observing the links among plants, animals, and habitats. Emergent properties of nature at higher levels of organization—species, families, orders, classes, kingdoms, ecosystems, and landscapes—become major concerns.

The notion of an ecosystem especially presumes an organized and persistent flow of energy and nutrients essential to the long-term survival of the creatures that make up its constituent parts. While not technically alive, ecosystems strike us as quasi-living entities with boundaries, patterns, and structural integrity persisting over time.[8] The most recognizable ecosystems usually contain some element of water—wetlands, swamps, rivers, ponds, watersheds, coral reefs. These areas often reveal distinctive borders, an extensive degree of species interdependence, and a stable character.

The ecosystem concept may seem quite modern and thus at odds with the previous assertion that a scientific/ecological outlook is a characteristic of all peoples and cultures throughout history. Many of the complexities of ecosystem structure and function have indeed emerged only recently under the gaze of contemporary science. Yet the recognition of systemic properties and relationships in nature represents an ancient understanding. The inclination and capacity for empirical study, precise observation, and systematic analysis of nature persist to some degree among all peoples and societies.

Three Adaptive Benefits

The scientific/ecological perspective developed in the human species because advantages accrued to those who nurtured this inclination to observe and understand even a fraction of nature's extraordinary richness and diversity. Three benefits, as noted, stand out in particular: intellectual growth and development; empirical knowledge and understanding; and a restraint and respect for nature and life. Collectively these functions fostered the emergence of a scientific/ecological perspective of nature as a genetically encoded tendency in the human species. Let us explore each benefit in somewhat more detail.

INTELLECTUAL GROWTH

The scientific/ecological perspective of nature can enhance human cognition. Precise observation and empirical study require care, patience, and a highly refined learning capacity. Nature's extraordinary diversity offers a limitless opportunity for building knowledge and sharpening mental acuity, especially among young people.

Intellectual growth requires critical thinking skills, problem-solving abilities, and an analytical capacity. Identifying, classifying, and understanding natural processes hones the inquiring mind. Few arenas of life provide so much opportunity for orderly and creative investigation. Intellectual maturation is enhanced by distinguishing one creature from another, by perceiving connections among diverse categories of life, by examining the characteristics of feeding, reproduction, survival, and more. Benefits accrue from developing this knowledge quite apart from their immediate utility and obvious application. Scrutinizing and analyzing the many complexities of our detailed and constantly changing world inevitably increases cognitive development and understanding.

The psychologist Benajamin Bloom has described a taxonomy of critical thinking skills characteristic of all peoples and cultures.[9] These cognitive abilities include knowledge, comprehension, application, analysis, synthesis, and evaluation. Studying natural processes offers people a challenging and accessible means for developing these intellectual capacities. For example, the ability to acquire knowledge, according to Bloom, requires a facility for assembling facts and figures—a capacity greatly enhanced by identifying and classifying aspects of the natural world. Comprehension stresses interpreting and understanding these empirical realities—a tendency fostered by translating specific knowledge of nature into categories of related functions and processes. Application puts this knowledge to use in varying situations—an ability stimulated by distinguishing one environmental feature from another. Analysis involves teasing apart elements or patterns nested within an overall structure, while synthesis is the reverse process of integrating distinctive objects into an overall whole. Dissecting and integrating elements and processes in nature offers considerable opportunity for developing these advanced cognitive capacities. Finally, evaluation emphasizes discerning worth and importance—an ability fostered by judging the relative significance of particular aspects of the natural world.

These cognitive and critical thinking skills can, of course, develop in other learning contexts. Yet nature provides a convenient, always stimulating, and unlimited stage for this process of building, refining, and honing our intellectual development, again especially for the young and inquiring mind. Nature offers a universal classroom for learning and instruction—a place where, independent of culture and history, intellectual capacity can be nurtured and developed, whether among the Foré of New Guinea, the Inupiaq of Alaska, or people in modern society. Our species' inherent inclination to engage in study and observation has always fed upon nature's never-ending mystery and diversity.

EMPIRICAL KNOWLEDGE

In addition to building intellectual capacity, the scientific/ecological perspective fosters an empirical understanding of the natural world. This knowledge becomes initially manifest in identifying differences among species, habitats, and other environmental elements.

Natural history remains an important aspect of this study today. It is reflected in such recreational and professional pursuits as birding, insect collecting, geological study, and others. Its ancient character is suggested by Jared Diamond's description of the "primitive" Kalam people's ability to distinguish among more than 1,400 plant and animal species.[10] Beyond identifying individual elements, scientific/ecological study also promotes an understanding of relationships among species and natural systems. This knowledge can be obtained by discerning visual affinities and functional connections among plants, animals, and habitats.

The scientific/ecological capacity often derives from studying "lower" creatures like insects and other invertebrates.[11] This stems from the greater number and diversity of these organisms and their role in such basic ecological processes as pollination and seed dispersal, predation and parasitism, decay and decomposition, nutrient and energy cycling. Invertebrates compose some one-half to two-thirds of the 10 to 100 million species on this planet. Of the 1.7 million species already scientifically identified, there are approximately 900,000 insects and spiders, including 300,000 beetle, 150,000 butterfly and moth, and more than 100,000 ant species.[12] By comparison, only 9,000 bird and 4,000 mammal species have been classified to date. Moreover, the small size of most invertebrates hardly diminishes their ecological importance. Comparisons of the biomass in a typical American northeastern forest—the weight of its organic matter—reveal some 1,000 kilograms per hectare of insects, spiders, and earthworms, compared to just 18 kilograms for all wild vertebrate species, and a similar figure for humans.[13]

These calculations reflect the significance of invertebrates as a stock of edible organisms at the base of most food and energy chains. Invertebrates also support the existence of many plant species through such critical life-support processes as pollination, seed dispersal, and protecting against the destructive impact of other organisms. Eliminating certain invertebrates can result in the disappearance of entire species whose survival depends on these connections. Coral reefs, for example, have been linked to the existence of perhaps one-third of all marine fish species. The role of insects in plant reproduction is illustrated by the 5,000 or so bee species involved in pollinating activities in North America alone, including many agricultural crops worth billions of dollars annually.[14] Parasitic and predatory insects help prevent pest infestations, and many invertebrates perform the critical functions of decomposing wastes and helping to maintain soil fertility. As indicated in Chapter 2, invertebrates decompose the great majority of human and livestock wastes. Worms and ants especially assist in disintegrating fibrous tissues, mixing organic materials, and increasing soil fertility and drainage.

Still, it appears that only a small number of people evince curiosity or sympathy for the spineless kingdom—people usually characterized by an especially refined scientific/ecological outlook on life. All expressions of biophilia, however, tend to emphasize the significance and appeal of certain species or natural elements. As noted in previous chapters, the utilitarian outlook emphasizes creatures of material significance while the aesthetic outlook stresses the larger, more colorful, and visually charismatic species. Subsequent chapters will reveal other expressions of biophilia emphasizing different species and natural processes, each constituting a special lens focusing on a particular slice of the biological spectrum. The scientific/ecological perspective merely trains its lens on a more obscure and generally less appreciated category of life. The cumulative result of all these perspectives of biophilia, however, embraces a remarkable proportion of life on earth.

Apart from the curiosity value offered by these creatures, why did a scientific/ecological interest in invertebrates become ingrained in the human species? Over time and purely by chance, the knowledge accumulated from studying these and other organisms produces tangible benefits for people and society. Astute observation and understanding of even a fraction of life's extraordinary diversity eventually confers adaptational gains and advantages. Knowing well any aspect of the natural world's vast developmental matrix inevitably leads to a recognition of how a particular creature or natural process can benefit individuals and society. In the short run, the empirical examination and study of oddities in nature may appear esoteric. In the long run, this tendency reveals how serendipitous gains lurk behind even the most obscure human proclivities for affiliating with nature and life.

RESTRAINT AND RESPECT FOR NATURE

Fascination for the natural world almost always produces respect and a desire for its healthy perpetuation and protection. The more we know of life and natural process, the more we seek to maintain its values—

both explicit and latent, both known and unknown.[15] Probing the mysteries of even a fraction of creation expands the realization of how much we can learn from nature: any distinctive expression of the living mosaic provides a perennial source of inquiry and discovery. Admiration and respect derive from recognizing the many advantages that accrue from understanding even obscure organisms and natural processes. Only the ignorant view a natural element as an irrelevant, superfluous, or dispensable aspect of the human experience.[16]

A scientific/ecological perspective, moreover, fosters a profound appreciation of life's diversity. The more we know about other creatures and environments, the more we become filled with an astonishing regard for the extraordinary ingenuity of the biological enterprise. This realization of the worth of even mundane expressions of life caused Scott McVay, executive director of the Geraldine R. Dodge Foundation, to observe: "Roman Vishniac found more wonder in a drop of pond water than in travelling to the most remote places on the planet. . . . Dr. Karl Von Frisch . . . said there [is] miracle enough in a single species to provide a life's work."[17]

The desire to preserve and protect living diversity derives from recognizing the many benefits that eventually flow from knowing even a fragment of all the survival strategies found in nature. Every species, every ecological relationship, reflects the fine-tuned consequences of countless adaptations occurring over unimaginable time intended to fashion some solution to life's continual challenge. Appreciating these specialized virtues engenders a view of other species as following paths parallel to our own within a great evolutionary stream. Reflecting this realization, the writer Henry Beston remarks: "In a world older and more complete than ours [other creatures] move finished and complete, gifted with extensions of the senses we have lost or never attained, living by voices we shall never hear. They are not brethren, they are not underlings, they are other nations, caught with ourselves in the net of life and time, fellow prisoners of the splendor and travail of the earth."[18]

The scientific/ecological perspective engenders an awareness and appreciation of nature's inherent value. Rarely do we harm the focus of our respect. Only fools damage processes they do not fully understand or that some day may prove beneficial. The informed recognize the advantages inevitably deriving from knowing nature well. Certain cultures and historical epochs have, of course, caused catastrophic injury to the natural world. Yet a deep-seated aversion to destroying life looms strong in the human species—especially when fostered by a scientific/ecological understanding of natural complexity and variability. The inclination to respect and protect life became embedded in the human psyche because we internalized the recognition of the manifold advantages ultimately stemming from our better understanding of life.

Chapter Five

Nature As Metaphor

Certain plants, animals, and landscapes prompt images, myths, and symbolic projections. This chapter considers the natural world as a source of communication and thought. This function of nature in many ways represents an outgrowth of all the expressions of biophilia, which induce both fantastic as well as realistic representations of the natural world. Aesthetic perspectives of natural diversity, for example, stimulate images of beauty symbolized by swans and ladybugs, roses and orchids, babbling brooks and meandering streams. A utilitarian outlook conjures up impressions of busy bees and beavers and occasions when we work like dogs. Symbols of power and strength bring to mind bulls, stags, and mighty mountains. Spiritual reflection inspires images of lotus blossoms and the miraculous metamorphosis of caterpillars into butterflies. Snakes, spiders, rats, and sometimes wolves prompt images of fear and occasional loathing. All expressions of biophilia offer analogous opportunities for image, metaphor, and symbol.

This chapter's focus on the symbolic meaning of nature views this tendency as yet another expression of our innate inclination to affiliate with the natural world. Other aspects of biophilia—the aesthetic, the scientific, the utilitarian, for instance—prompt images and symbols, but these originate in the realistic experience of the natural world—

primarily engaging nature on its own terrain and on its own terms. The symbolic expression of biophilia, by contrast, brings nature into ourselves and transforms it into something distinctively different. The natural world as symbol and myth originates in the human mind and thinking process.

Nature has always provided people with a rich source for creating, shaping, and giving expression to our species' remarkable capacity for communication and thought.[1] We employ the natural world as the raw material for developing and expediting the exchange of information and understanding among generations of our kind. We accomplish this through language, story, myth, fantasy, dream, and other communicative means. More than any other creature, humans use sound, speech, and sign to facilitate thought. This tendency relies on images, symbols, and stories—all creations of the human mind as much as reflections of reality. As the writer Kathryn Morton suggests: "What got people out of the trees was something besides thumbs and gadgets. What did it . . . was a warp of the simian brain that made us insatiable for patterns—patterns of sequence, of behavior, of feeling—connections, reasons, causes: stories."[2]

The anthropologist and veterinarian Elizabeth Lawrence uses the term "cognitive biophilia" to describe the place of the natural world in fostering human communication.[3] The French anthropologist Claude Lévi-Strauss suggests that nature offers people as much food for thought as for physical sustenance.[4] The ecologist Paul Shepard argues that symbolic images of nature, especially of animal life, provide a fundamental basis for the formation of human intelligence.[5] He contends: "Human intelligence is bound to the presence of animals. They are the means by which cognition takes its first shape and they are the instruments for imagining abstract ideas and qualities. . . . They are the code images by which language retrieves ideas from memory at will. . . . They enable us to objectify qualities and traits. . . . [They] are used in the growth and development of the human person, in those most priceless qualities we lump together as 'mind.'"[6]

This chapter emphasizes how nature as symbol and metaphor has promoted three areas of human maturation: language acquisition, psychological development, and everyday communication and thought. Each function reflects on how the natural and living world has helped shape human intellectual and imaginative capacity. But before we consider these impacts, let us look at some of the ways people use nature symbolically to express feelings, thoughts, and beliefs.

Symbolic Expressions of Nature

How does our symbolic use of nature typically reveal itself? Above all, we employ natural images to represent feelings and thoughts. Nature provides a vast reservoir of symbols for conveying meaning through metaphor, analogy, and abstraction. These images are sometimes trite, at other times profound, occasionally realizing levels of meaning beyond words. Richard Nelson suggests that nature as metaphor aspires to "images that hint of something much larger and deeper than we're . . . able to penetrate."[7] In his poem, *Leaves of Grass,* Walt Whitman invokes this power for symbolizing nature:

> I find I incorporate gneiss, coal, long-threaded moss, fruits, grains, esculent roots,
> And am stucco'd with quadrupeds and birds all over,
> And have distanced what is behind me for good reasons,
> But call any thing back again when I desire it.
>
> In vain the speeding or shyness,
> In vain the plutonic rocks send their old heat against my approach,
> In vain the mastodon retreats beneath its own powder'd bones,
> In vain objects stand leagues off and assume manifold shapes,
> In vain the ocean setting in hollows and the great monsters lying low,
> In vain the buzzard houses herself with the sky,
> In vain the snake slides through the creepers and logs,
> In vain the elk takes to the inner passes of the woods,
> In vain the razor-bill'd auk sails far north to Labrador.
> I follow quickly, I ascend to the nest in the fissure of the cliff.[8]

Animals play an especially critical role in this symbolic capacity.

These creatures simulate people and society because they possess eyes, move, form attachments, and on occasion become our friends as well as our adversaries.[9] We dress them in clothes, disguise our feelings within them, employ their image to express our many fears and fantasies. As Elizabeth Lawrence notes: "The human need for metaphoric expression finds its greatest fulfillment through reference to the animal kingdom. No other realm affords such vivid expression of symbolic concepts. The more vehement their feelings, the more surely do people articulate them in animal terms. . . . Indeed, it is remarkable to contemplate the paucity of other categories for conceptual frames of reference, so preeminent, widespread, and enduring is the habit of symbolizing in terms of animals."[10]

Animals emerge in our speech and idioms, in our fables and fairy tales, in our myths and dreams, helping to convey a multiplicity of feelings, thoughts, and imaginings.[11] We encounter in our everyday life the characteristics of familiar animals used to project images and reflect judgments: a wolf intimates seduction, a fox slyness, a snake treachery, a lamb innocence, a worm deceit, a crab cantankerousness. The list goes on reflecting the use of animal imagery in "thousands of figures of speech, phrases, colloquialisms, and neologisms."[12]

Nature as image and metaphor can take the shape of a single word, a figure of speech, a phrase, a character, a plot. We use these symbols to elicit understanding. The message can be as eloquent as a Walt Whitman poem or as ephemeral, but nonetheless relevant, as Elizabeth Lawrence's recounting of newspaper descriptions of the 1992 American presidential candidates:

> One columnist characterized George Bush as a dog, specifically a Corgi, "dashing around trying to please everyone," appearing "yappy," lacking true conscious awareness by being merely "focussed on the moment, the instant at hand," and having demonstrated "dogged determinism" in waging the Gulf War. Bill Clinton is seen as a cat, "fuzzy," with "feline smugness," a "weakness for pleasure," and possessing multiple lives as evidenced by "resurrecting himself at each new scandal." Jerry Brown is a

> ferret, a clever critter whose "existence is rather pointless." Paul Tsongas is a hamster, "cuddly and vaguely pathetic," who "runs really fast on that wheel, round and round," getting nowhere. Patrick Buchanan is a "vampire bat" who "usually comes out at night . . . and drinks from the veins of helpless liberals. Like the winged rodent . . . some of his ideas are rather batty."[13]

Nature can be the source of terms and expressions whose origins become obscured by time. The anthropologist Edmund Leach, for example, found that many words of profanity and verbal abuse, both in English and other languages, reflect names applied to domesticated animals.[14] A sample in English includes "bitch," "cock," "ass," "swine," "pig," "pussy," even the words "screw," associated with a pig's phallus, or "cunt," etymologically derived from the Old English word "cunny" for rabbit. The reasons for this connection seem obscure, but Paul Shepard, drawing on the work of Leach and Lévi-Strauss, suggests it reflects the "culturally unclear . . . perceived as unclean."[15] Domesticated animals exist ambiguously in a cultural limbo between the human and natural worlds, their taxonomic status conflicting with the human penchant for orderly categorization. A dog may technically be a subspecies of the wolf, but its symbolic status remains altogether different—and more ambiguous. The emotional and cognitive significance of such relationships to the natural world render these subjects a valuable source of mental imagery, even if we fail to recognize the psychological basis for these symbolic projections or their origins.

Nature as symbol figures prominently in the fables, myths, and tales of all cultures and historical periods. The human ability to convey stories relies heavily on the imagery of nonhuman creatures and natural landscapes.[16] Four characteristics of this storytelling should be noted. First, the creatures often assume bizarre and sometimes supernatural forms. Jonah's whale, the wolves of Remus and Romulus, the bears in Goldilocks, "Bambi" the deer, "Babe" the talking pig, "Kermit" the frog—all bear only passing resemblance to their counterparts in the wild. Second, children constitute the primary audience for these stories, although their appeal frequently cuts across all age groups and remains powerfully seductive throughout life. Third, the plots of many classic tales occur in a wide variety of cultures, though specific animal characters and landscapes may vary. For example, some five hundred versions of the Cinderalla story have been identified in diverse cultures.[17] And fourth, anthropomorphism runs rampant throughout these stories: animals frequently play the role of people in disguise. The complex and often threatening issues of authority, sexuality, power, maturation, and loss occurring in many of these tales appear to be rendered more tolerable when cloaked in a nonhuman creature's image.[18]

Three Adaptive Benefits

How does this all relate to the central issue of the adaptive significance of nature imagery and symbolism? Nature as symbol, as we will see, emerged because of its beneficial importance in human evolution and development. The remainder of this chapter, drawing particularly on the insights of Paul Shepard, will stress three of these benefits: language acquisition (especially among young children), psychosocial development (especially for adolescents), and everyday communication and thought (especially with adults).[19]

LANGUAGE ACQUISITION

Various illustrations have been offered of nature imagery used in language and speech. But why do we encounter so many words, phrases, idioms, slang, and other linguistic forms that draw on the natural world to convey meaning and thought? Is it mere convenience, or does it have a deeper and more functional significance?

The symbolic use of nature appears to be instrumental in language acquisition, especially among young children. The learning of language relies on the capacity to sort objects into progressively more refined classifications.[20] Language involves an extraordinary range of distinctions that organize meaning. The use of complex labels helps differentiate and describe objects, thoughts, and feelings. This linguistic facility depends on rendering ever more subtle distinctions, groupings, and taxonomies.

How does this vast sorting process occur? For the young child, developing classifications requires clear boundaries separating distinct objects. Where do we encounter numerous, conveniently available, emotionally significant, and unquestionably distinguishable subjects for these categorizations? When we look about us with the eyes of the growing child, the natural world, especially the living world, provides an obvious source for this diversity. Nature offers an endless template of opportunities for practicing the art of classification. Distinct boundaries separating natural objects fosters sorting, classifying, and, most of all, naming. Living diversity provides a magic well of emotionally compelling images for applying the art of ordering and labeling so integral to language development.

This use of nature remains prominent even in modern times when we rely so much on books and formal instruction for teaching children about language, counting, and other basic skills. When we examine, for example, children's preschool books, we find that most of the stories focusing on words and numbers use images of the natural world.[21] One tall giraffe, two big elephants, three fat hippos, four furry bears, five snarling wolves, six fuzzy peaches, and seven towering trees represents a far more compelling instructional set than one tall chair, two big boxes, three fat computers, four furry coats, five snarling telephones, six fuzzy shirts, or seven towering telephone poles. Such objects may be useful aspects of everyday life, but they lack the emotional power to captivate and enchant the growing child.

Instructing children depends not only on clearly distinguishable objects but also on movement and animation, emphasizing how often life stimulates and arouses other life. Sometimes we question the ecological and practical significance of charismatic creatures like wolves, tigers, or bears. But what this calculus overlooks is the symbolic importance of such species. Large and charismatic life forms fascinate and charm the young child. One can hardly find a more absorbing subject for facilitating the task of grasping, through language, the meaning of our large and complex world.

Classifying nature provides opportunities for more sophisticated linguistic groupings and sortings. Young children, for example, readily distinguish among bears, wolves, snails, and clams, but they also discern how these creatures can be further grouped into two categories: mammals and mollusks. This process progresses to ever more complex distinctions, offering additional opportunities for refined orderings and language learning.[22] The classification of birds, for instance, offers an illustration. The child initially observes birds as winged and feathered creatures and sets them apart from other objects. Many kinds of birds, however, soon become recognizable. Although the child may be able to name only a few of the more than seven hundred bird species found in the United States, ample opportunities exist for naming, identifying, and classifying. Moreover, many obvious affinities occur among these various species grouped as songbirds, ducks, raptors, shorebirds, woodpeckers, and so on—providing yet further opportunities for categorizing. The young child's capacity to render these distinctions may be limited, but these variations offer many chances for the ever more refined practice of naming and sorting.

The value of these subjects of being alive is often critical. The very animation of the creatures makes the process of identification especially appealing to the young child. As Paul Shepard suggests: "Hundreds of centuries of human experience have generated our drive to master the skills of category making as we learn to speak, first in nouns and verbs. Animals are the primordial ground for this endeavor because they are the most nearly perfect set of distinct but related entities, and perhaps because they are alive like us."[23] The utility of nature—living nature—in language development helped to create our inclination to respond to natural diversity through the use of images and symbols.

PSYCHOSOCIAL DEVELOPMENT

Symbolizing and fantasizing nature helps us to confront issues of human identity and selfhood, as well, especially during adolescence.

Living diversity figures prominently in the myths, fairy tales, and fantasies of the maturing child. These storytelling forms give children critical assistance in encountering, and then resolving, difficult aspects of emotional development.

Symbolizing nature enables people and cultures to confront basic dilemmas of authority and independence, order and chaos, good and evil, love and sexuality, parochialism and worldliness, in a tolerable yet compelling and instructive manner. This process has been described by Carl Jung in the symbolic use of dreams, Claude Lévi-Strauss in the case of totems and taboos, Joseph Campbell through myths and legends, and Bruno Bettelheim in fairy tales and children's stories.[24] Each describes how humans use nature's imagery to face and sometimes resolve fundamental issues of human maturation, identity, and selfhood.

We might take as an example Carl Jung's examination of a young woman's symbolic use of nature in her dreams. Laden with images of the natural world—particularly images of other creatures—this girl's dreams attempt to navigate the perilous journey of puberty, especially the problems of change, sexuality, and identity. Jung's recounting of the girl's highly disturbing visions illustrates the many ways she and others use natural symbols to seek psychological balance and restoration. Her dreams, according to Jung, included the following images:

1. The evil animal, a snakelike monster with many horns, kills and devours all other animals. But God comes from the four corners . . . and gives rebirth to all the dead animals.
2. An ascent into heaven, where pagan dances are being celebrated; and a descent into hell, where angels are doing good deeds.
3. A horde of small animals frightens the dreamer. The animals increase to a tremendous size, and one of them devours the little girl.
4. A small mouse is penetrated by worms, snakes, fishes, and human beings. Thus, the mouse becomes human . . .
5. A drop of water is seen, as it appears when looked at through a microscope. The girl sees that the drop is full of tree branches . . .
6. A bad boy has a clod of earth and throws bits of it at everyone who passes. In this way, all the passers-by become bad.

7. A drunken woman falls into the water and comes out renewed and sober.
8. The scene is in America, where many people are rolling on an ant heap, attacked by the ants. The dreamer, in a panic, falls into a river.
9. There is a desert on the moon where the dreamer sinks so deeply into the ground that she reaches hell.
10. In this dream the girl has a vision of a luminous ball. She touches it. Vapors emanate from it. A man comes and kills her.
11. The girl dreams she is dangerously ill. Suddenly birds come out of her skin and cover her completely.
12. Swarms of gnats obscure the sun, the moon, and all the stars, except one. That one star falls upon the dreamer.[25]

The young girl repeatedly invokes visions of other creatures to objectify the struggles of her psychological development. In trying to unlock the meaning of these dreams, Jung as therapist, seeks to comprehend the pattern of her painful transition and offers her hope of achieving its healthy resolution. All people and cultures similarly employ nature's imagery—usually in less extreme and disturbing ways—to work toward resolving difficult maturational dilemmas of psychosocial development and identity.

The French anthropologist Claude Lévi-Strauss similarly explores the mythological use of nature.[26] He has described how certain myths allow cultures to confront universal quandaries of life including unity versus differentiation, wholeness versus fragmentation, relationship versus diversity. Myths of nature help humans address the paradox of being apart from, yet integral with, the rest of creation. Totemic creatures provide the means for people to establish a unique identity within a society while integrating with a larger universe beyond the limits of culture, place, and time.

Bruno Bettelheim has explored the symbolic use of nature in fairy tale and children's story as a way of fostering psychological development.[27] Animal images especially allow the maturing child an oblique, disguised, yet powerful means for confronting basic issues of individual identity and relationship. This masquerade permits many taboo subjects—such as sexuality and parental authority—to be examined in an instructive, mysterious, yet enchanting manner. Paul Shepard elucidates the power of these stories and Bettelheim's valuable insights:

> The fairy tale dramatizes the intrinsic childhood worries which the youthful listener unconsciously interprets as his own story and his own inner self. . . . Bettelheim believes the problems to be universal, having to do with protection from malicious relatives, the uncertain intentions of strangers, one's verbal or physical limitations such as the skills of speech or strength, the bodily changes and functions associated with growth, frightening dreams, fear of the dark, oedipal feelings, sibling rivalry, jealousy and envy, and the child's sense of limited intelligence, information, or techniques which adults already possess. . . . Every story is a magic prophecy of personal transcendence. . . . Their message is that special skills, often the powers represented by different animal species, will come to the rescue, solve the problems, save the day, and guarantee a happy lifetime.[28]

These examples suggest how symbolizing nature in dream, myth, and fairy tale can assist us in facing basic issues of selfhood in a compelling yet bearable manner. In these stories, we encounter ourselves through a glass darkly—thus muting the anxiety and uncertainty of personal identity and social relationship. "Anthropomorphism" helps render the enigmatic and challenging issues of desire, need, and conflict more palpable and captivating.[29] Nature provides a symbolic methodology for psychological growth—as critical to human welfare as the use of the natural world for producing food and scientific understanding. Alluding to this evolutionary significance, Paul Shepard remarkes: "For five thousand human generations animals served our species as delicate signs of the way the world goes, as elaborate metaphors and symbols, as spiritual beings, and as themselves—beautiful and imponderable counterplayers in a mysterious cosmos. In the immensity of time, humans acquired, deep in their hearts, the expectation that animals signify."[30]

COMMUNICATION AND THOUGHT

Symbolizing nature is also a device for assisting everyday communication and thought, especially among adults. People employ the imagery of the natural world in the language of the street, in the metaphors of the marketplace, in oratory and debate. This ubiquitous occurrence suggests a universal and indispensable means for everyday interaction and discourse.

The earthy language of the street provides a banal example of nature as symbol. Daily conversation alludes to pigs, worms, cockroaches, bitches, weeds, mud, dirt, slime, and more. The modern world of advertising invokes many images of nature for a variety of product promotion purposes. Marketeers bombard us with stingrays, firebirds, mustangs, jaguars, foxes, eagles, bats, spiders, sharks, bears, bees, and a vast menagerie of creatures attempting to direct our material needs and patterns of consumption. A recent *New York Times* article focusing on the most significant marketing event of our time—the Super Bowl—reveals the extent of this reliance on symbolizing nature, especially animals:

> The Rams, Bengals and Eagles were missing from Super Bowl XXX along with the Colts, Jaguars and Cardinals. But in their absence, advertisers unleashed an ark's worth of animals upon the game's record estimated audience of 138.5 million viewers. The beasts conscripted into pitching products on what is considered the biggest day in advertising included frogs, buzzards, horses and a penguin, . . . cattle, . . . lions and elephants and zebras, . . . wolves, . . . a spunky goldfish, . . . not to mention the pigs, . . . the skeleton of a dinosaur, . . . and the animated panther and coyote. . . . Animals in fact accounted for almost a quarter of the 47 spots that ran nationally during the game. . . . These marketers were no doubt strongly influenced by the . . . popularity of animals in popular culture. . . . Clearly, most people love animals, particularly when they are portrayed in an anthropomorphically pleasing manner.[31]

Symbolizing nature can render everyday communication and discourse more vivid and persuasive. The imagery can sometimes be trivial, but its pervasiveness suggests an essential role. The symbols may also be eloquent and deeply moving. Consider Emily Dickinson's reference to the lowly fly at the boundary of life and death:

> I heard a fly buzz—when I died—
> The stillness in the room
> Was like the stillness in the air—
> between the heaves of storm—
>
> The eyes around—had wrung them dry—
> And breaths were gathering firm
> For that last onset—when the King
> Be witnessed—in the room—
>
> I willed my keepsakes—signed away
> What portion of me be
> Assignable—and then it was
> There interposed a Fly—
>
> With blue—uncertain stumbling buzz—
> Between the light—and me—
> And then the windows failed—and then
> I could not see to see—[32]

Moral discourse, too, can exploit the imagery of nature to enliven debate and provide powerful illustration. Often the ability to move others relies on the use of natural symbol. The Bible speaks, for example, of "laying waste the mountains and hills, and drying up all the herbage . . . turning the rivers into islands, and drying up the pools."[33] We may argue abstractly how eradicating other life inevitably compromises our moral reliance on the natural world. Or we can invoke the words of John Muir to suggest: "How narrow we selfish, conceited creatures are in our sympathies! How blind to the rights of all the rest of creation. . . . A numerous class of men are painfully astonished whenever they find anything, living or dead, in all God's universe, which they cannot eat or render in some way . . . useful."[34] These examples represent but a few illustrations of the many ways nature's imagery powerfully challenges our feelings, thoughts, beliefs, and behavior.

A Continuing Reliance?

But is the tendency to use nature as symbol to facilitate human communication and thought still important in modern life? Have stuffed toys, cartoon characters, and abstract logos replaced the natural world as the primary source of our symbolic imagery? People today confront a bewildering diversity of artificial images. Has our increasing reliance on these products of modern technology, large-scale manufacturing, and the mass media rendered superfluous whatever metaphorical dependence we might have once had on the natural world? Does it really matter that real-life counterparts do not exist for celicas, acuras, luminas, conturas, tercels, ultimas, and more?

The possibility of having dispensed with our ancient need for symbolizing nature seems remote. The fruits of large-scale manufacturing and artificial fabrication have been with us for only a few centuries. This small fraction of human existence could hardly have rendered irrelevant the biological impress of more than 99 percent of our species' evolutionary history. Most of our myths, dreams, and stories still invoke the imagery of the natural world. We reflect in countless ways Walt Whitman's recognition that "the press of my foot to the earth springs a hundred affections."[35] We are unlikely to have dispensed with a symbolic dependence on nature encoded over thousands of generations. As Edward O. Wilson reminds us: "The brain evolved in a biocentric, not a machine-regulated world."[36]

To think we have been released from our age-old dependence on symbolizing nature may even be an arrogant, even a dangerous, illusion. The human ability to communicate and think effectively depends on a rich tapestry of natural images. No other realm of life provides an equivalent degree of complexity and diversity. We should not confuse large-scale fabrication and artificial imagery with the *content* of all this activity: stuffed toys, plastic creatures, cartoon characters, company logos, and other symbolic inventions continuously draw on nature. Today's dragons depend on snakes and dinosaurs, flying ships on winged creatures, "wookies" on large carnivores. We need "Willys" to free, "Bambis" to protect, "Yogis" to mock, "Lassies" to emulate, "Jaws" to intimidate. The natural world offers the symbolic substrate for artificial creation, just as wildlife forms the biochemical template for laboratory synthetics. Nature still provides the clay from which we mold and fabricate our images and projections.

A world devoid of natural symbolism would be a world of emotionally and mentally stunted people. A society reliant solely on artificial creation would strike us as not only odd but oppressive. Our current anxiety about the diminished state of civil discourse and the intellectual sterility of the mass media perhaps reflects this growing concern. Children's books increasingly lack the emotional power of many traditional stories, few modern politicians seem to possess the rhetorical power of a Julius Caesar or a Winston Churchill, and the level of everyday conversation seems coarser and ever more inarticulate. An impoverished relation between people and nature may underlie this decline in imagery and effective rhetoric. Environmental destruction produces not only material injury but also a wounded intellectual and communicative capacity. As Elizabeth Lawrence ponders: "It is difficult to predict the ways in which our diminishing interactions with the natural world . . . will affect expressions of cognitive biophilia. . . . If we continue our current policy of destructiveness toward nature, does this mean that human language will contain fewer and fewer symbolic references to animals [and nature]—with consequent impoverishment of thought and expression?"[37]

Chapter Six

The Quest for Exploration and Discovery

Henry Beston describes a typical day during his year living in a small cabin overlooking the dunes and ocean of outer Cape Cod where this remarkable spit of land juts far out into the North Atlantic:

> From the moment that I rose in the morning and threw open my door looking toward the sea to the moment when the spark of a match sounded in the evening quiet of my solitary house, there was always something to do, something to observe, something to record, something to study, something to put aside in a corner of the mind. There was the ocean in all weathers and at all tides, now grey and lonely and veiled in winter rain, now sun-bright, coldly green, and marbled with dissolving foam; there was the marsh with its great congresses, its little companies, its wandering groups, and little family gatherings of winter birds; there was the glory of the winter sky rolling out of the ocean over and across the dunes, constellation by constellation, lonely star by star.[1]

Beston's narrative reflects on his passion for nature as a source of wonder and discovery. Despite the solitude and isolation, he never seems bored or lonely. He appears inspirited with an emotional and intellectual excitement, immersed in a multiplicity of intimate relations with the living and nonliving world that surrounds and engulfs him. He indulges in searching and exploration, possessed by curiosity and imagination, enchanted by the many mysteries of the various creatures and habitats of this world of sand and sea. Despite his age—a man in his late 30s—he exults in an almost childlike innocence and delight: taking long and tireless walks along stretches of pristine beach, continually pursuing wildlife and other natural curiosities, indulging his craving for adventure and discovery. He is consumed by the many fascinations of an ever sensuous and stimulating world.

Nature and living diversity function as an unrivaled context for engaging the human spirit for curiosity, imagination, and discovery.[2] We take pleasure in encountering and immersing ourselves in wild nature—particularly when it elicits feelings and rhythms seemingly timeless. Humans have always mined intellectual and emotional ore from nature's rich matrix of shapes and forms, above all its conspicuous and emotionally charged plants, animals, and landscapes.

But do these ancient pleasures hold much relevance for us in today's industrial society? Beston's experience represents an unusual luxury, and few of us possess the opportunity or desire to emulate him. Our contacts with wild nature often seem confined to vicarious and indirect encounters on the television set, trips to the zoo, visits to the nearby park.

Yet a growing number of people in modern society do seek regular contact with the natural world, especially young adolescents and adults.[3] We witness an expanding interest in the outdoors. Hiking, camping, birding, fishing, whalewatching, ecotourism, and more have captured the participatory interest of many, perhaps even a majority. Indirect encounters with natural diversity have mushroomed as well—in zoos, botanical gardens, museums, and nature centers; through magazines, field guides, and books; via television, film, and photography. Consider these statistics:

- More Americans visit zoos during an average year than attend all professional baseball, basketball, and football games together.
- A majority of Japanese, Germans, and Americans report watching at least one wildlife and nature-related television program during a typical year.
- Visits to national parks and protected areas have soared so dramatically that many of these areas are now afflicted by an excess of popularity and interest.
- Encounters with wild nature in urban areas have increased as well—in city parks, local forests, and along nearby rivers, lakes, and seashores.
- Sales of field guides about aspects of the natural world have been extraordinary—Roger Tory Peterson's guide to the birds alone has sold more than 5 million copies since its first printing.
- Three million people in more than twenty countries seek the chance to see whales and other marine mammals in the wild—an activity that was unknown fifty or sixty years ago.
- Ecotourism is now the fastest-growing segment of the international travel industry and one of the most significant sources of income for countries like Kenya, Nepal, Costa Rica, and Ecuador.

How can we explain this growing interest in recreational contact with the natural world? Why has it persisted into the modern age? This desire has endured because, like all expressions of biophilia, it still has functional significance in human evolution and development. Discovery in the natural world continues to offer an unrivaled context for physical, emotional, and mental growth and maturation.

Four Adaptive Benefits

In this chapter, we will consider four adaptive advantages to be gained from intimate contact with nature: enhanced physical fitness and vitality; expanded curiosity and imagination; increased self-confidence and self-esteem; and greater calm and peace of mind. We will consider how modern society has nurtured these benefits by keeping alive opportunities for intimate contact with nature and living diversity—particularly through an array of recreational pursuits such as fishing, birding, hiking, hunting, whalewatching, visiting zoos and botanical gardens, as well as the vicarious experience of nature on film and television. We will nonetheless conclude with the sobering realization that much of modern life has eroded our chances for spontaneous and everyday encounters with wild nature, especially for young people. But first let us consider some of the positive benefits derived from the human inclination for contact with the natural world.

PHYSICAL FITNESS AND VITALITY

The desire to experience nature directly often originates in the simple pleasures derived from extending and exerting ourselves.[4] An aliveness flows from exercising our physical and mental endowment—especially when it involves a special encounter in nature, whether confronting the crashing waves of a pristine beach, hiking in a remote wilderness, or pursuing fish in a mountain stream. Intense physical stimulation can occur in ordinary settings as well, even settings we have experienced many times before. Yet the more spontaneous the encounter with nature, the more gratifying it typically seems.

Physical fitness is an obvious benefit derived from immersion in nature. Hiking, backpacking, canoeing, cross-country skiing, and other outdoor activities often require strenuous exertion and enhance our physical health and well-being. Even walking urban trails in a nearby park or forest, or along a local river or lake, can produce the sense of having engaged our body and spirit.

Humans require activity and arousal as a condition of physical and mental health. Our increasingly sedentary existence, however, challenges us to find ways for maintaining this conditioning. Sometimes we employ artificial means to achieve this end—through health clubs, exercise regimes, organized sports, and manipulative devices. Yet these contrivances rarely elicit the stimulation, spontaneity, and convenience afforded by the outdoors. Rarely do they offer the pleasures and benefits of direct contact with a physically challenging and aesthetically pleasing landscape in the wild.

Beyond the physical fitness, a feeling of aliveness flows from the intimate experience of nature. Immersing oneself in natural settings produces a heightened vitality—a sense of becoming more attuned and receptive to the myriad details of time and place. The gray rocks assume a more vivid texture, the amorphous vegetation comes alive with meaning and definition, the stillness of the landscape is replaced by a profusion of sounds and sensations, even the air takes on a discernible quality.[5] Our absorption produces a sharpened awareness and experience of the world: time seems stretched out; a sensation emerges of *living* life rather than just passing through it. And the less spoiled the natural setting, the more intense the feeling of endless, eternal rhythms. We seem to step back in time, reliving the experience of our distant ancestors.

CURIOSITY AND IMAGINATION

Intimate contact with nature also stimulates our curiosity and imagination.[6] It is only the naive who confront a formless landscape, monotonous, devoid of detail and differentiation. The alert, however, by immersing themselves in natural diversity, encounter a world of many shapes, features, traits, and movements. With this increased sensitivity to detail and difference, we nurture our capacity for inquisitiveness, inquiry, and creativity.

Heightened awareness is prompted by our sense of adventure and desire for exploration, especially among young people.[7] Mystery and discovery emerge for the growing person from searching the woods, seashore, and other environs. The child ventures forth, unsure but aroused, the moment filled with possibilities: the chance of finding some treasure, of confronting something fascinating, even relevant and useful. Challenge and excitement lurk around the next bend, hidden under a rock, concealed within a covert or among the vegetation.

Engaging one's curiosity invites creativity and intellectual development. The inquisitive mind is immersed in detail. The more engaged we are, the more we seek involvement and long for discovery. The evolutionary value of this quest is suggested by the observation: "The surest way to enrich the knowledge pool that will keep the flywheel of cultural evolution turning is to nourish the human spirit of curiosity."[8]

Immersing oneself in nature often produces feelings of wonder and awe. This sense of connection with the natural world is manifest in many ways: wonder at the tencity of a barnacle on a stormy seashore, awe at the agility of a mountain goat on a nearly vertical ledge, amazement at the synchrony of a school of migrating fish, admiration of the spinning of a spider's web. Almost any aspect of nature offers opportunities for appreciation and respect. Deep affiliation with natural detail and process provides the key to unlocking this potential. The more we observe the intricacies of nature, the more we recognize its extraordinary potential for eliciting wonder and an urge to discover.

People have always used the natural world to arouse their capacity for imagination and inquiry. We readily exercise this inquisitive spirit in wilderness, but it can also emerge in the creek around the corner, the woods in the nearby park, even the trees in our own backyard. All of these encounters have the power to elicit the curiosity and wonder reflected in Edward O. Wilson's observation: "The living world is the natural domain of the most restless and paradoxical part of the human spirit. Our sense of wonder grows exponentially: the greater the knowledge, the deeper the mystery and the more we seek knowledge to create new mystery. . . . Our intrinsic emotions drive us to search for new habitats, to cross unexplored terrain, but we still crave this sense of a mysterious world stretching infinitely beyond."[9]

A world of imagination and discovery awaits those willing to immerse themselves in natural diversity, whatever their socioeconomic privilege and formal education. Intimate contact with nature offers all of us the opportunity for exercising imagination. The biologist Gary Nabhan describes how as a high school dropout he labored on the railroad tracks of a nearby steel mill, yet still encountered in himself a deep predilection for exploring the natural world—in this case, the world of herons:

> It was then that I had my own magnetic encounter with an encoded legacy—a continuity with former generations of my own kind—that had [been] buried deep within my own consciousness. I realized that no matter where I was, I had the capacity to see the world as freshly as any naturalist could. Even in the most damaged of habitats, in the drudgery of the most menial labor, whatever wildlife remained could still pull at me deeply enough to disrupt business-as-usual. The behavior of those birds had overtaken my imagination, even though I had never demonstrated any scholarly inclinations toward ornithology. The herons awakened capabilities in me that formal education had not yet cultivated, for I felt welling up within me a profound desire to know those birds better. I felt the weight of the spike mall in my hand and the burden of labor I had before me, yet my heart flew with the herons.[10]

SELF-CONFIDENCE AND SELF-ESTEEM

For our ancient ancestors, the acquisition of outdoor skills offered invaluable advantages. Climbing, orienteering, hiking, observing, scanning, tracking, collecting, capturing, trapping—in general, being proficient in nature—conferred many benefits in the struggle to survive and succeed.[11] But are these tendencies still relevant in a world of modern technology, mass production, and urbanization? The skeptic might view these abilities as interesting, perhaps quaint, but nothing more, really, than a dispensable pleasure.

To view these natural proclivities as trivial and obsolete would be simplistic. Many benefits still derive from exercising competence in the natural world. Advantages accrue in any experience that enhances our capacity to react quickly, resolve new and challenging situations, overcome difficulties, and consume with efficiency.[12] Even today, critical thinking and risk taking remain attributes of an adaptive and successful life. Outdoor challenge offers important opportunities for developing these capacities and, along with the achievement, feelings of personal competence and confidence, especially for young people. Demonstrating skill and accomplishment in nature fosters self-esteem and self-respect. Proving one's worth in natural circumstances can instill feelings of independence and self-reliance.

These character-building traits have been revealed in various studies of the outdoors and wilderness experience. Many outdoor adventure programs have been found to produce increased self-esteem and self-confidence among the majority of participants. These benefits especially derive from building skills in natural settings. Professor Richard Schreyer of Utah State University and his colleagues report: "While not unique in [their] ability to afford self-concept enhancement, wilderness [experiences] possess many attributes particularly well-suited to the development of self-concept . . . including the presence of obstacles, challenges, opportunity for solitude, freedom from social forces, and enhanced ability to focus on self."[13] Dr. Alan Ewert, formerly with the U.S. Forest Service, concluded after examining various outdoor programs that enhanced well-being, problem-solving skills, physical fitness, and coordination often result from these experiences.[14] Participants also report that these programs exerted a significant impact on their personal development—and an enhanced capacity for confronting challenge and problem-solving situations—years after the experience.

The environmental psychologists Stephen and Rachel Kaplan offer additional insight regarding the character-building effects of wilderness and outdoor experiences.[15] They carefully observed high school and college participants of an outdoor challenge program in northern Michigan over a period of years. These students hiked and backpacked in small groups in rough terrain with two leaders, followed by solo wilderness trips. The program emphasized survival skills, physical challenge, and personal development. The researchers compared participants with a matched group of nonparticipants and interviewed all subjects immediately before, just after, and six months following the experience. Each participant also kept a journal of impressions. Participants reported being able to acquire various wilderness and outdoor skills far more quickly and efficiently than they had anticipated, even though most lacked relevant knowledge or experience. Mastering these abilities enhanced their feelings of competence and self-esteem: they learned to "read" the landscape, identify various plants and animals, secure food and water, and orient themselves in unfamiliar places. These skills emerged as an integral aspect of their improved self-image. Based on such research, Stephen Kaplan and his colleague Janet Talbot conclude: "Wilderness inspires feelings of awe and wonder, and one's intimate contact with this environment leads to thoughts about spiritual meanings and eternal processes. Individuals feel better acquainted with their own thoughts and feelings, and they feel 'different' in some way—calmer, at peace with themselves [and, as one participant remarked,] 'more beautiful on the inside and unstifled.'"[16]

These character-building effects have also been reported among groups of poor and urban children who participated in similar outdoor programs. Recent studies among inner-city youth in Baltimore, Houston, and elsewhere suggest that outdoor adventure programs can enhance self-awareness and improve academic and social performance.[17] These outdoor skills may be only marginally relevant to the everyday world of many of these participants. But the benefits of increased self-esteem and self-confidence they derived from demonstrating their competence, adaptability, and problem-solving skills in new and challenging situations offer many advantages in learning to cope with life. For these youth, the outdoors functions, as it always has, as an arena for promoting self-worth and personal capacity.

PEACE OF MIND

Immersing oneself in nature can paradoxically produce feelings of both calm and arousal—a heightened awareness coincident with an increased sense of tranquility. The common denominator here is the experience of reduced stress and anxiety. Roger Ulrich reports in this regard: "A consistent finding in well over 100 studies of recreation experiences in wilderness and urban nature areas has been that stress mitigation is one of the most important verbally expressed and perceived benefits."[18]

Intimate experience of nature and the outdoors frequently provides a way to escape, at least temporarily, from the pressures and strains of society. We confront a world more authentic, simple, and focused. We have the opportunity for sorting out priorities, for gathering strength and resolve, for relieving tension and anxiety. The solitude of nature can be an antidote to the excessive stimulation of modern life. The unrelieved cacophony of the contemporary world often cries out for mitigation and relief. Loud sounds signify danger and threat for most animals, and perhaps humans have internalized a similar aversion. The outdoors presents a time-honored means for experiencing tranquility, peace, and perhaps, as a consequence, an increased capacity for coping with everyday life.

The natural world offers the chance for reconnecting with a simpler and more genuine experience of self. Even the most physically demanding activities—backcountry hiking, wilderness camping, mountain climbing, river running—can provide relief from the tensions and complexity of contemporary life. These activities offer a directness of purpose and a safety valve for relieving anxiety. Such benefits may have instilled in us the proclivity to seek out nature as a way of achieving greater calm and peace of mind.

A Contemporary Quandary

These four benefits suggest the importance of direct contact and immersion in nature for human physical, intellectual, and emotional development. But does modern society offer sufficient opportunities for this degree of intimate experience of natural diversity? It is discouraging to realize how rarely today we experience routine, convenient, and spontaneous access to healthy and stimulating natural settings. A distinguishing feature of modern, especially urban, existence is the diminishing role of wild nature as an integral aspect of our everyday lives.

Still, as noted earlier, more people than ever participate in an extraordinary range of organized nature activities. We may be experiencing fewer direct encounters with wildness in our daily lives, but deliberately planned excursions to nature have expanded enormously. Moreover, the vicarious experience of the natural world through zoos, nature centers, film, art, photography, and television has become a fixture of contemporary existence.

But do these organized and vicarious experiences provide an adequate diet of intimate affiliation and immersion in nature? Can they compensate for the decline of spontaneous everyday encounters with natural and living diversity, especially among urban and suburban youth? We will address this complicated question in Chapter 11, but for the moment let us explore the impact and popularity of such nature-related activities as recreational fishing and hunting, birding, whale-watching, visiting zoos, and watching nature programs on film and television.

FISHING, HUNTING, AND OBSERVATION

Fishing and hunting are among the most ancient of human activities. The hunting-gathering way of life predominated for much of human history and became the basis for most of our species' evolutionary development.[19] Large-scale agriculture accounts for perhaps 5 percent of our time on earth; the industrial age comprises but a moment in our species' existence. Although the hunting-gathering way of life as a primary means of subsistence has largely disappeared, both hunting and fishing continue to remain widely prevalent as a recreational pastime. Some 10 percent of the American public participates in recreational hunting today, and at least 25 percent of the population either fishes or hunts for recreation during an average year.[20]

Although many hunt and fish for the harvest, few depend on the meat for commercial purposes or subsistence.[21] For most, the chance for intimate contact with nature represents an important motivation. These hunters and fishers especially cherish the opportunities for deep participatory involvement in natural surroundings. Closely experiencing wildlife and the outdoors constitute major attractions of the activity. Hunting and fishing confer a heightened awareness of the natural world. The Spanish philosopher José Ortega y Gasset describes elements of this satisfaction in the hunting experience: "When one is hunting, the air has another, more exquisite feel as it glides over the skin or enters the lungs; the rocks acquire a more expressive physiognomy, and the vegetation becomes loaded with meaning. All this is due to the fact the hunter, while he advances or waits crouching, feels tied through the earth to the animal he pursues."[22]

Some hunters and fishers claim the activities produce a more pronounced awareness of the link binding creatures with one another and to the natural environment. Through hunting and fishing they enter into the lives and experiences of other animals and participate in the movement of energy and matter through nature. This participatory relation to the natural world often seems difficult to achieve when one is merely an observer or outsider. Fishing and hunting provide an organizing basis for deep immersion in natural surroundings.

Despite the kill, many hunters and fishers claim great admiration and even affection for the prey species—a respect that derives, it seems, from knowing the animal at its best. The sportsmen and conservationists John Madson and Ed Kozicky maintain: "The hunter deeply respects and admire the creatures he hunts. This is the mysterious, ancient contradiction of the . . . hunter's character—that he can at once hunt the thing he loves. . . . Part of the hunter's deep attachment to wildlife may stem from the fact that he sees wild creatures at their best—when they are being hunted. It is then they are strongest, freest and sharpest."[23] José Ortega y Gasset suggests the hunter can achieve an empathetic experience of the prey animal: how it reacts and responds to the landscape and, above all, its pursuer: "A sensing and presentiment . . . lead the hunter to perceive the environment from the point of view of the prey, without abandoning his own point of view. This is paradoxical in itself and appears to be contradictory. . . . The pursuer cannot pursue if he does not integrate his vision with that of the pursued. This is to say, *hunting is an imitation of the animal*. . . . In that . . . union with the beast a contagion is immediately generated and the hunter begins to behave like the game."[24]

Still, either for reasons of opportunity, skill, or motivation, relatively few people pursue hunting or fishing today. These activities, therefore, offer only limited occasions for frequent, direct, and intimate contact with nature and living diversity in contemporary society. Other means for encountering wild nature today include organized observation—birdwatching and whalewatching, for example. One-quarter of Americans claim they birdwatch each year.[25] Only a minority can be called active or committed birders, however, in the sense of regularly using a field guide or binoculars and being able to identify more than a handful of species. Whalewatching statistics reveal that some 3 million people participate in this activity annually in more than twenty countries, a million in the United States alone.[26] Commercial whalewatching first appeared along the California coast during the 1950s. Although birding's lineage dates back many centuries, it has become a popular recreational pastime just since the nineteenth century, mainly in the United States and northern Europe.

Only a small proportion of birders pursue the activity with much commitment, knowledge, and skill. For these active birders, however, a strong motivation is often the desire for deep contact with the natural world. Research reveals these birders to be exceptionally knowledgeable, appreciative, and concerned about wildlife and its conservation. This appreciation may be encouraged by three characteristics of the activity. First, birding focuses on the species rather than the individual animal—and this may produce a strong ecological awareness. Second, many bird species associate with particular habitats—and this may foster an enhanced appreciation of ecosystems and natural processes. Third, the high energy requirements of many bird species often render these animals especially susceptible to environmental stresses and disturbance—and this may engender a greater awareness of the effects of pollution and habitat degradation.

Birding appears to encourage a deeper appreciation and knowledge of the natural world. Yet, like fishing and hunting, active birding is pursued by only a small number of people in modern society. Its potential, therefore, for offering a widely practiced means for intimate contact with nature seems questionable. But unlike fishing and especially hunting, birding requires little equipment or training and can be pursued in many settings, even urban ones. Thus the activity does hold considerable promise as a way of increasing people's experience of the natural world.

The impact of whalewatching appears more ambiguous.[27] Positive indications suggest this activity's popularity has increased considerably and has expanded the public's interest in whales, their conservation, and the marine environment. Moreover, a sense of adventure and discovery derives from encountering these huge and mysterious creatures in their ocean world. Yet research also suggests that the impact of whale-watching may be transient and superficial. Perhaps the restricted opportunity afforded for close and sustained contact with whales, as well as the minimal demands of this passive activity, account for its limited impact. Moreover, most whalewatching operations are not distinguished for the quality of the information conveyed. The limited availability of whalewatching—and the lack of close involvement in the lives of whales and the ocean environment—suggest this activity produces only a restricted understanding of the natural world.

CAPTIVE WILDLIFE

Zoos, aquariums, nature centers, botanical gardens, and other largely captive and urban displays of plants and animals represent common experiences of nature and wildlife in modern society. The popularity of zoos is suggested by the fact that every year some 135 million Americans attend the country's more than one hundred zoos and another 10 million visit the thirty-five most popular aquariums. Worldwide, approximately 350 million people annually visit more than six hundred zoos and aquariums. A majority of Americans, Germans, and Japanese also report visiting a zoo at least once during a typical year.[28]

The remarkable popularity of zoos and aquariums intimates a desire for maintaining contact with wild creatures, no matter how fleeting and indirect. People attend these facilities for many reasons: for the aesthetic appeal of the animals, the desire to be with family and friends, the presumably safe and attractive environment, and various educational and scientific purposes.[29] Encountering wild creatures involves an element of authenticity that no degree of reading or vicarious observation can ever replicate.[30]

But does this contrived encounter with nature provide a sufficiently nourishing experience of the natural world? Do the modern zoo and aquarium offer a deep relationship with wild lives, or merely an ephemeral taste of the natural world? Moreover, could viewing incarcerated wildlife produce a distorted picture of the creature and its environment, compromising the potential for these animals to instruct and inspire people with meaning and deep satisfaction? The modern zoo and aquarium seem caught somewhere between, on the one hand, easy entertainment and escape and, on the other, an enriching encounter with the natural world. These institutions seem to float at the edge of potential, unsure of their impact on people or the creatures they imprison and exhibit.

The beneficial impacts of zoos and aquariums may be constrained by the motivation of the typical visitor who largely pursues an undemanding encounter with captive animals. Most visits represent a chance to be with family and friends as much as to experience wild animals. Most visitors seek out creatures reminiscent of humans—the young especially desire contact with animals, whether feeding, touching, or making faces, even when admonished not to do so. Despite the wall between creature and visitor, a vital element of mystery somehow persists, along with an interest in discovery and communicating with a life in the wild.

Even so, how much lasting impact do the average zoo and aquarium exert? Research results are not encouraging. The typical visitor appears only marginally more appreciative, better informed, or engaged in the natural world following the experience. The average time spent at most exhibits is less than a minute; only a minority bother to read the information provided; rarely do they share the information with others. Interest is usually restricted to the larger, more active, and entertaining animals. Many visitors leave the zoo more convinced than ever of human superiority over the natural world. The visit's positive effects appear to be largely emotional and aesthetic. Yet a small minority of visitors do reveal substantially greater appreciation and concern for wildlife—primarily at zoos devoting considerable resources to naturalistic design, education, native wildlife, and a wide diversity of species.

The popularity of zoos and aquariums intimates considerable potential for enhancing awareness and an affinity for the natural world. Yet, as institutions focusing on the forced and sometimes frivolous display of wild lives, they also can foster a sense of separation and even alienation from nature. Zoos and aquariums must strive for innovative ways to connect the natural world more closely with their visitors' lives, emphasizing how natural diversity can enhance the possibilities for people to achieve a richer existence both emotionally and intellectually.

FILM AND TELEVISION

With the advent of visual technology such as film and television, today more people than ever in human history are able to enter into the lives of distant animals and natural habitats. We now encounter a remarkable diversity of the world's creatures and environments from the comfort and security of our homes and communities. Moreover, this experience of the natural world has existed for less than a century—a profound and revolutionary change in the human relationship to nature and wildlife. Attesting to the extraordinary popularity of this technological change, three-quarters and more of the German, American, and Japanese publics report watching at least one nature-related television program or film each year.[31] Film and television now represent the most frequent form of contact between people and wild nature.

But what is the impact of this experience? Does encountering nature and living diversity through film and television exert a lasting effect on people's perceptions and experience of the natural world? TV and film, after all, confront nature in an essentially vicarious, artificial, and noninteractive manner in the confines of an entirely human-dominated environment. Can this anesthetized experience offer sufficient challenge, mystery, and immersion? Research offers an uncertain answer.[32] Positive impacts are suggested by a rapid growth in environmental awareness and interest during the past half century—concurrent, that is, with the appearance of nature-related film and television programming. Studies in Japan and the United States find that a majority of people report their appreciation and knowledge of the natural world have been greatly influenced by watching film and television. Studies of popular feature-length films (*Never Cry Wolf, Free Willy, Gorillas in the Mist,* various Jacques Cousteau specials, and others) suggest these viewing experiences can engender widespread admiration for large and charismatic species.[33]

Still, studies indicate a shallow and ephemeral effect. Sometimes there is greater attachment to certain species and habitats, but this rarely involves much increased understanding of wildlife, ecological process, or human impacts on the natural environment. Popular film and television also seem limited in their capacity for conveying complexity and dealing with conservation issues. This failure may reflect intrinsic limitations of the video technology, as well as people's ability to avoid watching complicated, less entertaining, and "depressing" programs. Such preferences may explain why nature-related television programming tends to focus on natural history, action, adventure, sentimentality, and anthropomorphism. The informative and sophisticated depictions of nature and conservation that do appear are usually restricted to a public broadcasting audience of affluent, educated, and environmentally concerned citizens.

Today more people than ever encounter the wonders of nature and wildlife through film and television. Indeed, the parallel development of these media and a vastly expanded public concern for the natural world intimate a subtle and perhaps powerful influence. Yet the depth and lasting impact of this encounter remain uncertain. The vicarious and unrealistic experience of nature on film and television can often produce distortion, sentimentality, and naïveté. It may also leave fundamentally unsatisfied the yearning for direct and intimate contact with the natural world.

Diminished Experience?

We return to where we began: the quantity and quality of spontaneous and intimate encounters with nature and wildlife in contemporary society, particularly among young people and especially in urban and suburban settings. Significant increases in organized outdoor and recreational experiences of nature offer encouraging trends. Yet most of these encounters with nature are sporadic and indirect. Moreover, increasing urbanization and large-scale development have diminished enormous areas of natural habitat and caused profound declines in biological diversity. Clearly such trends are reducing the extent of accessible nature we can encounter as a routine and integral aspect of everyday life.

Many of the benefits of experiencing nature directly, as we have seen, depend on ongoing and spontaneous experience. Curiosity, imagination, awe, discovery, physical fitness, calm, peace of mind, enhanced self-confidence—all require intimate contact and immersion in natural settings. Sometimes these benefits can be derived through organized recreation and vicarious viewing of nature on film and television, but direct and spontaneous contact with natural settings remains essential.

The modern world appears to be embracing two opposing trends. On the one hand, more people than ever encounter nature in spectacular, unusual, and biologically diverse ways—the thermal springs of the Yellowstone basin, the grandeur of the Alaskan tundra, the coral reefs of the coastal oceans, the splendor and diversity of the tropical rain forests. Yet, typically, these experiences occur in sporadic and artificial ways. On the other hand, the everyday, unplanned, and impulsive experience of nature in nearby fields, wetlands, forests, and other habitats is slowly disappearing. Our contact with the natural world—an essential dimension of normal life—is eroding. The biologist Robert Pyle refers to this condition as "the extinction of experience."[34] Reflecting on his own childhood, he describes the need for more mundane encounters with nature:

> When people connect with nature, it happens *somewhere.* Almost everyone who cares deeply about the outdoors can identify a particular place where contact occurred. . . . My own point of intimate contact with the land was a ditch. Growing up on the wrong side of Denver to reach the mountains easily or often, I resorted to the tattered edges of the Great Plains on the back side of town. There I encountered a century-old irrigation channel. . . . Without a doubt, most of the elements of my life

> flowed from the canal. From the time I was six, this weedy watercourse had been my sanctuary, playground, and sulking walk. It was also my imaginary wilderness, escape hatch, and birthplace as a naturalist. Everyone has at least a chance of realizing a pleasurable and collegial wholeness with nature. But to get there, intimate association is necessary. A face-to-face encounter with a banana slug means much more than a Komodo dragon seen on television.[35]

Opportunities for young people to nourish their desire for engaging the natural world with imagination, adventure, exploration, and discovery have receded. This loss represents not so much a question of declining wilderness as the erosion of semi-wildness in the scattered plots of local neighborhoods, communities, and cities. Children deprived of these everyday opportunities for unstructured immersion in natural settings confront a world profoundly lacking in the power to instruct and equip them with the many adaptive benefits described in this chapter. The biologist Gary Nabhan remarks on the importance of these daily encounters with nature and living diversity—especially for young people:

> Over time, I've come to realize that a few intimate places mean more to my children, and to others, than all the glorious panoramas I could ever show them. . . . There are still many children in this world [who] have primary contact with wild nature. . . . Yet the percentage of children who have frequent exposure to wildlands and to other undomesticated species is smaller than ever before in human history. . . . While many children may visit zoos, watch nature films, or cuddle with pets and stuffed animals, their responses to other species [have become] less grounded on their own visceral experiences. . . . We need to return to learning about the land by being *on* the land, or better, by being *in* the thick of it. That is the best way we can stay in touch with the fate of its creatures, its indigenous cultures, its earthbound wisdom. That is the best way we can be in touch with ourselves.[36]

We will confront these complex issues again in the concluding chapters after we have examined all the ways natural diversity continues to assist in our physical, emotional, and intellectual growth and development. Two conclusions should already be evident from this chapter. First, direct contact and intimate affiliation with the natural world remain an important basis for engendering creativity, imagination, physical fitness, peace of mind, and self-esteem. Second, while modern society has retained and even enhanced opportunities for experiencing nature through outdoor recreation and innovative technology, everyday and spontaneous encounters with the natural world have greatly diminished.

Chapter Seven

Yearning for Kinship and Affection

All expressions of biophilia foster elements of thinking, feeling, and belief to varying degrees. The scientific/ecological perspective, for example, especially encourages intellectual growth and development. This outlook largely approaches nature from a dispassionate point of view: creatures are viewed more as representatives of their kind than as individuals eliciting loyalty, attachment, and affection. In this chapter, we will examine a more emotional outlook on life—a prespective stressing passionate affinities and attachment to other creatures. Just as with other expressions of biophilia, kinship and affection for the natural world have been critical in human evolution. In this case, they emerge as a basis for people's emotional maturation and development.

The Nature of the Bond

The proclivity to bond with elements of nature often depends on identifying humanlike feelings and attributes. Rather than seeing other species or even inanimate aspects of the natural world in anonymous terms, this perspective values them most for their individuality and emotionally appealing qualities. Strong affection and attachment prevail for certain animals, plants, and landscapes. This attitude toward nature focuses above all on the opportunities for emotional bonding and companionship—a connection so intense it sometimes engenders feelings of love. The orbit of human fellowship is extended to incorporate other creatures and landscapes into the intimacy of the human experience.

A degree of emotional connection can occur with many aspects of nature, but pet animals represent the most common focus of bonding to the nonhuman world.[1] Although this chapter will consider strong feelings of affection for wildlife and natural settings in general, the emphasis will be on the "companion animal"—the dogs, cats, parrots, gerbils, fish, and other creatures that become our intimates and presumed friends. These creatures frequently serve as sources of deep affection, personal responsibility, and feelings of kinship. The English historian Keith Thomas describes three characteristics of this kind of human/animal relationship: the creature receives a name; it becomes part of the human household; and, above all, it is never eaten.[2]

Emotional vulnerability can also accompany this degree of intimacy and affection. Our companions suffer hardship, illness, and death. Sometimes they even become burdens of dependency and disappointment, for humans routinely outlive two, three, and more generations of cats, dogs, and other companion animals. This can also extend beyond the companion animal to the wild. Forests, rivers, even inanimate cliffs and canyons, can become the objects of great affection as well. The destruction of these creatures and landscapes can produce feelings of profound loss and grief.

For most of us, the benefits of emotional attachment to the nonhuman world outweigh the burdens. Bonding and companionship constitute highly cherished qualities of the human experience, welcomed whether the source of these affections be human or nonhuman. As highly social animals, we crave intimacy and affiliation. With rare exceptions, we hunger for connection and kinship. The companionship of other creatures and even landscapes offers an invaluable source of friendship, relationship, and a means for expressing and sometimes receiving affection. The companion animal and natural feature can provide an antidote to isolation and aloneness.

The companion animal especially has become a feature of modern life. Americans alone possess some 130 million cats and dogs, most enjoying the status of quasi-family members receiving more food, comforts, and conveniences than many of the world's most impoverished peoples.[3] During the past half century or so, pet ownership has multiplied dramatically in much of the industrial world, despite the burdens of keeping animals in an increasingly urban and mobile society. Various aspects of modern life help explain this interest in companion animals. Despite our vastly expanded numbers and likelihood of residing in congested areas, we increasingly encounter isolation and loneliness today. An erosion of traditional communities, a shift from the extended to the nuclear family, increasing mobility and impermanence—all have contributed to feelings of separation and diminished social ties. In this social context, the companion animal fills a growing need for relationship, familiarity, and affection.

Certain species and landscapes possess attributes that seem to encourage strong emotional bonding and attachment. These animals and natural features often elicit empathetic responses because we can distinguish them individually by their distinctive color, shape, pattern, and size. In the case of animal life, these creatures often demonstrate affection in some pronounced and particular way—a dog's tail, a cat's purr, a bird's movements and sounds. These creatures strike us as intelligent: sometimes they can be trained, occasionally they appear to make "rational" decisions. Many reveal a distinct sociability, tolerate others, and form strong bonds. Vertebrates often comprise the bulk of these animals—especially mammals, although sometimes birds, turtles, or even fish will suffice. This inclination to extend strong attachment and even affection to a segment of the living world might seem a narrow relationship to nature. Yet, as we have seen in previous chapters, nearly every expression of biophilia places a spotlight of interest on only certain species and natural features.

Sometimes people do form too strong an emotional dependence on the nonhuman world. Sometimes we are unduly inclined to impute human attributes to other creatures. An indiscriminate extension of human thought and feeling to other life forms can encourage an exaggerated anthropomorphism. Other creatures may become viewed as kindred spirits rather than unique beings with distinct characteristics and evolutionary histories of their own. We may attribute humanlike reason and morality to the behavior of other animals. "Bambi," "Lassie," "Willy," and the like can emerge as beasts with the human inclination to perceive evil, punish wrongdoing, and foil greed and malice. Celebrating other creatures as friends and companions is indeed commendable. But extending the presumption of moral judgment and human rationality to these species can sometimes distort the animal as well as the human dependence on other life.

These problems should not distract us, however, from recognizing other creatures and landscapes as a critical basis for nurturing the human capacities for affection, bonding, and companionship. Emotional dependence on nature has been vital in human development—as critical as the intellectual benefits derived from a scientific/ecological outlook, the material needs provided by a utilitarian relationship, the inspirational advantages offered by an aesthetic view, or the creativity fostered by intimacy and immersion in nature.

Four Adaptive Benefits

The evolutionary and maturational benefits of emotional bonding to the natural world appear in four areas: emotional sustenance and security; sociability and affiliation; self-esteem and self-respect; and physical healing and mental restoration. Each of these benefits will be examined here in more detail—as well as stories offered as a way of bringing these advantages to life, imaginary situations derived from accounts in the scientific literature of the emotional impact of bonding with nature.

EMOTIONAL SUSTENANCE AND SECURITY

Studies offer evidence to support the role of companion animals and, more generally, nature in encouraging our emotional development and sense of security. The research of Boris Levinson, Sam and Elizabeth Corson, Aaron Katcher, Alan Beck, and James Serpell, the many publications of the journal *Anthrozoos,* and the work of the Delta Society elucidate how close relationships with other creatures and landscapes can foster our personal maturation and well-being.[4]

The impact of companion animals derives from their capacity to give and receive affection, to form close ties of attachment, and to bond with people. Few elements in life provide as dependable and seemingly unqualified affection as the companion animal. The veterinarian James Serpell describes the significance of this human/animal relationship:

> By seeking to be near us and soliciting our caresses, by their exuberant greetings and pain on separation, by their possessiveness and their deferential looks of admiration, [companion animals] persuade us that they love us and regard us highly. . . . People need to feel liked, respected, admired; they enjoy the sensation of being valued and needed by others. . . . Our confidence, our self-esteem, our ability to cope with the stresses of life and, ultimately, our physical health depend on this sense of belonging. . . . Pets don't just substitute for human relationships. They complement them and augment them. They add a new and unique dimension to human social life.[5]

Kinship and companionship offer intimacy and friendship, a way of feeling trusted and needed. Isolation constitutes a heavy burden for a largely social species such as the human animal. Separated from other life for prolonged periods of time, we often suffer mental and sometimes physical deterioration. Intimate and secure relationships with other creatures can counter feelings of separation and aloneness. The uncritical attention and devotion of another animal can offer assurance and convey a feeling of being wanted. This nurturing relationship can be especially critical during times of emotional and physical insecurity.

While companion animals provide the most reliable means for achieving this degree of intimacy and bonding, analogous feelings of emotional connection can derive from strong attachment to other aspects of nature. A potted plant, a garden shrub, a backyard tree, a nearby river, a local forest, experienced with intimacy and familiarity, can become subjects of special fondness and regard. Their health and seeming permanence may emerge as a critical basis for a reassuring sense of place; injury to them can provoke feelings of loss and even despair.

The growing child can be especially sustained by learning to receive and extend affection through developing close ties with nature and life. The elderly can find in the companion animal and natural feature a source of consolation when confronting death and disease, especially of family and friends. The shepherd and hunter can enjoy the company of other creatures to counter feelings of loneliness and separation as much as to protect livestock and secure game. These represent but a sample of the many ways nature gives people the emotional strength to confront life's vicissitudes. As a species, we developed our inclination to seek out and bond with other life in the pursuit of emotional sustenance and security. Perhaps the following story will make this connection with other life more vivid and compelling.

At first, Mrs. Trent had a great deal of trouble adjusting to the nursing home. She had entered the facility some six months before. At ninety-two, she was no longer able to take care of herself in the house she had lived in for more than half a century. Overwhelmed by arthritis, she feared becoming an oppressive burden to her two daughters who lived nearby and had children and full-time jobs.

She hated the nursing home at first—its sick and decrepit inmates (as she called them), the ugly and anonymous furnishings, the antiseptic decor and odor. Life changed markedly for the better when, after some insistence, she was permitted to introduce one of her ancient bird feeders. She hung it from a branch of a tree just beyond the sliding glass doors of the common room where many of the nursing home residents assembled each day for cards, conversation, and television. It made all the difference, not only for her, but eventually for the others as well. They took special delight in seeing and feeding the birds that gathered. They got to "know" some individually, and sometimes attracted an unusual species or two. They named a few and even held a writing contest about the birds and their life in the wild.

This small pleasure brought vitality, color, and diversion into Mrs. Trent's life. It became a way for her to make new friends and establish common interests. Although it did little for her painful arthritis, the exercise of filling and tending the feeder did make her feel better. Most of all, she loved the feeling of helping other creatures despite her many infirmities. Her act of charity gave added importance to her life. Seeing the feverish activity of all those beautiful creatures engendered in her a special delight.

SOCIABILITY AND AFFILIATION

The extraordinary success of the human species has occurred despite our relative lack of speed, strength, stamina, stealth, or other physical attributes possessed by many other creatures. What we do possess to an unusual degree are attributes of cooperation, ingenuity, and social inventiveness. Social bonding and affiliation have been critical in the human achievement. We have thrived by nurturing our cooperative capacities for producing food, shelter, and security. This highly developed social, organizational, and communicative capacity springs from many sources, but clearly it has been facilitated by our ability to give and receive affection. We cultivate our relationships; we assume responsibility for the well-being of others; we count on and gratefully receive their commitment and caring response. We teach one another mutual dependence and the virtues of cooperation.

Our family and friends represent the primary means for developing these social capacities. Still, caring for other creatures and nature can be a highly effective way of expressing and receiving affection, intimacy, and companionship. The human/nature bond fosters our potential for relationship, connection, and stewardship. Humans developed an inclination to form close ties with nature, in part, because of the benefits of increased sociability, cooperation, and affiliation. These nurturing ties are often critical for the young, the vulnerable, and the isolated.[6] This facility for shared relation through connecting with nature and life is dramatized in the following story.

John and Emily Livingston were married a little over a year. As ambitious young professionals living in Toronto, they sometimes worked ten- to fifteen-hour days and usually dined out, occasionally seeing friends and family when they got the chance. They delighted in the fullness of their city existence, with its diversity and many attractions, yet often felt exhausted, looking forward to the day when they might have a more settled life with children and a house in an established neighborhood. Despite their happiness with one another and their work, the frenetic and often disconnected character of their existence sometimes made them uncomfortable and anxious.

About this time, they acquired "Jimbo" and then "Cloey," two playful and affectionate cats. Soon they came to regard these animals as close friends, even family members. They especially enjoyed being with them at the end of a long day. The pets injected a spark of life into their apartment, making their existence fuller, more settled, more satisfying.

When they had their first child a year later, they worried that the cats might react jealously and even harm the baby. They also fretted about their pets becoming a superfluous burden to them. After some initial tension, however, they returned to their former intimacy with their pets. The baby, after all, had become just another member of a larger and extended family.

SELF-ESTEEM AND SELF-RESPECT

The affection of another creature can enhance self-confidence and self-esteem. The belief in being intrinsically worthy can derive from caring for others, giving and receiving affection, and developing bonds of loyalty and commitment. Caring for animals and other aspects of nature may provide opportunities for feeling wanted, valued, necessary, and special.

This building of self-respect and self-esteem inspired the development of "pet-facilitated psychotherapy."[7] This clinical strategy uses pets to promote, as James Serpell suggests, "self-respect, independence, and self-confidence." The companion animal offers the disturbed and disabled a reassuring sense of worth, goodness, and ability to relate to others. These creatures have helped transform mental patients, as James Serpell notes, citing the work of psychiatrists Sam and Elizabeth Corson, from "irresponsible, dependent psychological invalids into self-respecting, responsible individuals."

Companion animals also help us build skills that enhance feelings of self-confidence and autonomy. The product of a different evolutionary line, these creatures possess their own diverse abilities and attributes. The dog has the capacity for tracking and discovery; the horse, speed and power; the cat, agility and stealth. Such characteristics have become refined through years of genetic manipulation. Although people cannot incorporate these features, through training and instruction we can use them to advantage and even occasionally emulate them. Intimate familiarity with wild animals and nature can also foster this increased competence and confidence. Barry Lopez, for example, describes an analogous experience among wolves:

> The wolves moved deftly and silently in the woods and in trying to imitate them I came to walk more quietly and to freeze at the sign of slight movement. At first this imitation gave me no advantage, but after several weeks I realized I was becoming far more attuned to the environment we moved through. I heard more . . . and my senses now constantly alert, I occasionally saw a deer mouse or a grouse before they did. . . . I took from them the confidence to believe I could attune myself better to the woods

by behaving as they did—minutely inspecting things, seeking vantage points, always sniffing the air. I did, and felt vigorous, charged with alertness.[8]

Enhanced self-worth and competence has always been a facet of the human/nature relationship—in the process improving people's chances for survival and success. The human disposition to affiliate closely with nature offers both company and an increased capacity for coping with life's trials and challenges. The following story illustrates this effect.

Rickey had been arrested many times. In fact, he was viewed as a violent career criminal by the time he was a teenager. He didn't feel like a particularly vicious person, but violence was a "normal" and expected part of the drug-dealing business. Raised in a family of alcoholics in rural Maine by a father who needed little prompting before beating his children, Rickey had grown up inured to brutality. Now twenty-one, he was behind bars for a minimum of five years and faced a grim and unpromising future.

The prison was infamous for its savagery and ugliness. The prisoners included some of the most violent criminals in the system. Rickey's initial eighteen months were a nightmare of brutality and demoralizing boredom. Little occurred of any particular value or purpose—beyond affirming his meanness and self-sufficiency, occasionally fighting, and allying himself with one or another of the prison's many gangs.

It would be an exaggeration to claim that a bird saved Rickey's life, but from the perspective of many years later it sometimes seemed that way. The creature, without question, injected a measure of happiness and meaning into his existence. It certainly made him calmer and gentler, and eventually offered a way of defining himself more positively.

Rickey was given the bird after vocational tests indicated he had an affinity for animals and might be rehabilitated as an animal keeper or veterinary assistant. They gave him custody of a young parrot as a temporary measure, but Rickey took to the creature immediately, gave it excellent care, and eventually taught the bird to "talk." The prison li-

brary, linked by computer to the state university, enabled him to become something of an expert on "psittacines," the parrots and macaws.

After some initial hazing as the new "Bird Man of Alcatraz," Rickey's obsession was accepted and then respected. He presented a number of fascinating lectures to his fellow inmates and started corresponding with scientists about various aspects of his observations, communicating along the Internet about parrot biology and behavior.

Rickey's problems remained far from resolved, but his knowledge and attachment to the bird brought meaning, companionship, and pride into his life. He looked forward to the day when as a free man he could witness in the wild the splendor of these glorious creatures. He took special pleasure in realizing he would be able to carry with him his new understanding and competence wherever he went for the rest of his life.

PHYSICAL HEALING AND MENTAL RESTORATION

An intimate bond with nature has been linked to emotional security, sociability, self-confidence, and self-esteem. Although these benefits accrue under normal circumstances, they become especially critical during times of mental and physical stress and disorder. Studies by Aaron Katcher and Alan Beck have been particularly instructive in this regard.[9] These two doctors present an impressive body of evidence demonstrating nature's therapeutic value for the sick and disabled. They especially stress the healing impact of the companion animal: "If the loving devotion, the soft touch, the constant companionship, the attentive eye and the uncritical ear of the pet are so attractive to so many of us, they should be even more important to those who have been wounded by other people or deprived of the comfort that friends, family and children bring."[10] Other researchers have demonstrated the healing effect of horses, dogs, cats, birds, plants, water, and certain landscapes on the mentally disturbed, the handicapped, and the sick.

Aaron Katcher and his colleague Gregory Wilkins, focusing on brain-damaged and autistic children, recently reported: "In patients with chronic organic brain damage and autistic children with congenital brain dysfunction . . . the entry of animals into a purely human environment resulted in focused attention, increased social responding, positive emotion, and, critically, speech."[11] They describe a particularly fascinating study of nine- to fifteen-year-olds afflicted with attention deficit disorder, half of whom were diagnosed with "conduct disorders" and "opposition defiant disorders." They randomly assigned fifty children to two kinds of voluntary after-school programs—an outdoor nature program (involving rock climbing, canoeing, and water safety) and an animal care program (requiring pet management, learning about animal biology, and animal care). These assignments persisted for six months and then the children were switched to the other program. The animal care experience, they discovered, exerted significant therapeutic effects. Caring for other creatures consistently captured and maintained the children's attention. More important, 80 percent of the children experienced substantially reduced symptoms, including greater impulse control, enhanced attention, and improved speech and emotional behavior.

These emotional benefits especially derive from interactions with highly responsive and intelligent animals. Yet analogous therapeutic benefits derive from "lower" animals and plants like tropical fish, butterflies, flowers, and trees. Patients undergoing dental treatment, for example, including oral surgery, have reported significantly less pain and distress when observing aquarium fish than those who looked at pictures of animals and landscapes—or the walls of a lifeless and antiseptic office.[12]

Even nonliving nature—water, mountains, savannas—can exert a significant healing impact. After an extensive review of the research literature, Roger Ulrich concluded: "Exposure to unthreatening natural settings [can] promote recovery from mild and even acute stress." As reported in Chapter 3, Ulrich compared the postoperative recovery rates of surgical patients who had a window view of trees and a lake with those who had no window or looked out on a brick wall. He found that patients exposed to the natural settings required significantly less pharmaceutical assistance, had reduced hospital times following surgery, diminished adjustment problems, and fewer postsurgical complications.[13]

What explains the apparent healing effect of nature on people experiencing mental distress and physical disorder? As noted earlier, the affection of a close and caring companion can be especially comforting. Intimate ties may be especially critical when people confront vulnerability, weakness, and disorder. The experience of natural beauty and living diversity can be revitalizing. Exposure to the vitality of any living creature, the bright colors of a flowering plant, the splendor of a mountain, or the life-giving quality of water can be inspiring and restorative. We feel drawn to nature's drama and animation. Paradoxically we feel calmer but more invigorated. Our sense of vulnerability and mortality is replaced by the reassurance of life-sustaining process. The following two stories reflect these healing effects of nature.

Peter would have been diagnosed a schizophrenic if not for the logic of his behavior. The nine-year-old's severe depression came on suddenly following the death of his father in a plane crash. All at once the boy's world lost meaning and predictability. He became so withdrawn, he barely spoke with anyone, not even his mother, sisters, or friends. Peter remained partially aware and responsive, but much of the time he stared sullenly and impassively into space. He even stopped watching television. No amount of coaxing or indulgence seemed to alter his drift toward isolation and withdrawal.

The absence of a complete break with reality meant that Peter could remain at home. This allowed his sister, Cathy, on a whim and a hunch, to purchase "Joffrey," a ten-month-old Labrador retriever. Immediately an intense affection developed between the dog and the boy. Peter focused almost all of his attention on the animal, showering it with affection, taking the dog for long walks, even to bed with him. The dog returned Peter's devotion with unqualified loyalty, renewing the boy's sense of worth and meaning.

Taking care of Joffrey prompted Peter to become more communicative, and gradually he climbed out of his shell. Before long he had regained his old confidence and joy. His mother exalted in the miracle of the little Labrador—despite a twinge of jealousy. She knew that henceforth a dog would always be part of her life.

Connie's mother frequently pronounced, "There's nothing more important than your health." It had always struck Connie as just another aphorism of Mom's. It held little meaning for an active, optimistic, and successful thirty-two-year-old who felt invulnerable and even at times immortal. Cancer afflicted the old following a lifetime of marriage, children, work, and retirement. Connie, therefore, had little chance to adjust to the reality of first the lump, then the diagnosis, and finally the need for immediate surgery.

She thought back on all this as she lay numb and debilitated in a recovery room just three weeks after her diagnosis. She looked around at the bright white walls, the slowly descending fluid of the catheter, the incomprehensible blinking of the machines. The hours passed like days, a nurse or doctor occasionally wandering by, as she struggled to climb out of a world of suffocating drugs and painkillers.

Eventually they moved her into a brighter, more comfortable room, where she remained for a week. The absence of a window and the abstract painting of criss-crossed lines at the foot of her bed nearly drove her insane. After repeated complaining, her mother was allowed to cover the painting with a poster of a mountain scene in the tropics. The bright orchids, vivid hummingbirds, riotous foliage, swirling clouds, and brilliant hues of the setting sun filled her with pleasure and fascination. She felt drawn to the painting, projecting herself into its wondrous world of mystery, animation, and beauty.

Her health really improved when she was moved again—this time to a room overlooking a park with a lake. She especially enjoyed seeing the ducks and geese on the water, the squirrels and songbirds in the trees, the mothers with babies, the older children at play floating boats on the lake. She sometimes felt as if an umbilical cord connected her with this vibrant energy and that she sucked life and optimism from its vitality. The doctors offered a guarded but reassuring prognosis. Soon she would be able to partake of the simple everyday treasures of the park across the street.

Four benefits resulting from the inclination to bond closely with other creatures and nature have been described here: emotional sustenance and security; sociability and affiliation; self-esteem and self-respect; and physical healing and mental restoration. Each reveals the many adaptive advantages stemming from the company of nature and other life. These ties especially offer us the means to cope with the challenges and vagaries of human existence. Perhaps this is why they encouraged the biological encoding in our species of an inclination to seek in other life a nurturing and sustaining relationship.

Chapter Eight

The Urge to Master

We explored in the previous chapter how emotional bonding and attachment to nature can play a pivotal role in human growth and development—how the capacities for sharing, cooperating, forming allegiances, developing affections, and creating kinships can be shaped and honed through our various ties with the natural world. This loving and caring side of the human personality should not prevent us from recognizing our equally powerful tendency to hone our mental and physical skills by subduing and mastering nature. Just as we covet kinship and affection in our lives, so too do we strive to compete, outwit, and overcome challenge and adversity. The natural world has always presented an unrivaled context for developing these competitive traits in the human species.

Modern society no longer relies on besting or overcoming prey, eluding menacing predators, or surviving wilderness. Yet the physical and mental strengths we derive from such outdoor challenges remain an important pathway for developing competitive fitness and adaptive capacity. Although these activities rarely seem necessary today, and sometimes involve considerable risk and danger, these characteristics constitute a major reason why so many people continue to seek adventure and confrontation in nature. This chapter describes features of this urge to challenge and best the natural world and explains how the benefits of this relationship led to the biological encoding of a disposition to seek in nature the opportunity for honing various competitive and aggressive skills.

The competitive aspect of biophilia emphasizes above all the urge to master and control nature. From this perspective, we value nature as an arena of contest and contention. We dote on images of boats battling high winds, finding our way through wild country, traversing rugged terrain, besting (with gun, rod, or camera) elk or trout, running wild rivers, climbing steep mountains. Such experiences nurture our capacities for ingenuity, perseverance, strength, and prowess in the age-old quest to overcome challenge. From the accomplishment flow confidence, pride, and self-worth. In this relation to nature, we seek the chance to be tested, to demonstrate physical stamina, to evince mental fortitude.[1]

Mastering nature once meant obtaining food, sustenance, and security. Controlling the natural world focused on locating safe and secure havens, establishing boundaries and territories, securing food and prey, avoiding and besting predators. Many outdoor activities today endeavor to retain, simulate, and recreate these challenges through backcountry camping, river running, mountain climbing, fishing, hunting, and more. Such outdoor activities persist because vital benefits continue to accrue.[2] These advantages often defy easy explanation or obvious relevance to modern life. Yet people feel stronger by having been tested and having persevered. They feel stimulated by the struggle, proud to have marshaled the inner resources and outward skills to master challenging circumstances, pleased at having overcome hardship and outwitting treacherous situations and cunning competitors.

Living creatures, especially the large predators, evoke strong images of competition and strife. Wolves, bears, lions, tigers, crocodiles, sharks, and others often signify conflict and struggle. These creatures conjure impressions of dread and awe, fright and excitement, challenge and competition, escape and conquest. Persevering in areas where they exist—or even successfully besting them—suggests our own strength and prowess.

Despite our modern triumphs over the natural world, apprehension toward these large predators endures. Among our most primal fears are fantasies of being victimized by one or another of these creatures. Yet a far greater chance exists of dying from an automobile crash, electrocution, or gunshot than being mauled by a grizzly bear, attacked by a shark, or bitten by a snake.[3] Indeed, we stand a greater chance of serious injury from an automobile accident in Yellowstone National Park (1 in 4,600) than suffering injury or death from a grizzly bear (1 in 1.5 million).[4] Even so, most campers and hikers express anxiety regarding the possibility of encountering grizzlies. The story of human fatalities inflicted by bears in Glacier National Park more than a decade ago continues to generate extraordinary sales of books and magazines. Moreover, campers and photographers (and not long ago hunters) express considerable satisfaction and pride in having successfully navigated grizzly country. We value these large predators not only because they seem scientifically fascinating or aesthetically pleasing but because they provide us with opportunities for demonstrating prowess, courage, and skill.

The Satisfactions of Challenge

The satisfactions derived from challenging nature can perhaps be grasped by examining three activities: outdoor adventure, fishing, and hunting. Later in the chapter we will consider how the human inclination to wrestle with nature confers certain advantages.

OUTDOOR ADVENTURE

Wilderness and outdoor challenge programs have become popular in modern society, especially among young adults. One of the best-known programs is Outward Bound, established by Kurt Hahn following World War II because he believed thousands of seamen had lost their lives lacking the endurance, hardiness, and survival skills characteristic of people in the past.[5] Outward Bound's motto—"To Serve, to Strive, and Not to Yield"—reflects its "educational philosophy [of] developing a student's inner resources through physical as well as mental challenge."[6]

Overcoming adversity constitutes a critical dimension of this outdoor program. Outward Bound encourages the belief that by testing ourselves in nature we achieve competence, fitness, confidence, and courage. These sentiments emerge in the following account by a participant:

> I was hotter, colder, more afraid and more alone than ever before in my life . . . and I wouldn't trade that experience for anything in the world. I . . . hiked twelve to fifteen hours some days, canoed eight hours on others, climbed five hundred feet of solid, vertical rock, fell off a one hundred fifty-foot cliff. . . . I didn't know about the daily runs at 5 A.M., or the nine-mile race, or that I would be the hottest I'd ever been in my life, and the coldest, and the most afraid. . . . I didn't know that I could survive for three days on top of a mountain all by myself, or that I could face fear and apprehension without panicking. Or that despite the pain and agony, I wouldn't want the course to end.[7]

Another participant recalls:

> I felt the panic climbing up from the pit of my stomach as I looked down from the ledge high on the summit. . . . Everything in my past told me there was no way I could throw myself off into that yawning nothing, trusting only to the clumsy, unfamiliar ropes cinched about my waist. . . . I shook my head in disbelief at what I was about to do, gulped hard and leaned out over the precipice.
>
> The glassy surface of the mountain's granite face slid by in a blur and my heart stopped for that instant before I felt the "whump" as the ropes caught me. The panic passed as I looked back up at the ledge above. The drop had been only six feet but I felt it had been a mile. "I did it!" I whooped. "I really *did* it!" . . . In that split second of committing myself to leap off that wind-swept cliff, I had finally learned what Outward Bound is all about: Pushing yourself beyond your own limits and finding you can do far more than you had ever dreamed.[8]

These participants acquired outdoor skills but, more significantly, they increased their sense of self-worth, adaptive capacity, and the belief they could cope with life's adversities.[9] As another participant explains, this experience offered "[the] chance to challenge and test oneself and thereby discover hidden potential . . . learning to attempt difficult physical tasks with minimal training, and discovering that, in fact, we can accomplish if not master them. [This] can be both instructive and applicable to the less physical challenges faced at work and in life."[10]

FISHING AND HUNTING

Fishing and hunting often necessitate outwitting and mastering other creatures. Seeking, capturing, killing, processing, transporting, and consuming prey takes prowess and skill. And defeating a challenging opponent can be a critical element of the experience.[11] Important motivations include competition, conquest, and achievement. Successfully securing game can involve not only skill but courage and fortitude.[12]

These activities often evoke expressions of power and endurance. Frequently they are valued for the opportunities afforded for demonstrating strength and virility. As one hunter remarked: "An important drive is the maleness of it . . . a symbol of machismo, strength. Cats kill birds not [just] because they want [to eat] the bird. They kill it to confirm their prowess and ability. I think they share the same exultation in their prowess as the [fisher and] hunter." Excitement flows from having exercised physical dominance and superiority through competition and challenge. In the process we experience feelings of power, strength, and toughness.

Modern fishing and hunting occur in a primarily recreational context rather than out of necessity. And as the motivation has shifted, the acceptance of these activities has waned. Some now regard sport fishing and hunting as reprehensible—a cruel inflicting of death in the absence of sufficient justification or necessity.[13] Recreational killing strikes some critics as an act of destruction debasing the perpetrator as much as the prey. Moreover, the contest seems unfair: today's modern weaponry and equipment have obscured the competitive dimensions of these activities.

The recreational killing of other life should not prevent us, however, from recognizing the advantages people gain from exercising their prowess and mastery over the natural world. The satisfactions and benefits of sport fishing and hunting can be comprehended whether we approve of the activities or not. Moreover, the achievements and skills experienced in besting and consuming nature can also be obtained through "hunting" clams, mushrooms, or berries. A deer may revel as much in finding good browse as a wolf or human hunter rejoices in downing the deer.

Modern humans struggle to keep this aspect of our character alive, even when it appears superfluous. The continuing utility of challenging wild nature is suggested by the environmental philosopher Holmes Rolston: "The pioneer, pilgrim, explorer, and settler loved the frontier for the challenge and discipline. . . . One reason we lament the passing of wilderness is that we do not want entirely to tame this aboriginal element. . . . Half the beauty of life comes out of it. . . . The cougar's fang sharpens the deer's sight, the deer's fleet-footedness shapes a more supple lioness. . . . None of life's heroic quality is possible without this dialectical stress."[14]

The allure of wildness persists because it offers opportunities for expressing hardiness, strength, endurance, and skill. Through challenging and mastering wild nature we demonstrate competence and enhance our self-worth. These conditions may be less evident today than in our pioneering past, but their significance remains pertinent and powerfully seductive even for modern humans. Sport fishing, hunting, outdoor challenge, and other activities reflect the continuing attraction of the natural world as a source of contest and competition. Even today, the urge to control nature remains enticing.

Yet many question the continuing relevance of a perspective that encouraged the destruction of so much wildlife and wilderness. Can we still afford this urge to dominate nature? Does our desire to master elements of the natural world address critical human needs, or is it just an obsolete romanticizing of the past? Does it make any sense in an age of modern technology and burgeoning human numbers? Ridding ourselves of a "conquest over nature" mentality might eliminate a dangerous anachronism. Perhaps we could dampen these lingering tendencies by channeling them into more benign pastimes like video games or movies such as *Jurassic Park* and *The Terminator.*

To do so, I believe, would be a misguided understanding of our humanity and persisting dependence on the natural world. Courage, strength, agility, competitiveness, and the ability to master nature continue to confer adaptational significance. Self-esteem and confidence derive from challenging involvement in the natural world. Young people, especially, look to nature and wildlife for opportunities for testing and proving themselves in an age of complexity and confusion.

The inclination to compete with nature represents neither an intrinsic wrong nor an unworthy pursuit. All expressions of biophilia confer advantages, but they can also become distorted and dysfunctional. At one extreme, we can incline toward an excessive and cruel dominance over nature; at the other, we can love animals too much as an excuse for not loving humans enough. At one extreme, we can overexploit the natural world; at the other, we can escape into wildness to avoid coping with everyday life. Mastering nature represents less a problem than a channeling of this tendency in positive and functional ways.

Four Adaptive Benefits

Each expression of biophilia has been shaped, fashioned, and tested during the long course of human evolution. The brief span of contemporary life has hardly rendered irrelevant the tendencies we have developed during much of our history. Nor should our potential for excess deter us from recognizing this urge's many potential advantages. We still rely on an occasional adversarial relationship with the natural world. The adaptive advantages accruing from this relationship may become more evident by considering four potential benefits derived from mastering nature: physical strength and mental prowess; self-reliance and independence; exploration and adventure; and courage and heroism.

PHYSICAL STRENGTH AND MENTAL PROWESS

People develop physical health and competence through testing themselves in nature. Bodily fitness constitutes the first, most obvious, and most compelling reason for seeking challenge and competition in the outdoors. This capacity undoubtedly contributed to human survival during much of human history. Yet, even today, the motivation for many outdoor activities—whether hiking, backpacking, climbing, canoeing, kayaking, cross-country skiing, fishing, or hunting—originates in the desire to cultivate physical fitness, stamina, and strength. These attributes foster the will to persevere in the face of hardship and adversity, as well as a belief in one's personal hardiness and prowess.

Mental skills, too, can derive from the experience of outdoor challenge. Cleverness and technique translate into a more efficient and effective expression of strength—whether carrying a canoe across a difficult portage, skiing over a high plateau, or hiking with a heavy pack across rugged terrain. Pursuing another creature well, whether with camera or fishing rod, depends on more than power and perseverance. We also need to comprehend the creature's habits, develop the guile and dexterity to follow it unobserved, and acquire the proficiency to cast a rod or shoot a snapshot effectively. These skills demand mental refinement as much as physical strength and durability. Together the body and mind generate the capacity for physical grace and mental dexterity.

Through testing ourselves in nature, we extol the virtues of strength and hardiness. By confronting and besting another creature, we achieve fitness and security. This emphasis on power and agility often celebrates the characteristics of the predator. Some deride this predatory emphasis as encouraging a destructive mentality. In its place they advocate a more benign attitude of kindness and kinship for life. These opposing tendencies represent contrasting qualities in the human animal. They reflect the complexity and sometimes contradictory character of our species' biology, alternating between predatory fierceness and peaceful tranquility. The Spanish philosopher José Ortega y Gassett reflects on this seeming duality: "Do not forget that man was once a beast. His carnivore's fangs and canine teeth are unimpeachable evidence of this. Of course, he was also a vegetarian . . . as his molars attest. Man, in fact, combines the two extreme conditions of the mammal, and therefore he goes through life vacillating between being a sheep and being a tiger . . . a confrontation between two systems of instincts."[15]

Human survival necessitates *both* inclinations for affiliating with the natural world. This chapter has celebrated the virtues of competition and challenge, of demonstrating physical capacity and mental strength. Power, mastery, and toughness have been emphasized as ingredients of human adaptability and success. Contesting nature provides a time-honored proving ground for evincing physical and mental competence, fitness, and well-being. Wilderness survival may no longer be a facet of everyday life, but wildness remains an unrivaled setting for building physical strength and mental fortitude.

SELF-RELIANCE AND INDEPENDENCE

We have seen how our social capacity can be nurtured through intimacy and bonding with nature. But people also seek independence and autonomy, and this too can be developed through our interactions with the natural world. Again this duality reflects the complexity of the human experience: vacillating between the craving for group acceptance and an equally vigorous longing for individuality and distinctiveness.

Personal identity and autonomy can be enhanced through coping with nature. A feeling of self-reliance derives from testing oneself in unfamiliar situations. Outdoor activities offer opportunities for demonstrating self-sufficiency and the capacity to function effectively in challenging circumstances. We emerge surer and more confident of our inner reserves—and our ability to prove our skill and fortitude in even the most demanding situations.

The developing adolescent especially seeks a greater sense of autonomy and independence. Unfamiliar nature offers the young the opportunity for exhibiting competence and self-sufficiency. They encounter the chance for demonstrating skills taken for granted during the course of everyday life—building fires, gathering food, securing a place to sleep, cooking and cleaning, orienteering. Modern life with its comforts and conveniences often trivializes these essentials. Experienced in the wild, these achievements can provide the young person with a reassuring sense of autonomy and accomplishment.[16]

At earlier stages in human evolution, the natural world provided the primary means for achieving these displays of independence and self-reliance. Today we emphasize more culturally refined and artificial methods for distinguishing ourselves individually. Yet the complexity and interdependence of contemporary life often thwart the realization of personal distinctiveness. The natural world continues to afford important opportunities for people to achieve feelings of autonomy and individuality.

EXPLORATION AND ADVENTURE

An adventurous spirit can also be fostered through confronting and mastering nature. By pushing the limits of the known, we learn to adapt to the unfamiliar and uncertain. Wild nature provides the chance for dealing with the unexpected, for testing our knowledge, for coping with the rarely experienced and seldom encountered. Pioneers attest to the many dangers and risks associated with challenging the unknown, but exploration and discovery have always been integral to the success of the human animal. Nature has always served as a context for nurturing this pioneering and adventurous spirit.

People seek novelty as much as stability and security. Because of this innovative and exploratory urge, our species colonized much of the globe, despite possessing a physical endowment seemingly restricted to a narrow subtropical climate. Our willingness to explore and take risks permitted us to adapt to new and unfamiliar circumstances, as well as defy danger and adversity. Today we climb mountains, run rivers, camp in wilderness, activities that often seem impractical and even dangerous. But advantage derives from any pursuit that pushes the unknown and increases our ability to persevere in the face of hardship. Contesting wild nature cultivates our inclination for exploration and instills in us the willingness to take risks and cope with adversity.

COURAGE AND HEROISM

Attributes of daring and boldness can derive from the inclination to take on and master elements of the natural world. A heroic image emerges when we dare to take risks and display fortitude in the pursuit of worthy and noble objectives.

Many outdoor participants cite deep satisfaction from testing and proving themselves in nature. They recall moments of intense pride and pleasure when they demonstrated to others—and to themselves—the capacity for resourcefulness, courage, and sacrifice.[17] They especially covet the memory of times when they discovered their ability to help others in distress and pushed the limits of what they thought possible for themselves. They dwell on heroic moments even if experienced temporarily.

The concept of the hero figures prominently in the work of the nineteenth-century German philosopher Friedrich Nietzsche.[18] The precariousness of human existence prompted him to assert the necessity of mastery and dominance. According to Nietzsche, people achieve superiority by heroically struggling to surpass others and nature through the exercise of power and will: "The true meaning of evolution [stems from] an aggressive 'will to power' to dominate the environment. . . . The strongest and highest Will to Life does not find expression in a miserable struggle for existence, but in a . . . Will to Power, a Will to Overpower!"[19] To Nietzsche, success requires the unrelenting willingness to master opposition and adversity. These heroic qualities, produce the "superman"—the kind of individual who, according to Nietzsche, generated much of human progress and creativity.

This notion of the hero can also foster arrogance and authoritarianism. The heroic ideal can be used to justify excess and extremism pursued in the name of particular ideologies or a desire to master and control. One group's heroic construction can become the excuse for persecuting and destroying another, including elements of the natural world. Nietzsche's philosophy of the "superman" became, for example, strongly associated with the ideology, barbarism, and cruelty of Nazi Germany.[20] This presumption of heroic certitude also prevailed during

America's historic attempt to exterminate the wolf. As Barry Lopez describes: "Civilized man . . . came to measure his own progress by his subjugation of the wilderness. . . . The act of killing wolves became a symbolic act, a way to lash out at that enormous, inchoate obstacle: wilderness. Man demonstrated his own prodigious strength as well as his allegiance to God by killing wolves."[21]

Despite these tendencies, a core of positive meaning and functional significance prevails in the heroic capacity to confront, challenge, and endure. The attributes of courage and daring often accompany this ideal. Would our species have ventured forth, taken risks, innovated, and pursued the hope of a better world lacking the image of the hero? The human potential for excess dooms a certain proportion of heroic endeavor to the scrapheap of misguided exaggeration and delusion. Still, progress and goodness depend on the pursuit of ennobling ideals. Our affinity for the wild has much to do with nature's ability to bring out the best in us through testing ourselves in the natural world.

Chapter Nine

Seeking Meaning and Transcendence

The extraordinary richness and diversity of the natural world, particularly its living creatures, constitute a source of endless fascination and wonder. We are awed by the dazzling variety of plants, animals, fungi, mosses, lichens, algae, protozoa, bacteria, and viruses inhabiting this small planet. The animal kingdom alone embraces a stunning assortment of mammals, birds, reptiles, amphibians, fish—and, far more than all else, invertebrate insects, spiders, mollusks, worms, and others. Beyond the sheer diversity of life, we encounter in every creature an astonishing and almost endless wealth of detail and mystery.

Our knowledge of the number of creatures inhabiting the earth is remarkable for its incompleteness despite centuries of study.[1] As we noted in Chapter 4, the total number of scientifically described species is approximately 1.7 million. But recent studies in the tropics, oceans, and other areas of the planet now suggest the actual number of species may be 10 to 100 million, possibly more. Ten million represents the generally accepted figure for the number of species on earth—five times more, that is, than those identified to date. Variability among insects alone staggers the imagination: some 900,000 identified and an astounding 8 to 100 million species yet to be discovered. Among identified insects, there exist some 300,000 beetle species, more than 100,000 butterfly and moth species, and an equal number of ant species. Moreover, an estimated 99 percent of all species that ever existed on earth are now extinct. During the Permian age alone, 250 million years ago, an astonishing 96 percent of the earth's life disappeared.[2] This diversity leaves one in awe of the capacity of living matter, in all its many forms, to gain a unique adaptive foothold on the ladder of existence.

In the face of all this incredible variability, the essential similarity uniting so much of this diversity seems equally remarkable. Much of life on earth shares a fundamental unity: a common molecular and genetic structure, certain cellular characteristics, analogous circulatory and reproductive processes, and parallel bodily features.[3] An extraordinary web of relationship appears to connect a beetle on the forest floor, a fish in the sea, a bird in the air, an elephant on the savanna, and a human in the modern city. Edward O. Wilson, commenting on the origins and implications of all this living affinity, suggests: "All higher eukaryotic organisms, from flowering plants to insects and humanity itself, are thought to have descended from a single ancestral population that lived about 1.8 billion years ago. . . . All this distant kinship is stamped by a common genetic code and elementary features of cell structure. Humanity did not soft-land into the teeming biosphere like an alien from another planet. We arose from other organisms already here."[4]

A kind of unity, then, binds much of life on earth. Although this relationship can be rationalized in the language of modern science, its intuitive realization seems quite ancient, indicative of a universal perspective in the human species. The perception of a unifying life force is indeed a cornerstone of the religious perspective, what the writer Aldous Huxley termed the "perennial philosophy."[5] This outlook regards creation as reflecting patterns of interrelationship and underlying order. At the foundation of life is seen a basic symmetry and association. The words of the anthropologist Loren Eisley reflect this recognition:

> It is said . . . that the smallest living cell probably contains a quarter of a million protein molecules engaged in the multitudinous coordinated activities which make up the phenomenon of life. At the instant of death, whether of man or microbe, that ordered, incredible spinning passes away in an almost furious haste. . . . I do not think, if someone finally twists the key successfully in the tiniest and most humble house of life, that many of these questions will be answered, or that the dark forces which create lights in the deep sea and living batteries in the waters of tropical forests, or the dread cycles of parasites, or the most noble workings of the human brain, will be much if at all revealed. Rather, I would say that if "dead" matter has reared up this curious landscape of fiddling crickets, song sparrows, and wondering men, it must be plain even to the most devoted materialist that the matter of which he speaks contains amazing, if not dreadful powers, and may not impossibly be, as Hardy suggested, "but one mask of many worn by the Great Face behind."[6]

The recognition of an underlying web of connection in nature can foster a belief in a fundamental meaning and harmony governing human existence. Transcending the distinctiveness, separateness, and aloneness of the single individual, species, and moment in time, an ultimate unity and purpose is discerned. A picture of overall coherence emerges, even the possibility of some functional and meaningful end. Life is viewed from the vantage point of a basic and underlying integrity, harmony, even goodness of purpose.

This outlook confers an array of benefits and advantages in human evolution and development. It offers us a unifying and motivating sense of purpose, instilling in us the will to persevere and the capacity to face adversity. It fosters a feeling of kinship, as well, inspiring group loyalty and an inclination to share, cooperate, and help one another. It creates a willingness to conserve nature, to protect it, and to sustain our natural resource base for present as well as for future generations. Later in the chapter we will explore the benefits of this perspective of nature more fully. For now, let us examine its expression in aspects of human religion, mysticism, science, and ethics.

Religion and Mysticism

A feeling of profound connection binding humans with the rest of creation characterizes the religious convictions of many peoples, perhaps most. Among tribal cultures, one encounters a view of all living beings sharing a similar consciousness and experience.[7] The anthropologist Richard Nelson describes a belief among indigenous peoples that all creatures, "no matter how small and inconspicuous, carry the luminescence of power."[8] As the words of a Native American, Luther Standing Bear, suggest, a basic affinity unites humans with the natural world: "We are of the soil and the soil is of us. We love the birds and beasts that grew with us on this soil. They drank the same water as we did and breathed the same air. We are all one in nature. Believing so, there was in our hearts a great peace of mind and a willing kindness for all living, growing things."[9] This view intimates a common social order shared by humans and nonhumans alike. Mutual obligation and associated responsibilities govern the relationship among species. Only respectful conduct by humans toward the rest of creation ensures peace and harmony.

The notion of a unifying connection between people and nature can similarly be discerned within the great religious tradition of Buddhism-Hinduism and, though less apparent and more controversial, in Judeo-Christian thought. The Buddhist-Hindu perspective especially emphasizes a concept of shared relation linking the human and nonhuman worlds.[10] Endless cycles of birth, death, and rebirth bind every living being. All creation strives for peace and harmony through repeated cycles of struggle and existence. No fundamental difference distinguishes human life from the strivings of other creatures. All existence shares an analogous field of experience—a view reflected in the Buddhist notion that "all beings, even the grasses, are in the process of enlightenment."[11]

The Judeo-Christian perspective, by contrast, is sometimes depicted as emphasizing a strict duality distinguishing people from nature.[12] Only humans, in this view, possess the capacity for rising above their natural limits in the search for salvation and eternal life. This religious tradition is said to assert human superiority over the rest of creation: people alone exhibit the capacity for reason and moral judgment. A tree, an insect, even a mammal, lack sentience, a mental life, and ethical standing. Stripped of any moral worth or sacred status, nature can make no claim on human morality. This indifference toward the interests of nature invites arrogance, mastery, and dominance.

Such an interpretation ignores a more positive tradition of respect, stewardship, and reverence for the natural world in Judeo-Christian thought. We may discern in this strand of theology a view of nature as God's creation and the idea that humans are obliged to treat the creator's works with respect, kindness, and compassion. As the Christian philosopher John Passmore explains: "Genesis, and after it the Old Testament, generally, certainly tells man that he is, or has the right to be, master of the earth and all it contains. But at the same time it insists that the world was good before man was created, and that it exists to glorify God rather than to serve man."[13] From this perspective, Christian love of God cannot be separated from goodwill and kindness to all creatures. The Christian theologian and physician Albert Schweitzer suggests: "Kindness to animals [is] an ethical demand on exactly the same footing as kindness to human beings."[14] The historian Roderick Nash describes Schweitzer's religious outlook on nature: "The powerful and privileged status humans enjoyed in the natural community entailed for Schweitzer not a right to exploit but a responsibility to protect [nature]."[15] Central to this Christian theology is a concept of "reverence for life" embracing an awe and humility before the miracle of God's creation.

These Christian, Buddhist, and tribal views all assert a fundamental connection binding life and nature, a mystical union uniting all of creation. A similar mysticism can be found among many nonreligious persons as well. John Steinbeck describes this profound feeling of awe toward the unity of creation:

> It seems apparent that species are only commas in a sentence, that each species is at once the point and the base of a pyramid, that all life is related. . . . And then not only the meaning but the feeling about species grows misty. One merges into another, groups melt into ecological groups until the time when what we know as life meets and enters what we know of as non-life: barnacle and rock, rock and earth, earth and tree, tree and rain and air. And the units nestle into the whole and are inseparable from it. . . . And it is a strange thing that most of the feeling we call religious, most of the mystical outcrying which is one of the most prized and used and desired reactions of our species, is really the understanding and the attempt to say that man is related to the whole thing, related inextricably to all reality, known and unknowable. This is a simple thing to say, but a profound feeling of it made a Jesus, a St. Augustine, a Roger Bacon, a Charles Darwin, an Einstein. Each of them in his own tempo and with his own voice discovered and reaffirmed with astonishment the knowledge that all things are one thing and that one thing is all things—a plankton, a shimmering phosphorescence on the sea and the spinning planets and an expanding universe, all bound together by the elastic string of time.[16]

Walt Whitman reveals similar mystical sentiments toward nature in his epic poem *Leaves of Grass:*

> I believe a leaf of grass is no less than the journey-work of the stars,
> And the pismire is equally perfect, and a grain of sand, and the
> egg of the wren,
> And the tree-toad is a chef-d'oeuvre for the highest,
> And the running blackberry would adorn the parlors of heaven,
> And the narrowest hinge in my hand puts to scorn all machinery.
> And the cow crunching with depress'd head surpasses any statue,
> And a mouse is miracle enough to stagger sextillions of infidels.[17]

These tribal, religious, and mystical expressions of a perceived order and harmony uniting people with the natural world reflect a universal inclination in the human species. Like all such inclinations, this biological tendency is rooted in the well-being of our species.

Science

The notion of an underlying unity in nature can also be discerned in modern science. Ironically, science has been linked with the tendency to demystify nature through subjecting the natural world to precise observation, quantitative measurement, and empirical study. Moreover, applied science and engineering have been linked to the manipulative control of nature through the use of technology. As the historian Keith Thomas describes: "The purpose of science was to restore to man dominion over creation. . . . Civilization and science were synonymous with the conquest of nature. . . . The whole purpose of science was that [nature] may be mastered, managed, and used in the services of humanity."[18]

Despite these tendencies, an equally compelling characteristic of modern science is the idea of an underlying commonality and relationship connecting humans with the rest of life and its processes. Earlier we noted that science has discovered an extraordinary degree of genetic, chemical, physiological, and morphological relation among life on earth suggesting a common biological origin and thus a basic affinity. This modern evolutionary and scientific knowledge intimates, as Edward O. Wilson suggests, a view of "other species [as] our kin."[19]

Modern ecological knowledge, too, stresses basic connections among living and nonliving elements of air, water, soil, plants, and animals.[20] Some scientists have even portrayed the sum total of life in quasi-organismal terms, arguing that conditions for life's perpetuation are maintained through ecological and chemical feedback loops and self-correcting mechanisms. Lynn Margulis and Dorion Sagan invoke the "Gaia" concept to describe such associations of life and nonlife: "On earth, the atmosphere-hydrosphere, surface sediments, and all living beings together (the biota) behave as a single integrated system with properties more akin to systems of physiology than those of physics. . . . In its strongest terms, the Gaia hypothesis claims that the mean global temperature, the composition of reactive gases in the atmosphere, and the salinity and alkalinity of the oceans are not only influenced but regulated, at a planetary level, by the flora, fauna, and microorganisms."[21]

Modern science does not explicitly endorse a spiritual interpretation of nature. Yet we find in contemporary science strong expressions of an underlying order and relation in the natural world despite extraordinary propensities for change and diversity. Modern science increasingly allies itself with ancient assumptions of commonality and connection binding humans with the rest of creation. The environmental philosopher Holmes Rolston intimates this coupling of modern science with traditional religious concepts of unity and order:

> The sciences describe much natural *diversity* and also much *unity*. . . . The physical sciences have revealed the astronomical extent of matter coupled with its reduction into a few kinds of elements and particles. . . . The biochemist has found only the materials of physics organized everywhere in parallel chemistries, such as glycolysis and the citric acid cycle or DNA and RNA at the core of life. Evolution has traced every life form back to monophyletic or a few polyphyletic origins, while ecology has interwoven these myriad forms to connect them at present as fully as they have been related by paleontology. . . . The story of science is the discovery of a bigger universe with more things in it, and the finding of laws and structures to explain their common composition and kinship.[22]

Ethics

Modern ethics, as well, increasingly links human society with morally acceptable behavior toward other life and nature in general.[23] Feelings of compassion and ethical responsibility emerge from the view that other creatures share a basic biological kinship and experience with humans. The moral circle of human society is broadened from families, communities, and nations to include nonhumans, particularly those like ourselves, and sometimes even lower life forms and nature more generally.[24] Aldo Leopold invokes the image of a "land ethic" in extending the focus of human moral interest from people to the whole natural realm: "All ethics evolve from a single premise: the individual is a member of a community of interdependent parts. The land ethic enlarges the boundaries of the community to include soils, waters, plants, and animals. . . . We can be ethical only in relation to something we can see, feel, understand, love, or otherwise have faith in."[25] From this vantage point, to harm nature is to injure oneself. Despite Leopold's assertion, most people's ethical obligations to nature are confined to creatures reminiscent of ourselves. These species strike us as possessing human-like capacities for pain and suffering.[26] Kindness, compassion, and respect concentrate on creatures who reveal attributes of sentience and self-interest similar to our own.

The ethical debate regarding modern sport hunting and fishing illustrates some of the issues involved in connecting closely with other life. Many people who object to recreational hunting and fishing do so because of their compassion for other animals.[27] Deliberately killing another creature for entertainment and nonessential purposes is viewed as ethically repugnant, even evil. As the writer and naturalist Joseph Wood Krutch argues: "Killing for sport is the perfect type of that pure evil for which metaphysicians have sometimes sought. . . . Most wicked deeds are done because the doer proposes some good to himself. The liar lies to gain some end; the swindler and burglar want things which, if honestly got, might be good in themselves. . . . The killer for sport, however, has no such comprehensible motive. He prefers death to life, darkness to light."[28]

In Chapter 6, we noted how the desire for intimacy with nature, ironically, can be a powerful motivating force for hunting and fishing. According to this view, hunting and fishing offer an unrivaled chance for entering into another creature's world and achieving a heightened awareness of human dependence on, and connection with, nature. Lacking evil intent, human hunters and fishers were depicted as no more morally culpable than a lion, wolf, or spider pursuing and killing prey. The ethics of recreational hunting and fishing defy easy resolution. The point is how often a strong compassion for nonhuman life produces a moral objection to activities that inflict harm and suffering on other creatures.

Tribal societies often possess strong spiritual and moral affinities for the natural world but rarely object to killing wildlife. Is there a difference between the tribal hunter and the person who hunts for recreation? The critical difference may be the tribal hunter's pragmatic justification for this exploitation, as well as the degree of compassion expressed by the human predator toward the prey. A feeling of moral connection and ethical responsibility for the natural world may be the distinguishing characteristic of the thoughtful person and caring society. Reverence and respect for other life constitute an essential condition for human spiritual relationship to the nonhuman world, whether the person's objective be exploitative or not.

Three Adaptive Benefits

Pronounced ethical concern for nature has sometimes been dismissed as unrealistic—at odds, that is, with the competitive demands of human fitness and survival. All expressions of biophilia, however, emerged because of the advantages they conferred during human evolution and development. Let us see how a yearning for unity and connection with nature may have encouraged three adaptive benefits: group loyalty and cooperation; personal confidence and security; and an inclination to conserve and protect life.

GROUP LOYALTY AND COOPERATION

The shared belief in an underlying meaning and purpose to life represents a powerful basis for group loyalty and commitment.[29] These convictions offer a foundation of collective morality that gives order, definition, and shape to our social existence. We take comfort and spiritual sustenance in sharing our moral and ethical beliefs. Common convictions promote loyalty and allegiance. People strive in common to find explanations to the meaning of life. And the answers to these questions have always involved the idea of connection to the rest of creation. As Holmes Rolston observes: "Humans are programmed to ask why, and the natural dialectic [is] the cradle of our spirituality."[30]

Group bonding encourages cooperative and helping behavior. Human survival and well-being depend on sharing, compassion, and a sense of social obligation. In their common interdependence, people achieve safety and security. This capacity for cooperation, empathy, and altruism is enhanced by the shared belief in a common moral order. We achieve cohesion and group commitment through recognizing life's enduring unity and our mutual connection with the rest of creation.

PERSONAL CONFIDENCE AND SECURITY

People also derive advantage from recognizing an underlying order binding humans with the natural world. We reap personal faith and confidence in believing that life possesses intrinsic meaning, value, and purpose. This conviction imbues in us the calming assurance that the world is fundamentally good, harmonious, worthwhile.

These beliefs can become particularly sustaining in times of crisis and adversity. A feeling of profound connection with nature offers a sense of relationship and enduring value in the face of individual separation and aloneness. We derive faith and optimism from our belief in a unity that transcends our lone and often vulnerable selves. This commitment musters in us the will to persevere in the face of setbacks. By connecting with the rest of creation, we find the trials of life somehow less overwhelming. This wisdom can be fathomed in an Ojibway expression: "Sometimes I go about pitying myself, and all the time I am being carried on great winds across the sky."[31]

CONSERVING AND PROTECTING NATURE

We have been sustained, as well, by our willingness to conserve and protect nature and treat its various creatures with kindness and respect. This claim may seem doubtful given the many times humans have reaped considerable reward from callously exploiting the natural world and even eliminating entire species. Nevertheless, there are few historical examples of the long-term utility of overexploiting nature. We confront instead the carcasses of many failed societies who heedlessly destroyed life and debased nature.[32]

Most successful cultures behave over the long term with restraint and respect toward natural diversity. These social orders assure the sustainability of their resource base by establishing ethical standards and moral conventions, not just by restricting access and property rights and developing formal rules and regulations.[33] Moreover, periods of excessive and highly destructive environmental exploitation often follow times of social and moral disintegration. North America's indigenous peoples overexploited the continent's wildlife, for example, largely after the cultural and moral breakdown caused by the devastating effects of conquest, colonization, and introduced disease.[34]

Ethical restraint and respect remain today an essential element in protecting and conserving nature. Too often we rely on law, regulation, and enforcement as the only means for protecting our natural resources. We underestimate the human inclination to act prudently and conservatively toward nature when motivated by a shared ethical commitment. History has frequently demonstrated a willingness to protect nature when people are motivated by common moral principles. The Indian ecologist Madhav Gadgil reports that ancient India conserved 6 percent of its land as "sacred groves"—nearly double the area tenuously set aside as protected area today.[35] Similiarly, many aboriginal peoples continue to prohibit large-scale resource extraction for moral and spiritual reasons, despite lucrative incentives to behave otherwise.[36]

Overexploiting our resources, both living and nonliving, can be prevented by strongly held moral beliefs, whether among traditional or modern peoples. The power of these convictions even today can be illustrated by our behavior toward surplus pets. Each year we incinerate millions of homeless cats and dogs, thereby, "wasting" much potentially edible protein. Yet proposals to ship this excess to hungry people around the globe elicit almost universal scorn and rebuke in our society. Whatever practical arguments may be offered to the contrary, we view the consuming of these creatures as ethically repugnant. Proposals for sustainably harvesting "surplus" whales similarly provoke widespread opposition.[37] For many people, whales no long represent a material resource. A growing affinity and ethical respect for these creatures has largely displaced scientific and utilitarian perceptions. We can see, then, that the desire to protect nature often derives as much from moral principle as from any calculated empiricism.

An attitude of ethical regard and spiritual connection with nature has more often than not sustained humans materially and physically as well as religiously. This tendency emerged in our species because, on balance and over time, it has served us well. We need to recognize the continuing relevance of an ethical affinity and moral respect for the diversity of life. We depend on this moral compass more than ever. Our capacity to destroy nature and life today threatens the survival of many thousands of creatures and habitats and, eventually, our own existence. The willingness to divine spiritual and moral connection with the rest of creation can help to stem and reverse this tide of ultimately self-defeating destruction.

Chapter Ten

Of Fear and Loathing

So far this book has emphasized the positive side of our inclination to affiliate with nature and life. We have explored how nature's utility, beauty, and wonder have nurtured our physical, emotional, and intellectual evolution. We have examined various facets of our admiration, affection, and even reverence and love for nature. We have largely ignored, however, our equally compelling and functional tendency to avoid and fear elements of the natural world. We must now confront the many expressions of our powerful inclination to reject nature. Human fascination for natural diversity is a two-edged sword—one side enriching and inspiring; the other, the source of great dread and disdain.[1] The tendency to repudiate and suppress elements of nature constitutes the other side of the same biological coin as our disposition to affiliate positively with it. In both cases, we derive advantage from our various inclinations to react and respond to natural diversity.

The natural world is a powerful source of human fears and anxieties. High winds, stagnant swamps, large predators, snakes and spiders, stinging invertebrates, and a host of other creatures and situations frequently strike terror and revulsion in us. These species and landscapes often provoke aversive behavior with only slight stimulus and under widely varying conditions.[2] Not only do such situations inflame acute and antagonistic passions but, once aroused, these emotions are often difficult to erase. Certain creatures and environments exert a particularly negative fascination for us, although these passions can sometimes be channeled into feelings of awe and admiration. What remains constant is the intensity of our instinctive inclination to react strongly to certain elements in nature.

This chapter explores this tendency to fear, avoid, and reject aspects of the natural and living world. We will consider various characteristics of our aversive reactions and the presumed benefits of this response. We will also examine how dread and avoidance of nature can inspire hateful and destructive acts but also, sometimes, feelings of awe and respect. The inclination to fear nature does not represent an intrinsically wrong or evil tendency. Like all expressions of biophilia, it has the potential for both functional advantage and harmful exaggeration.

Let us start by imagining two situations where sentiments of fear and aversion toward nature might be strongly manifest: a powerful storm at sea and a dark and forbidding swamp.

Late fall brought Jack and Betty Kane to the North Atlantic sailing their sturdy sixty-foot sloop to Bermuda. They were joined by another retired couple—the Glynns, old friends from Boston, where the Kanes had lived before Jack retired from a large insurance company.

The sailing had been idyllic: beautiful weather, occasional sightings of whales and dolphins, fresh fish almost every day, all in a boat that glided over the surface of the ocean as if floating on a large and peaceful lake.

Then, with little warning, the barometric pressure dropped precipitously, the sea boiled into heavy swells and long rolling waves, and strong winds and rains fell viciously on them.[3] *An intense storm had developed, one that had largely eluded the forecasters. They hardly had time to furl the sails and tie down the various lines. The wind and rain intensified, blinding them to all but an encircling whiteness. They remained on deck for as long as they could, tying lines and securing sails, before being forced below for fear of being swept overboard.*

Yet the ferocity of the storm kept escalating, great waves crashing down and over the boat. The force of the water and bitter cold left them terrified, huddled in corners. The once spacious cabin now felt like a crowded cell, the claustrophobic space contributing to an ever increasing sense of horror. The howling wind and violent waves reached nearly unendurable heights. They had become a speck of irrelevance before a savage, malevolent, and insatiable beast.

For six hours it continued unabated, each moment an eternity of dread. The boat's continuous creaking and moaning warned that it might break apart at any moment. Then the almost inconceivable occurred.[4] *A great wave struck, the boat shuddered, and then, incredibly, rolled over. Though the rolling seemed to go on forever, they could have been upside down for only a minute or two. As time moved in slow motion, they tumbled upon one another, pots, pans, gear, clothes, shoes, and other objects flying past, sometimes striking them, seawater swirling about despite the watertight hatches. Then, miraculously, the sixty-foot-boat, little more than a toy in a boiling cauldron, ever so slowly righted itself.*

The storm continued for hours, producing moments of intense fear and anxiety, but nothing could rival that upside-down moment of pure and unmitigated terror. Then, as if in anticlimax, the cyclone suddenly abated as quickly as it had arisen.

It took another two days before they finally reached Bermuda, bruised, battered, but incredibly thankful for being safe and alive. The Kanes eventually returned to the sea, again relishing the joy of riding the ocean waves, mainsail, jib, and genie full before a sturdy breeze. But it took six months on land before the thought of even sailing a boat produced anything more than a sickening dread.

When Peter proposed to Larry the idea of canoeing a tributary of the Amazon, it struck them both as a rare chance for exploration and adventure in one of the world's last great remaining wildernesses. They had canoed many rivers in North America together and regarded themselves as experienced outdoorsmen and naturalists.

Half the battle, they knew, was in the preparation. So they devoted many months to the tasks of gathering gear, assembling maps, planning routes, getting medical equipment, and accumulating knowledge of the fauna, flora, hydrology, weather, geology, human cultures, and other features of the region. They prided themselves on being neither naive nor reckless regarding the many challenges and dangers of venturing into the largest rain forest in the world.

Still, the reality they encountered was altogether different from what they had anticipated despite all their elaborate preparations. They had not imagined being quite so disturbed by the dark and foreboding waters. Less than a river, the tributary often spread out in all directions like an endless swamp. They felt like a floating island in a vast marsh. Its frequently putrid stench seemed unhealthy. They encountered patches of dry land, but when they stepped onto the surface, they would often be confronted by great clouds of mosquitoes and other biting insects. Thereafter they canoed fully clothed, despite the heat, humidity, and almost daily torrential rains.

For two weeks, they moved through a wet, shadowy, sullen world. Though they marveled at the wondrous flowers, trees, butterflies, birds, and other creatures, more often than not the dense foliage prevented them from seeing very far, and they ominously sensed, especially at night, hidden and watchful eyes.

Despite the almost constant anxiety and discomfort that enveloped them like a blanket, there were few major incidents. One of their worst moments was the time a boa constrictor fell on Peter from an overhanging branch. Seized by pure and irrational panic, he jumped and in the process capsized the boat. As they swam to shore, they dreaded the attack of alligators and piranha. Later they laughed at how the four-foot snake in fact posed no danger whatsoever.

Yet the incident epitomized how the haunting swamp had filled them with the fear of forces malignant and uncontrollable. In time they came to appreciate the river, but not before a certain arrogance and certainty had been replaced by awe of its vast strength and mystery. They now confessed to deep-seated fears in themselves—fears that helped in-

still a greater regard and respect for the rain forest and its many powers. They came to recognize in this immense wetland their capacity to be humbled and, in acknowledging this, developed a new appreciation for nature's many faces.

Bugs, Rats, and Dread

Anxiety, fear, and sometimes terror are still part of our relationship with the natural world. Particular environmental features and events elicit fear and avoidance under widely varying circumstances with little provocation. Although our fears and anxieties may be out of proportion to the actual risks involved, the inclination to avoid certain creatures and landscapes is motivated by more than careful calculation alone. We seem predisposed to evade certain features of the natural world almost independent of their immediate and obvious danger.

The work of the Swedish psychologist Arne Öhman examines this tendency.[5] He and his colleagues discovered an inclination among many "normal" persons to avoid snakes, spiders, and other commonly feared natural elements—even when subliminally shown pictures for just 15 to 30 milliseconds. Roger Ulrich cites various findings suggesting far greater fears of ancient natural threats like snakes and spiders than contemporary dangers like handguns and frayed electrical wiring.[6] Other research reveals pronounced inclinations among human infants and other primates (even laboratory-raised monkeys) to withdraw from "ugly, slimy, and erratic" moving animals, even in the absence of an overt or obvious threat.[7] Once aroused, moreover, these aversive tendencies frequently persist and are hard to erase.[8]

Distancing oneself from certain creatures and landscapes does not necessarily produce intense fear or dislike. Insulating oneself from threatening objects by minimizing, repressing, or denying their relevance or even existence can sometimes accomplish the same purpose. Often we practice "out of sight, out of mind" as a way of coping with anxiety and threat. Modern urbanization and separation from nature make this kind of apathy all too easy to achieve. Yet people who acknowledge only indifference when questioned about snakes, large predators, and other common dangers of the wild frequently reveal highly aversive and fearful reactions when actually confronted by these same creatures and landscapes.

These deeply ingrained fears may be illustrated by the reaction of many to the proposal to reintroduce wolves into Yellowstone National Park. Wolf restoration has provoked some to exclaim that "there'll be a dead child within a year," although no known wolf attack on humans has ever been reliably recorded in North America. Others have predicted: "The wolf is like a cockroach and will creep outside of Yellowstone and devour wildlife." Still others have remarked: "Only a brain-dead son-of-a-bitch would favor reintroduction of wolves. . . . It's like inviting the AIDS virus."[9] Even historically well-known advocates of wildlife protection, such as President Theodore Roosevelt and William Hornaday (founding president of the New York Zoological Society), have described the wolf as "the beast of waste and desolation" and condemned it: "Of all the wild creatures of North America, none are more despicable than wolves. There is no meanness, treachery or cruelty to which they do not cheerfully descend."[10] The wolf nowadays has its many proponents, however, equally passionate in their defense and admiration of this creature. The common link between those who love wolves and those who loathe them is the intensity of their feelings and reactions to this animal. The wolf reflects how certain natural elements, such as large predators, tend to provoke strong passions.

Our common aversive reactions to large predators may reflect our atavistic fear of being killed or eaten by another creature. Avoiding injury and death in nature represents one of the most deeply rooted tendencies of the human or any animal. As Öhman remarks: "Behaviors . . . associated with fear are pervasive in the animal kingdom. . . . One could argue that systems for active escape and avoidance must have been among the first functional behavior systems that evolved."[11] As a hairless ape of limited speed, endurance, and defensive capabilities, we still feel vulnerable no matter how insulated and protected from nature we have become in the modern age. Fearing injury and death represents a basic element of the human emotional and behavioral response to the natural world.

Avoiding and fearing nature can become so extreme it assumes irrational proportions not only in people but in cultures. The philosopher and animal rights advocate Peter Singer coined the term "specicide" for describing how our loathing for certain organisms can become so intense it provokes a willingness to exterminate the creature altogether.[12] Rats, snakes, sharks, ticks, and mosquitoes offer but a sample of species that have generated this degree of hatred and destructive antipathy. And with modern technology, such fears can create devastating levels of destruction. Even higher vertebrates like wolves can become the object of such excess. The writer Barry Lopez offers some insight regarding this kind of motive for exterminating wolves in North America during the nineteenth and early twentieth centuries: "Killing wolves [had] to do with fear based on superstitions. It [had] to do with duty. It [had] to do with proving manhood. . . . The most visible motive, and the one that best explains the excess of killing, [was] a type of fear: theriophobia. Fear of the beast as an irrational, violent, insatiable creature."[13]

Many insects and spiders provoke such fears and antipathy. In a study I conducted with colleagues, we examined attitudes toward insects, spiders, and other invertebrates among the general public, farmers, scientists, and environmental organization members.[14] The great majority of respondents, with the exception of scientists, expressed strong dislike of bugs, beetles, ants, crabs, ticks, cockroaches, and especially biting and stinging invertebrates such as wasps, spiders, mosquitoes, and scorpions. Indeed, a majority of the general public indicated a willingness to eliminate mosquitoes, cockroaches, fleas, moths, and spiders altogether. Invertebrates were generally viewed as mindless; incapable of emotion and rational decision making; and possessing little ethical, ecological, or practical value. Only a minority supported making economic sacrifices to protect endangered spiders or mollusks. Some species elicited more positive responses—mainly butterflies, "shellfish" (shrimps, lobsters, clams), and bees. These more sanguine attitudes appear to be related to the presumed beauty, food value, or practical significance of these creatures. Moreover, a majority of scientists expressed favorable and more informed views of insects, spiders, and other invertebrates, although these were largely organic (biologists, ecologists) not inorganic scientists (physicists, geologists).

What accounts for this widespread aversion, anxiety, and hostility toward many invertebrates, especially insects? Why do so many people lack awareness or appreciation of the various ecological, scientific, and utilitarian benefits of these creatures? Why do certain invertebrates provoke a willingness to exterminate them altogether?

Antipathy toward invertebrates often originates in the association of these animals with agricultural destruction and disease.[15] Destroying invertebrates has been linked to protecting crops and preventing illness. Producing food surpluses has been achieved by creating vast monocultures and eliminating insect "pests," often through the widespread use of toxics and biocides. The availability of inexpensive and plentiful food has been partly a result of our unrelenting "war on the bugs."

Notions of disease transmission and prevention similarly focus on the dangers of various invertebrates and other microorganisms.[16] Mosquitoes are associated with malaria, fleas with plague, ticks with fever, worms with intestinal problems, cockroaches with hygiene-related diseases, and so on. Entire medical specialties like parasitology have been built around the role of insects and other invertebrates as vectors of disease. To many people, these organisms intimate illness and disorder. Frequently they are victims of guilt by association.

Human antipathy toward invertebrates sometimes extends beyond the rational to levels of extreme fantasy and antagonistic projection.[17] What other attributes do these creatures possess that elicit such hateful feelings? Perhaps people feel threatened by the radically different biological and behavioral characteristics and survival strategies of these creatures. Insects and other invertebrates strike many of us as otherworldly and bizarre. They possess too many legs, move in odd and disturbing ways, boast strange and bewildering body shapes, typically come in small, even microscopic, packages. They can also reproduce in staggering numbers in a remarkably short period of time.

Insects, spiders, and other invertebrates often defy human notions of normality. They stretch our empathetic capacity and acceptance. Perhaps most disturbing, these creatures appear to lack a mental life: they reveal neither humanlike emotions of warmth and affection nor the intellectual characteristics of rationality and choice. The mind and soul appear irrelevant to their existence. Sometimes the peculiarities of invertebrates strike us as strange and exotic, the source of great mystery and curiosity. More often, they provoke the inclination to dislike the grotesque, fear the monstrous, and reject the alien and incomprehensible.

The psychologist James Hillman has suggested that invertebrates threaten our cherished assumptions of individuality, selfhood, and identity.[18] The enormous numbers of invertebrates imply the insignificance of the individual; the seeming absence of a mental life implies the irrelevance of personal consciousness. The sanctity of a single human life appears threatened by the idea that a single bee hive contains tens of thousands of organisms, a single ant colony hundreds of thousands, or that the number of beetle species numbers in the millions. Hillman remarks: "Imagining insects numerically threatens the individualized fantasy of a unique and unitary human being. Their very numbers indicate insignificance of us as individuals."[19]

Invertebrates lack the characteristics most people associate with moral standing: feelings, autonomy, rationality, choice, ethical responsibility. These creatures seem to respond only to the dictates of a rigid genetics, forsaking all selfhood for the sake of the species. Appearing mindless, lacking emotion and intellect, they emerge as symbols of madness and irrationality. Hillman notes: "Bug-eyed, spidery, worm, roach, bloodsucker, louse, going buggy, locked up in the bughouse—these are all terms of contempt supposedly characterizing inhuman traits. . . . To become an insect is to become a mindless creature without the warm blood of feeling."[20]

Invertebrates threaten by being so indifferent to our desires and presumptions of importance. Our homes, offices, buildings, even hospitals, are routinely invaded by insects and spiders, defying our notions of human sanctity and omnipotence. Most mammals, birds, and other vertebrates flee from human presence; insects and spiders frequently seem unaware, possibly disdainful, of our existence. They live in our homes and workplaces, and we cringe at hearing that seldom in our lives will we be more than five feet from a spider.

Three Adaptive Benefits

Like all expressions of biophilia, these tendencies of anxiety, aversion, and avoidance toward aspects of nature developed over the long course of human evolution. Although these inclinations can assume irrational proportions, they remain largely beneficial and adaptive elements of human existence. These tendencies can also form the basis for the more positive sentiments of awe and respect for the natural world. Let us consider three potential benefits associated with the human tendency to dislike aspects of nature: safety and survival; avoidance and defense; and awe and respect.

SAFETY AND SURVIVAL

Avoiding injury, harm, and death represents a basic tendency in every organism. As the previous quote from Arne Öhman suggests, this inclination probably emerged early in human development. People have an ingrained disposition to respond aversively to aspects of nature that, in our evolutionary past, proved threatening. Roger Ulrich reports: "Findings from many laboratory conditioning experiments support the notion that humans are biologically prepared to acquire and especially to not 'forget' adaptive biophobic (fear/avoidance) responses to certain natural stimuli and situations that presumably have presented survival-related risks throughout evolution."[21]

We can imagine how dislike of certain dangerous creatures and threatening landscapes might have developed. Large predators—particularly the great solitary, nocturnal cats and pack-hunting canids, for example—clearly presented a significant challenge to human security and survival. Aversive responses to certain meteorological events (lightning strikes, hurricanes, earthquakes), certain arthropods (biting and stinging invertebrates), or poisonous organisms (snakes, mushrooms) similarly conferred adaptive advantages and, consequently, became statistically preponderant in the human population. Even today, many thousands of people die each year from bee stings, lightning strikes, snake bites, crocodile and shark attacks, and other natural events.[22]

Avoiding injury and death in nature remains a basic aspect of human emotion, intellect, and behavior. Our tendency to fear certain creatures, like snakes, spiders, and large predators, and certain environmental features should be neither surprising nor necessarily unwelcomed. When rationally manifest, advantages accrue from isolating and occasionally removing threatening aspects of the natural world.

Our ambivalence today reflects uncertainty: how much do these anxieties represent realistic responses to the world we normally confront? And with technology at our command, as noted earlier, our formidable powers of destruction can assume awesome proportions. Can we still afford the consequences of a disposition to dislike certain species and landscapes? People do not just avoid snakes, spiders, scorpions, mosquitoes, ticks, large predators, and other commonly feared elements in nature. They also, at times, indulge in their wholesale and indiscriminate slaughter. Should our aversions to the natural world be viewed as largely anachronistic and dysfunctional and, if possible, be discouraged?

In fact, we are still vulnerable to various known and unknown threats in nature. Tornadoes, earthquakes, plagues, and other natural elements will no doubt continue to challenge our security and survival. A rational inclination to avoid and even remove threatening aspects of nature should be neither entirely repressed nor discouraged. Our well-being depends on skills and emotions associated with a healthy distancing from injurious elements in the natural world. Our emotional health and intellectual capacity will continue to depend on recognizing life as a struggle against odds—no matter how removed we become from nature.

Our fears and anxieties, as noted in Chapter 5, can also serve as a rich and valued source of human imagery and myth. Consider the snake.[23]

The subject of story and legend throughout human history, snake tales assume both realistic and fantastic proportions. The snake's emotional power derives from its capacity to bite, poison, and sometimes suffocate people—a fear likely originating in the particular vulnerabilities of a largely terrestrial primate. Moreover, other primates, including gorillas, chimpanzees, various Old World and New World monkeys, express fear of snakes, even laboratory primates who had never previously seen a snake.[24]

Our dislike of snakes makes these creatures an especially powerful source of fascination and symbolic projection. As the image of the snake can be easily molded and shaped, it has emerged in human legend and belief in many ways. Images of snakes entwining and entering humans have long figured in the collective myths and individualized fantasies of many people. As Edward O. Wilson suggests: "People in diverse cultures dream more about serpents than any other kind of animal, conjuring as they do so a rich medley of dread and magical power. When shamans and religious prophets report such images, they invest them with mystery and symbolic authority."[25]

Fascination, even veneration, can also accompany our fears and anxieties. The emotional power of snakes and other creatures permits us to regard them, not only as objects of loathing, but also as subjects of enchantment. Without the capacity to frighten and intimidate, such a creature would be symbolically ill-equipped to function in either our positive or negative myths and projections.

AVOIDANCE AND DEFENSE

Defending against danger has played a pivotal role in our inclination to respond aversively to certain creatures and landscapes. As noted in Chapter 8, humans reflect the characteristics of both herbivore and carnivore. As a predator, we display a certain aggressiveness and inclination to master and control. As a herbivore, we seek to avoid conflict, find shelter and security, remain elusive and out of harm's way. Essentially, then, we are a divided creature—one moment dominating and controlling; the next, avoiding conflict and strife.[26] We exalt in conquering other people, species, and environments; yet at the same time we relish the image of a peaceable kingdom where lions lie down with lambs.

Our avoidance strategies include an advanced capacity for climbing, hiding, and camouflaging. We remain visually alert, capable of discerning threat and risk from afar. We possess an especially developed capacity for constructing shelters and manipulating environments. We frequently choose to locate near promontories where we can see for long distances and escape easily. We routinely clear forests and contrive open spaces to ensure orientation and clear lines of sight. We erect obstacles and establish boundaries for minimizing risk and uncertainty. We remain especially furtive and evasive. We are steadfast in the face of adversity and misfortune. Like many other herbivores, we seek safety in numbers.

These highly refined capacities for avoidance and defense developed in the company of fearsome creatures and dangerous landscapes. Even today, our ability to achieve safety and security continues to be nurtured through our aversive affiliations with the natural world. Often we seek the image and even the reality of threatening nature—in our recreational choices, our stories, our fantasies. Lacking natural risk and uncertainty, we construct flimsy structures in places where they do not belong—on floodplains, along earthquake fault lines—and remain naive about our continuing vulnerability in an always uncertain and unpredictable world.

AWE AND RESPECT

We should not presume that our apprehensions about nature always breed contempt or destructive tendencies. Indeed, some of nature's most feared elements can also provoke feelings of awe and wonder, even reverence. Deference and respect for nature can arise as much from recognizing nature's power to overwhelm us as from appreciating its capacity to sustain our well-being. The dictionary defines awe as "an emotion of mingled reverence, dread, and wonder . . . respect, tinged with fear." We develop respect and a healthy distancing from sources of great power. Most godlike entities possess not only the capacity for great love and benevolence, but also the potential to terrify and destroy. Our dread of nature, similarly, can reflect a recognition of the power to humble and even crush us.

The great American landscape painters—Bierstadt, Cole, Church, Homer, and others—emphasized these qualities of strength and grandeur in nature.[27] Their depictions of mountains, seas, predators, and other natural elements exaggerated the mighty, the fearsome, and the sublime. Much like the great European cathedrals, these landscapes inspired awe and admiration. They intimated both wondrous and ferocious powers. They humbled humans in the presence of godlike authority. They drew strength and inspiration from the positive aspects of risk and danger. Stripped of these fearsome elements wildness often becomes merely pretty: a place for idle sightseeing but rarely for glimpsing great and inspiring truths.

The grandeur of nature, then, can engender a respectful appreciation. We keep a healthy distance from those natural elements presumably capable of exacting retribution for presumed wrongdoing. We may even temper our tendencies toward excess when it might invite retaliation. In cultivating an ethic of reverence for life, fear of nature can be as essential as deep affection.

Balance or Distortion?

We return once more to the intrinsic worth of any expression of biophilia—even a biophobic response. The inherent tendency to affiliate with nature and living diversity has functional value and benefit, whether positive or negative. The various strains of biophilia emerged because they offered some degree of adaptive advantage in human evolution and development. Each expression of biophilia can be weakly or strongly, functionally or dysfunctionally, manifested in individuals and societies. Indifference, fear, and dislike of nature—like the other aspects of biophilia—can assume both beneficial and harmful forms. A disturbing feature of modern society is our extraordinary capacity to dominate and destroy the natural world. This potential should not prevent us, however, from recognizing the many benefits that flow from our tendency to avert, fear, and dislike aspects of nature.

As we have seen, our anxieties can also be the source of a healthy distancing and respect for nature. The survival of tigers, bears, mighty rivers, and wilderness will depend as much on our avoiding and fearing these species and landscapes as on our willingness to shower them with affection. Fearing snakes, bears, wolves, lions, great heights, mighty winds, dark caverns, and other natural elements may well remind us of the need for humility and deference before the natural world. Nature subdued and utterly mastered inspires little appreciation and no respect. Wonder and inspiration follow moments of great insecurity and anxiety—how frequently we forget experiences lacking challenge and risk! A leopard pacing behind a cage or a snake curling on the other side of a wall of glass possess far less emotional power to inspire and instruct than their counterparts in the wild. Stripped of their menace, powerful creatures and landscapes become little more than objects of amusement and condescension.

Nature's capacity to intimidate captures our attention and commands our respect. Wildness must possess what Richard Nelson called "the luminescence of power."[28] Our respect and appreciation depend on fear and awe of the grizzly bear, the mighty storm, the great swamp, even the lowly bug.

This concludes our exploration of the nine expressions of biophilia and their role in human evolution and development. In the final two chapters, we will consider the conditions essential to the healthy realization of these basic inclinations to affiliate with nature and living diversity. We will consider, too, how modern life has increasingly compromised these connections and will examine alternatives to the current wave of environmental destruction and human disaffection.

Chapter Eleven

Diminishing Nature, Self, and Society

The previous chapters explored the role of biophilia in human evolution and development. We progressed from the material utility people derive from exploiting the natural world to the less obvious role of symbolizing nature to foster human communication and thought. Along the way we examined how the intimate experience of contact with living diversity can enhance our capacities for kinship and bonding, curiosity and discovery, critical thinking and inquiry. We considered, too, how the urge to master and control, avert danger, and even defy nature can strengthen our confidence and ability to sustain ourselves in the face of hardship and adversity.

These diverse expressions of biophilia have proved instrumental in building self-concept, developing a nurturing connection to others, and creating a harmonious relationship to the vast and varied universe. Collectively, these affiliations with the natural world have nourished the progress of our species' physical and mental health, our intelligence and emotional capacity, and a sense of spiritual hope and well-being. These various adaptations suggest why the multiple threads of biophilia have become encoded as genetic tendencies in the human animal over the long course of human history. In the process, these proclivities have passed through the individual, entered into the beliefs and behavior of human groups, and eventually diffused into the values and norms of cultures and societies.

As emphasized repeatedly, these expressions of biophilia represent, to varying degrees, weak biological tendencies that are greatly dependent on learning, experience, and social support for their full and functional realization. Without this reinforcement these inclinations become frustrated and atrophied, although, as elements of human biology, they continue to be fitfully manifest in various dispirited ways. Moreover, we must remember that any expression of biophilia can also be inordinately stressed—these tendencies, that is, can become exaggerated, distorted, and dysfunctional.

This chapter explores the conditions for the healthy realization of human biophilia. We consider circumstances accompanying people's effective experience of the natural world and examine how, in many ways, modern society has compromised and diminished our need for connecting with nature and living diversity. But first, let us examine some of the conditions necessary for the healthy expression of these tendencies. How do people integrate the experience of nature into their individual and collective lives? Like all complex phenomena, biophilia is "contextually driven"—that is, it depends on varying interactions and experiences to become stable and functionally manifest. The many expressions of biophilia develop only after adequate learning occurs in a variety of supportive situations and circumstances.[1]

Every expression of biophilia comprises a complex of feelings, thoughts, and beliefs about the natural world.[2] In more formal terms, people perceive and process their understanding of nature in different emotional, intellectual, and evaluative ways. Sometimes we view nature with fear, desire, or need. At more complex levels of experience, we reveal interest, fascination, curiosity, imagination. At even more sophisticated planes of perception, we form attitudes, judgments, and beliefs. This progression reflects how nature initially engages our feelings—

mainly emotions of attraction, fear, and affection. As we relate more intellectually, seeking knowledge and discovery, curiosity and an inquisitive spirit usually follow. Having become secure in our ideas and emotions, we then build assumptions and beliefs, rendering opinions and forming values about the worth, significance, and moral and ethical qualities of the natural world and our relations to it.

This development implies an evolutionary sequence. Emotions represent our most spontaneous and earliest responses to nature. Intellectual and cognitive reactions follow. Values and beliefs emerge last. All the expressions of biophilia, to varying degrees, involve a mix of these emotional, intellectual, and evaluative orientations to nature and life. To understand how this sequence might work in everyday terms, imagine a family traveling to Africa for the first time to see its wildlife.

Chou Chang and his wife, Lee, signed up for a trip to Kenya and Tanzania organized by their alumni association at the University of California at Berkeley. Chou and Lee were physicians in San Francisco who had long been fascinated by wildlife. They had always wanted to visit Africa and thought their kids were about the right age—fifteen, fourteen, and eleven—to benefit from the experience.

Arriving in Africa they were initially struck by the extraordinary beauty of the savanna, its seeming familiarity, its rolling hills, punctuated by the tall spreading acacia and baobab trees dotting the undulating plains. The wildlife especially awed and astounded them—the enormous herds of zebra, gazelle, antelope, wildebeest, and other ungulates; the great predators, particularly the cats, hyenas, and crocodiles; the often amusing hippos, rhinoceroses, and giraffes; even the large and colorful birds, above all the huge flocks of flamingos, pelicans, and avocets. Not only splendor but also a sense of timelessness pervaded this brilliant profusion of life. Fascinated and aroused, their feelings and fantasies took imaginative flight.

They were especially enthralled by the great caldera of the Ngorongoro crater. As they sat around the fire in their tented camp one night, they wondered why it affected them so. Perhaps it had something to do with the enormous size of the crater; or the abundance and diversity of its wildlife; or its magnificent lake, which, seen from the rim, seemed to capture the very clouds, sky, and air within its liquid depths.

The next day, they visited the Olduvai Gorge, just over the crater's rim, the place where "man was born." The landscape radiated wonder, felt rich with possibilities, offered powerful images that burned into their memories.

Upon leaving Africa, they reflected on their shifting reactions. Initially they had largely responded with fascination, wonder, pleasure, awe, and sometimes fear. Eventually their responses became more informed, more organized, reflecting a diversity of emerging interests and understandings. At the conclusion of their two-week visit, they started to form convictions about the significance of this land and how its wonderful natural diversity might be sustained and protected for present as well as for future generations.

Over time, most people's reactions to landscapes and wildlife follow this progression from largely emotional to more intellectual to, eventually, relatively complex judgments and beliefs about nature. An analogous developmental sequence has been observed in the formation of children's attitudes toward nature.[3] The preschool period from four to six years of age marks the time when children largely express feelings toward nature and animals—particularly desire, attraction, fear, and aversion. During this developmental period, children focus mainly on gratifying and protecting themselves in their relations to the natural world.

The next stage, usually from six to nine years of age, involves a greater appreciation of the feelings and needs of other creatures. Children begin to recognize nature apart from themselves, realizing other creatures can experience pain and distress, and why nature should be left alone—regardless of whether or not they might be punished for harming it.

The stage that follows—the middle school years—marks the time when children reveal a dramatic increase in knowledge, interest, and curiosity about nature and life. A rapidly developing intellectual concern for nature occurs, along with growing fascination about how the nonhuman world functions and works.

Finally, in late adolescence, children express more abstract and conceptual orientations to life and nature, becoming much bolder and more exploratory in their experience of the natural world. Children at this stage form ecological and moral judgments about nature, as well as views about human responsibilities and ethical obligations. These children push the boundaries of the natural world, seeking new and bolder contacts with wildlife and unfamiliar landscapes.

These stages of childhood development do not imply the irrelevance of adult experiences of nature. Other research we conducted revealed profound changes in values and perceptions of the natural world among the college-educated.[4] Studies in the United States, Germany, and Japan found that college-educated persons expressed the greatest interest, appreciation, and concern for nature and wildlife of any demographic group examined. Moreover, this attitude had nothing to do with the person's major in college. Still, childhood represents the most critical period in the formation and development of the various expressions of biophilia. A certain hardening of perspectives of nature often occurs during adulthood and especially old age.[5] As in so many other areas of human experience, childhood constitutes the most opportune time for cultivating an affinity, appreciation, awareness, knowledge, and concern for the natural world.

What social and environmental conditions might promote or impede the development of biophilia during childhood? Three factors especially stand out: a healthy and diverse natural environment; satisfying and attractive places of residence and work; and a reinforcing social and cultural milieu. Before considering each of these factors, let us imagine how two young children growing up in a contemporary American city might encounter difficulties in this regard.

John, nine, and his sister Denise, ten, lived in a new condominium situated near a picturesque river in a historic section of a city of some 100,000 on the New England coast. The family had moved from Ohio a little more than a year ago.

Their mother and father worked as biological researchers at a nearby medical school. Their complicated work kept them in the laboratory for hours at a time, often well into the late afternoon, after John and Denise had returned home from school. Their parents debated the costly step of after-school day care, but decided to see if John and Denise could take care of themselves for the few hours before they got home. With fondness the parents recalled a rural childhood in the Midwest when they routinely spent long periods of time playing on their own.

The experiment was initially a success. John and Denise had few problems. Indeed, they reveled in the chance to play on their own. Before long these late afternoon interludes became the high point of their day. Their classes often seemed boring, oppressive, and their school building had high sealed windows with only a view of the asphalt playground and the teachers' parking lot. The average class size was forty, courses mainly focusing on the basics of reading, writing, and arithmetic taught exclusively through books full of facts and formulas. Their time outside consisted of thirty minutes after lunch, mainly involving organized sports and playing on the asphalt. Although there was a large park nearby, its trees and meandering river an inviting distraction, the possibility of playing there was precluded by the teachers' lack of interest, union contracts, and liability concerns.

John and Denise's time after school, thus, became their magical time of day. They played various card and board games, worked on puzzles, drew and painted. Their favorite activity, though, was playing outdoors—especially exploring the banks of the nearby river. At first their parents were apprehensive about the river. After considerable discussion and debate, however, the children were allowed to play there so long as they promised to remain close to home, periodically checked in with a helpful neighbor, and never entered the water itself.

John and Denise indulged in the many wonders and mysteries of the riverbank. Their home base consisted of a "secret cave" located in a particularly tall patch of marsh grass. After hollowing it out, they filled it with various "treasures"—a bouquet of purple loosestrife and pink marshmallows, a collection of oyster shells, bones from a long-departed muskrat, the feathers of various birds, an occasional live frog and turtle, some dragonflies, the skin of a snake, and, their favorite treasure of all, a set of deer antlers they found. They even caught a fish on two occasions, using fishing lines of their own construction, some hooks they discovered, and worms found in the muck. And although they suspected their parents would disapprove, they built a fire and ate some of the fish, before its peculiar taste prompted them to discard it.

They spent considerable time exploring elements of the river. They pushed the frontiers of their universe, exhilarating in their many discoveries, occasionally being set back by fear and anxiety. Each exploration, each imaginative search and foray, carried the promise of new and special discoveries.

Once they stumbled onto a skunk. At first, they marveled at its brilliant black and white coat, so much more resplendent than the pictures in their books or on television. But the novelty quickly evaporated when the skunk turned suddenly and sprayed them. The rest of the afternoon they spent scrubbing, showering, and struggling to remove the offending smell before their parents came home.

Another time, the bank caved in and Denise went sliding into the swollen river, cold and fast from the previous day's rain. Horrible moments ensued before John managed to pull his sister back onto the bank. They shivered, cried, and hugged each other. They had bad dreams for weeks afterwards, and neither of them ever forgot the experience. In the mythological retelling that followed, John took special pride in overcoming his panic and having "saved" his sister's life.

The episode instilled in them a new respect for the river, as well, and a view of it as more than just a place for fun and amusement. A few weeks after the incident, they performed a ceremony in their "cave" promising the river they would never harm it if, in return, it would never hurt them.

Their world of magic, splendor, and play, however, came to a sudden end. Three events conspired to remove the river from their lives, replacing it with another school, until their parents eventually abandoned the condo altogether.

The first problem stemmed from the festering sores that developed on parts of their skin. After much diagnostic confusion, the doctors eventually decided, following various tests, that the sores were caused by chemical pollution originating in upstream factories, landfills, and abandoned hazardous waste sites. A medical alert soon followed: no one was to consume any fish caught in the river, and children were not to play in or beside it.

Even if this incident had not occurred, John and Denise's access to the river would have been greatly constricted by the decision to build an office complex and marina on the condominium's riverfront property. Although there was plenty of vacant space in various downtown office buildings, the success of the condo and easy access to urban development funds persuaded a group of speculators to invest in a twelve-story office building, restaurant, marina, and boardwalk. Somehow various wetlands provisions and other environmental statutes were bypassed. The promise of new taxes, employment, and federal subsidies had proved too great a temptation for local officials.

The final incident involved a crime wave. The historic waterfront district, like much of the city, had experienced steep economic and social decline for more than two decades, and many of its middle-class residents had fled to the suburbs. Although the condominium complex helped revive the area, most of its residents were single and retired. The complex lacked the family atmosphere and amenities of a stable and prosperous community.

Moreover, a public housing project had been constructed about a mile away. This meant little in itself, but the project had become notorious for its drugs and accompanying violence. Eventually these problems spilled over onto the condominium, as groups of teenagers discovered the easy prey living nearby. Although the police responded quickly, the constant sirens and ensuing restrictions contributed to an atmosphere of fear that blanketed the neighborhood. The condo's management hired private guards, but the complex still lived in terror. Most people stayed inside, especially at night, behind locked doors and newly installed alarms. The few children living there, including John and Denise, were prohibited from wandering alone and playing outside.

Overwhelmed by these events, John and Denise, now a year older, were placed by their parents in an afternoon day care program. They did not dislike the program so much as its many restrictions. It seemed just like another school. Their opportunities for play, fantasy, and spontaneity had been replaced by a rigid and narrow regime. They remained mostly indoors. Their time outside consisted largely of being told by adults what to do and see.

Ultimately their parents sold the condo and moved them all to the suburbs. They took a substantial financial loss from the plunge in property values following the publicity over the polluted river and the crime wave. But the promise of a new start proved irresistible.

This story illustrates the three conditions for the functional development of biophilia noted earlier: a healthy and diverse environment; attractive places of residence and work; and a supportive social and cultural milieu. Let us examine each of these dimensions and its apparent status in contemporary society.

A Healthy and Diverse Environment

Our physical, emotional, and intellectual capacity relies greatly on the health and diversity of the natural, especially living, environment. This natural context remains an irreplaceable stage for performing and partaking in the drama of life's mystery and discovery. Even within the biologically impoverished context of modern life, we are drawn irresistibly to certain habitats, waters, soils, rocks, and especially living plants and animals. The natural fabric offers a magic well of connection. In this vibrant arena, we enter into a world of learning, experience, imagination, and play. The varying expressions of biophilia depend on a complex and subtle mix of environmental opportunities for human growth and development. Through these media of natural relationship, we experience utility and sustenance, searching and discovery, attraction and beauty, affection and companionship, mastery and control, understanding and comprehension, awe and reverence, fear and respect, myth and mystery, and more.

These affinities for nature emerged in adaptive response to the demands of survival and effective living. Each adds to a nourishing diet of vitality necessary for human maturation. All expressions of biophilia depend on healthy, abundant, and attractive natural environments for their full and functional realization. This learning context means repeated and spontaneous opportunities for interacting with richly diverse and accessible habitats and life forms.

What would it be like if we lacked the chance for interacting with healthy natural environments? What would happen if all we encountered were artificial realities? Such a world would conflict with everything we recognize as emotionally, intellectually, and spiritually normal and meaningful. Edward O. Wilson offers a picture of such a place: "Visualize a beautiful and peaceful world, where the horizon is rimmed by snowy peaks reaching into a perfect sky . . . except for one thing—it contains no life whatever. . . . This is a world where people would find their sanity at risk. Without beauty and mystery beyond itself, the mind . . . is deprived of its bearings and will drift to simpler and cruder configurations."[6]

Yet increasingly we embrace a biologically impoverished, artificial, and environmentally degraded existence. During the past several centuries, we have witnessed a profound diminution of life on earth, greater pollution, and the rapid spread of manufactured and human-dominated landscapes. The capacity of many creatures to survive has declined precipitously as a consequence of huge increases in human population, industrial and technological advance, excessive resource exploitation, and escalating consumption of space and materials. This loss has now reached intolerable levels exceeding the capacity of normal evolutionary processes to fill an ever widening biological void.[7] The overall quantity and quality of life on earth has diminished, and myriad human material and psychological dependencies on nature have suffered as a consequence of this biological hemorrhaging and environmental degradation.

THE SCALE OF DECLINE

Let us briefly review the scope of this decline before turning to its likely consequences.[8] The scale of the loss can be measured in various ways: increasing rates of pollution, eroding natural habitats, the endangerment and extinction of life, and more. By way of illustration, suppose we focus on the accelerating scale of contemporary species extinctions and endangerment. We might begin with a historical perspective of North America during the past millennium. An estimated six vertebrate species suffered extinction on this continent during a 500-year period, 1100 to 1600; in the next 250 years, 1600 to 1850, this figure increased to twenty extinctions; during the following 125 years, from 1850 to 1975, some five hundred extinctions occurred; the final quarter of the twentieth century and the first quarter of the next century will likely witness tens of thousands of vertebrate and invertebrate species extinctions.

The plight of certain species illustrates the magnitude of this loss. Since the time of the European settlement of North America, one out of every five freshwater fish species has disappeared or is currently in danger of extinction. Nearly all of the continent's large carnivores are endangered, including seventeen of its more than seventy marine mammal species and almost all of its large whales. Approximately half of North America's freshwater mollusk species (an animal group distinguished for its evolutionary development on this continent) have disappeared or cling precariously to survival. The U.S. government lists some one thousand American species as currently endangered or threatened with extinction—and another three thousand candidates are awaiting possible endangered species protection.[9]

The scale of planetary extinction remains just as distressing. One-fifth of the world's bird species, for example, have disappeared during the past thousand years, due mainly to human factors.[10] The destruction of the tropical rain forests threatens the existence of some 15,000 to 30,000 species each year. Based on a figure of 10 million species on the planet, half in the tropics, and assuming an annual tropical deforestation rate of 1 to 2 percent (due to agricultural clearing, human settlement, logging, mining, road building, and so on), Edward O. Wilson estimates that more than 25,000 tropical forest species are lost every year.[11] Professor Jay Savage of the University of Florida, employing a more conservative figure of 2 million tropical forest species, offers a somewhat lower estimate of 2,000 to 16,000 extinctions annually.[12] But a higher number of worldwide extinctions can be projected if we consider other biomes and include in our calculations species loss due to such factors as the introduction of nonnative species (responsible for an estimated 15 to 20 percent of extinctions) and overharvesting of various plant and animal species (the primary factor in some one-third of vertebrate endangerments). All these factors combined suggest the possibility of a million or more extinctions worldwide during the next half century, including an estimated 100,000 species in North America alone.

Three factors are primarily responsible for all this loss of life: habitat destruction, harmful introduction of nonnative species, and unsustainable levels of exploitation. Destruction of natural habitat constitutes, by far, the most important factor.[13] Particularly damaging activities include large-scale agriculture and forestry, excessive livestock herding and grazing, various water impoundments and diversions, extravagant mining and energy production, spreading urbanization and industrialization—and, underlying all of these, rapid human population growth. These forces are eradicating other life as our technology, our consumption, and our numbers preempt an ever increasing proportion of the world's available stock of energy, space, and materials. This disturbing decline in numbers and populations of species reflects the inevitable consequence of humans capturing an ever larger proportion of the planet's available energy and biological capital—some suggest as much as 40 percent.[14] This impact is magnified by our increasing fragmentation and simplification of natural systems, a process that is insidiously damaging the reproductive and survival strategies of many creatures.[15]

The introduction of nonnative organisms and diseases is another activity that contributes significantly to the decline and extinction of life.[16] Species that evolved in relative isolation (on islands, in isolated bodies of water, on mountaintops) are particularly susceptible to this impact. These creatures often specialize in exploiting particular habitats or food sources and frequently do not compete well with introduced species, especially predators. The estimated one-fifth of the world's bird species that disappeared during the past thousand years includes large numbers of island species—frequently victims of introduced predators and disease. Many fish species that evolved in isolated environments reveal similar patterns of decline.[17] A majority of America's endangered and extinct freshwater fish, especially in the western United States, have been victims of introduced species. A sampling of fish life in Arizona's Salt River, for example, revealed fourteen native and no nonnative fish species in 1900 and seven native and two alien species by 1920; by 1950, all the native fish had disappeared, entirely replaced by twenty exotic species.[18]

Species are introduced both deliberately and by accident. Deliberate reasons include food and commerce (in the case of nutria and gypsy moths), sport (carp and pheasants), aesthetics (swans and starlings), and to control the damaging impact of other species. Accidentally introduced species include creatures escaping from captivity and those stowing away on boats and airplanes. Whether accidental or deliberate, these introductions usually occur with little understanding or consideration of their potentially harmful impact. The biologist Walter Courtenay refers to the introduction of nonnative species as a game of "ecological roulette" with the benefits few and the damaging impacts many.[19]

The third primary cause of species extinction and endangerment has been excessive exploitation for various material purposes. Although typically associated with activity in the past, overexploitation still accounts for some one-third of vertebrate species endangerment today.[20] Even in our modern context of science and regulation, the forces of human greed, ignorance, technology, and apathy contribute to the unsustainable exploitation of various species.

Sustainable wildlife utilization is a very elusive ideal when a species has great economic value.[21] Commercially valuable species tend to be viewed as inexhaustible, substitutable, or likely to be replaced by future technologies that will render their elimination economically or materially irrelevant. People often ignore the future. Current profits and human ingenuity, they assume, will eventually compensate for the risks of a creature's extinction. The rhetoric of sustainable utilization implies strong incentives to conserve a species, but the reality has often been otherwise. Excessive profits and the ability to reinvest them in other areas of economic return often make a species' elimination a logical option.

The combined effects of habitat loss, species introductions, and excessive exploitation can sometimes contribute to the decline of entire groups of life. A particularly tragic example is provided by the forest birds of Hawaii.[22] At the time of Captain Cook's discovery of the Hawaiian Islands in 1786, more than eighty forest birds occurred there and nowhere else. These birds included one family, the honeycreepers, consisting of forty-seven species possessing an extraordinary range of shapes and bills for exploiting Hawaii's diversity of habitats and food sources. As Hawaii is the world's most geographically isolated environment, most of its plant and animal life was found only there. Hawaii contained no large predators. The only mammals were species of seal, bat, and whale.

All three of the major extinction factors played a significant role in the decline of Hawaii's unique plants and animals, especially bird life. Extensive habitat destruction resulted from large-scale agricultural clearing, urban development, fire, widespread military activity, pesticide use, and other activities. Excessive species exploitation occurred as a consequence of feather gathering, hunting, egg collecting, and the pet trade. Both accidental and deliberate species introductions resulted from stowaways on boats, domestic livestock escaping into the wild, and species introduced for reasons of food, pest control, sport, and decoration.

Sometimes Hawaii's exotics behaved in unexpected ways—a predatory wasp introduced to control an agricultural pest turned instead on a native insect that provided the primary food source for an indigenous bird species; mongooses, which were expected to eliminate harmful rabbits, instead began feeding on endemic flightless birds. Even wildlife enthusiasts such as hunters and birders, along with government officials, sometimes introduced species to enhance their recreational interests. These groups recognized that, while Hawaii had unique creatures, like most isolated islands it contained few overall numbers of species. Moreover, its hospitable climate and absence of predators offered an inviting setting for new forms of life. Rarely did these groups recognize the potentially harmful impacts of these introduced creatures.

Together, all these factors devastated Hawaii's bird life. In the two hundred years following Captain Cook's discovery of the islands, twenty-three forest birds disappeared and another thirty are currently endangered. Among the honeycreepers, two-thirds have been eliminated or presently are in peril of extinction. One Hawaiian honeycreeper, the palila, offers an interesting and relevant example.[23] The palila occurs on the big island of Hawaii in its unique Mamani-naio forest, a habitat restricted today to the slopes of Mauna Kea in Hawaii Volcanoes National Park. The bird's decline resulted from eliminating its forest habitat, mainly due to the feeding of introduced goats and sheep. Because Hawaii contained no land mammals, sportsmen and government officials promoted these introduced animals as game species. Ultimately a landmark lawsuit, *Palila v. the Hawaii Department of Land and Natural Resources,* forced the state to remove the feral animals.[24] The court declared that destroying the palila's habitat represented an illegal "taking" of the species. This ruling greatly expanded the government's ability to prevent destruction of an endangered species' habitat on both public and private lands.

THE SIGNIFICANCE OF THE DECLINE

The worldwide decline in biological abundance and diversity is reflected by the experience of Hawaii's birds, the freshwater fish and mollusks of North America, tropical forest species, and other cases. Does the prospect of all this extinction represent a serious threat to human welfare? After all, most tropical forest extinctions will affect mainly insects—many of them not scientifically described let alone meaningfully connected to human economics and well-being. The demise of America's freshwater fish, mollusks, marine mammals, or large carnivores strikes closer to home, but does this decline exert much impact on the lives of most Americans?

Even if we assume 15,000 to 30,000 extinctions every year, this figure represents but a small fraction of the planet's estimated 10 to 100 million species. Even if this rate of extinction continued unabated for the next half century it would still account for only a minority of species on earth. Moreover, the extinction of 25,000 or even a million species, or the decline of an obscure animal group like America's freshwater snails or desert fish, may seem like an acceptable loss if it helps improve the living standards of impoverished peoples around the globe. Many of our poorest nations, after all, are found in the same tropical areas rich in biological diversity.

The significance of the current extinction crisis can be minimized or even trivialized when viewed from the perspective of a single species or obscure plant and animal group. Does losing a palila, an inconspicuous mollusk, a tropical insect, or even a grizzly bear and tiger carry much importance? Moreover, the prospect of 25,000 extinctions a year represents an abstraction difficult for most people to fathom or appreciate. Putting aside for the moment the ethical question of a species' intrinsic right to exist, would this degree of extinction serve the ultimate interests of humanity? Can people experience lives replete with physical, material, emotional, intellectual, and spiritual meaning if these lives are built upon the destruction of so much of the natural world? I have endeavored in this book to indicate how, in so many ways, this would be impossible. Living nature shapes our identity, defines our values, and offers the possibility of experiencing beauty, meaning, and purpose. The natural world is an irreplaceable source of material gain, empirical truth, aesthetic worth, intellectual inspiration, emotional bonding, physical skill, spiritual grace, and more. We draw nourishment from healthy and diverse natural environments.

Yet the significance of nature as a whole should not diminish our appreciation of the value of even a single creature. Every species has the power to enhance our capacities for compassion, respect, moral judgment, and self-interest. Human existence is enriched by its connections with the life of every creature. Consider the extinction of the passenger pigeon.[25] This bird once numbered in the billions, regarded by some as the most abundant bird species in North American history. The pioneering Scottish ornithologist Alexander Wilson estimated one flock in 1810 in the Indiana Territory at 2.2 *billion* birds.[26] These huge flocks could turn the daytime sky dark. Like the bison, their remarkable numbers offered a compelling symbol of the New World's extraordinary biological abundance and richness.

The pigeon's demise resulted not only from intolerable levels of commercial hunting but also from clearing its oak–hickory forest for lumber and agriculture. The slaughter may be difficult to conceive of by today's standards, but the report of one Kentucky hunt in 1827 by the well-known ornithologist and artist John James Audubon provides some perspective on the devastation:

> Few pigeons were to be seen before sunset; but a great number of persons, with horses and wagons, guns and ammunition, had already established encampments on the borders. . . . Suddenly, there burst forth a general cry of "Here they come!" The noise which they made, though yet distant, reminded me of a hard gale at sea, passing through the rigging of a close-reefed vessel. As the birds arrived, and passed over me, I felt a current of air that surprised me. Thousands were soon knocked down by polemen. The current of birds, however, still kept increasing. The fires were

> lighted, and a most magnificent, as well as wonderful and terrifying sight, presented itself. The Pigeons, coming in by thousands, alighted everywhere, one above another, until solid masses, as large as hogsheads, were formed on every tree, in all directions. Here and there the perches gave way under the weight with a crash, and, falling to the ground, destroyed hundreds of the birds beneath, forcing down the dense groups with which every stick was loaded. It was a scene of uproar and confusion. I found it quite useless to speak, or even to shout, to those persons who were nearest to me. The reports, even of the nearest guns, were seldom heard. . . . The uproar continued . . . the whole night. . . . Toward the approach of day, the noise rather subsided. . . . The howlings of the wolves now reached our ears; and the foxes, lynxes, cougars, bears, raccoons, opossums, and pole-cats were seen sneaking off from the spot, whilst eagles and hawks, of different species, accompanied by a crowd of vultures, came to supplant them, and enjoy their share of the spoil. It was then that the authors of all this devastation began their entry amongst the dead, the dying, and the mangled. The pigeons were picked up and piled in heaps, until each had as many as he could possibly dispose of, when the hogs were let loose to feed on the remainder.[27]

The killing, timber felling, and agricultural conversion continued throughout the seventeenth, eighteenth, and nineteenth centuries. Even so, the impression of unlimited abundance of pigeons persisted. The writer Peter Matthiessen, quoting an Ohio county commissioner in 1857, captures the reasoning behind failed attempts to restrict the killing: "The passenger pigeon needs no protection. Wonderfully prolific, having the vast forests of the North as its breeding grounds, traveling hundreds of miles in search of food, it is here to-day and elsewhere tomorrow, and no ordinary destruction can lessen them or be missed from the myriads that are yearly produced."[28]

By the 1870s, the passenger pigeon had been eliminated from Ohio. An enormous flock of some 136 million birds still persisted in Michigan, occupying some 750 square miles, but this was the last of the great flocks. Too late it became apparent that the pigeon's survival depended on enormous aggregations for triggering its reproductive, feeding, and predator evasion strategies. The last wild pigeons disappeared at the end of the nineteenth century. The final member of the species, a captive bird named "Martha," expired in the Cincinnati Zoo in 1914. The pioneering wildlife ecologist Aldo Leopold offered eloquent words at a ceremony some decades later, expressing some of the benefits lost to humanity by the extinction of this single species:

> We have erected a monument to commemorate the funeral of a species. It symbolizes our sorrow. We grieve because no living man will see again the onrushing phalanx of victorious birds, sweeping a path for spring across the March skies, chasing the defeated winter from all the woods and prairies. . . . Men still live who, in their youth, remember pigeons. Trees still live who, in their youth, were shaken by a living wind. . . . There will always be pigeons in books and in museums, but these are effigies and images, dead to all hardships and to all delights. Book-pigeons cannot dive out of a cloud to make the deer run for cover, or clap their wings in thunderous applause of mast-laden woods. Book-pigeons cannot breakfast on new-mown wheat in Minnesota and dine on blueberries in Canada. They know no urge of seasons; they feel no kiss of sun, no lash of wind and weather. . . . Our grandfathers were less well-housed, well-fed, well-clothed than we are. The strivings by which they bettered their lot are also those which deprived us of pigeons. Perhaps we now grieve because we are not sure, in our hearts, that we have gained by the exchange. The gadgets of industry bring us more comforts than the pigeons did, but do they add as much to the glory of the spring?
>
> It is a century now since Darwin gave us the first glimpse of the origin of species. We know now what was unknown to all the preceding caravan of generations: that men are only fellow-voyagers with other creatures in the odyssey of evolution. This new knowledge should have given us, by this time, a sense of kinship with fellow-creatures; a wish to live and let live; a sense of wonder over the magnitude and duration of the biotic enterprise. . . . The pigeon was a biological storm. He was the lightning that played between two opposing potentials of intolerable intensity: the fat of the land and the oxygen of the air. Yearly the feathered tempest roared up, down, and across the continent, sucking up the laden fruits of forest and prairie, burning them in a traveling blast of life. . . . Today the oaks

still flaunt their burden at the sky, but the feathered lightning is no more. Worm and weevil must now perform slowly and silently the biological task that once drew thunder from the firmament."[29]

Leopold's words stir all but the most cynical and apathetic. He reveals how even the loss of a single creature can compromise a host of the values we cherish. We no longer delight, for example, at the pigeon's incredible abundance, signaling the triumphant return of spring, diving by thousands, while "sucking . . . the laden fruits . . . in a traveling blast of life." We no longer benefit by the pigeon's role in the cycling and propagating of the seeds and fruits of the land contributing to the region's remarkable fertility and agricultural abundance. We no longer feel enlightened and inspired by the extraordinary evolutionary success of this adaptive and prolific bird. Lifeless pigeons remain in museums, but they offer little more than ghostly reminders and an unrelieved source of guilt. A deepening disquietude emerges, perhaps our realization of a lesser and shrunken world.

Leopold did not object to killing pigeons. He advocated the virtues of hunting as a way of sustaining our knowledge, appreciation, and dependence on the land. The pigeon's numbers would have encouraged him to support its sustainable harvest for the plate, as well as for the opportunities it afforded for achieving competence through immersion in the outdoors. He might even have blanched at the naming of a pigeon, "Martha," yet he would have recognized how this species contributes to our understanding and respect of ourselves and the natural world.

Biotic diversity insinuates itself into our lives in so many subtle, complex, and indirect ways. Natural health and variability may seem a restricted and dispensable phenomenon when viewed from the perspective of a single creature, a single benefit, or a single point in time. But the irreplaceable role of nature in human development and well-being becomes evident when we calculate its significance across a wide diversity of species and in relation to all the expressions of biophilia. From the perspective of evolutionary time, we may appreciate the many ways nature and life continue to contribute to our physical, emotional, intellectual, and spiritual well-being.

Attractive and Satisfying Places to Live and Work

Natural abundance and diversity alone provide an insufficient basis for the effective development of the various expressions of biophilia. Tropical forests, coral reefs, and deep sea vents contain more species than any other biomes on earth, yet few people have a sustained and spontaneous connection with these areas. These biological communities offer invaluable ecological and material benefits to humanity, but they rarely function as meaningful places of residence and work. Certainly they do not offer everyday places for the ongoing experience of nature and living diversity.

The various expressions of biophilia depend on repeated and spontaneous, not transient and sporadic, connections with natural variety. Healthy development means encountering nature in a way that is physically stable, psychologically significant, and socially secure. This means places of residence and work linked meaningfully to natural diversity within relevant cultural and human-built environments.

When we refer to "great places" to live, we typically mean areas rich in sustainable relationships between the social and natural worlds.[30] This combination provides attractive, healthy, and bountiful experiences of nature integral and relevant to people's lives. The environmental philosopher Mark Sagoff elucidates this notion of place: "The concept of place combines the meaning we associate with nature and the utility we associate with environment. [The result is an idea of] surroundings that arises from harmony, partnership, and intimacy."[31]

Effective communities, whether villages or cities, constitute powerful carriers of human biophilia. These places offer meaningful and appealing access to abundant and healthy nature. They provide a matrix of opportunities for personal development and, as well, a culture of significance and security. People sink deep roots in these places, for here they can achieve enduring and confident lives. The word "roots" connotes a firm and settled foundation instrumental in both natural and human development. The writer Simone Weil explains:

> To be rooted is perhaps the most important and least recognized need of the human soul. It is one of the hardest to define. A human being has roots by virtue of his real, active and natural participation in the life of the community, which preserves in living shape certain particular expectations for the future. This participation is a natural one in the sense that it is automatically brought about by place, conditions of birth, profession and social surroundings. Every human being needs to have multiple roots. It is necessary for him to draw well-nigh the whole of his moral, intellectual, and spiritual life by way of the environment of which he forms a part."[32]

Environmentally degraded and biologically impoverished places offer stunted opportunities for sinking deep and sustainable roots. As noted earlier, the entomologist Robert Pyle suggests that these communities embrace an "extinction of experience" as much as an erosion of biological capital: "The extinction of experience is not just about losing personal benefits. . . . It also implies a cycle of disaffection. . . . The extinction of experience sucks the life from the land, the intimacy from the connections."[33]

The decline of healthy, attractive, and accessible places inevitably limits our human maturation and development. Effective places of residence and work call for biologically rich, socially familiar, and culturally relevant nature. When we degrade our environments, we jeopardize more than the existence of pretty neighborhoods or convenient recreational sites. We also compromise our possibilities for healthy personal development and a setting for shared values and secure communities. Again Mark Sagoff offers us some perspective: "Much of what we deplore about the human subversion of nature—and fear about the destruction of the environment—has to do with the loss of places we keep in shared memory and cherish with instinctive and collective loyalty. It has to do with loss of . . . security one has when one relies upon the characteristic aspects of places and communities one knows well. What may worry us most is the prospect of becoming strangers in our own land."[34]

Meaningful and attractive places possess abundant and healthy natural diversity. This does not necessarily mean spectacular vistas or charismatic creatures. A beautiful mountain range is little more than pretty scenery if access is denied or its existence remains irrelevant in our life. Brilliant colors do not assure the experience of natural beauty if they are encountered in a degraded or artificial way—a sunset seen through polluted haze or nature observed only through a television set.

Even ordinary and unspectacular nature can assume a deep and relevant meaning if intimately, repeatedly, and spontaneously encountered as an integral aspect of our life. The woods in a city park, the estuary of a busy river, even the ditch in a backyard can convey wonder, beauty, and enchantment if experienced with regularity. Nearly any expression of the natural world encountered with intimacy and understanding can offer endless fascination and satisfaction.

We depend on trusted and familiar places. Healthy childhood development, especially, relies on some degree of exhilarating and instructive immersion in natural settings, whether beside a nearby river or in the bushes and woods of an attractive apartment complex. By contrast, pollution, habitat destruction, and overexploitation offer nothing but severed connections with the natural world. Confronted by serious degradation, our allegiance to such places quickly dissipates. Before long we begin looking for a better place to live, work, and raise a family. When we lack deep roots linking culture and nature, we tend to abandon these communities in the face of crisis and uncertainty.[35]

What makes people state with conviction and pride that their village, city, or country constitutes a "great place to live"? Decent work, safety and security, recreation and entertainment, education and culture—certainly these are some of the answers. Yet all these conditions must be nested within a context of attractive, healthy, and meaningful natural diversity. To be whole we need deep and dependable connections between culture and nature, between the human-built and the natural environments.[36] Personal and social pride ultimately mirror the esteem people hold for their physical surroundings. Nature and society represent interlocking and mutually reinforcing elements of healthy human maturation and development. The mark of a degraded place is a vicious cycle of disaffection and disconnection between people and nature. The critical links between geography, biology, and society become tenuous and frayed, replaced by separation and alienation. These conditions characterize many places and communities today.

Certainly, modern society has attained unprecedented levels of material abundance and technological prowess. We draw sustenance and strength, as well, from our rich cultural and political traditions. Freedom of choice abounds in our society, as do recreational and aesthetic opportunities. Yet, we also confront widespread uncertainty and disappointment , even anxiety, about the quality of everyday life. Many cities, suburbs, and rural areas have become burdened with symptoms of decay, insecurity, transience, and pollution.

Countrysides once treasured for their inspiring landscapes have been replaced by sterile monocultures, uniform habitats of filled wetlands and eliminated groves, and increasingly contaminated soil and water from excessive use of fertilizers and biocides.[37] Many of our cities have become centers of crime, dependency, environmental ruin, and hopelessness. The promise of a better life in the suburbs has frequently witnessed the growth of cultural sterility, congested transportation corridors, and environmentally fragmented landscapes of shopping malls, housing developments, and highway strips.

We often hear complaints today of eroding values, declining communities, and a general deterioration of stability and pride in place. Our everyday experience corroborates the feeling of growing alienation. Extensive loss of natural areas, pollution, and an impoverished biota are integral to this decline. Accessible and enjoyable interactions with nature have greatly diminished. Aesthetically appealing villages, downtowns, and rural landscapes have been replaced by unattractive architecture and ubiquitous consumerism. Monotony and artificiality have pushed aside once distinctive communities and environments. The geographer Edward Relph describes elements of this declining sense of place:

> If places are indeed a fundamental aspect of existence in the world, if they are sources of security and identity for individuals and for groups of people, then it is important that the means of experiencing, creating, and maintaining significant places are not lost. . . . There are signs that these very means are disappearing and that "placelessness"—the weakening of distinct and diverse experiences and identities of places—is now a dominant force. Such a trend marks a major shift in the geographical bases of existence from a deep association with places to rootlessness.[38]

The feeling grows that economic and material affluence constitute a necessary but insufficient basis for a secure and satisfying existence. A crisis of values besets us. Healthy physical and mental functioning depends on the soundness of our connections with the natural and living world. The erosion of our relationships to nature has placed at risk many values that rely on a rich and satisfying experience of environmental health and diversity. Our material, emotional, intellectual, and spiritual well-being demands living abundance and variety. Our physical and mental fitness remains vitally dependent on intimate and sustainable connections between the social and natural worlds.

Villages, towns, and cities recognized as "great places" to live possess not only vibrant economies and cherished cultural attributes but also healthy and attractive landscapes. In the United States, such areas include Denver and the Front Range, Seattle and Puget Sound, San Francisco and the Bay Area, Boston and Cape Cod, Salt Lake City and the Wasatch Mountains, Tucson and the Sonoran Desert, among others. These places share both socioeconomic and biogeographical health. They offer nurturing connections between culture and nature.

In the final chapter, we will consider the characteristics of such "great places" of residence and work. For now, we need to recognize that both human-built and the natural environments have suffered a general decline during the past half century and more. It is hardly a coincidence that the drastic erosion of natural abundance and diversity has been accompanied by a widespread weakening of stable, secure, and satisfying communities. In many of our cities, towns, and rural areas, reassuring ties of nature and culture have become increasingly threatened.

A Supportive Cultural Milieu

What are the characteristics of a socially and culturally supportive society? To address this complicated question fully is beyond the scope of this book, yet some important attributes can be suggested.

A well-functioning society provides the majority of its citizens adequate and rewarding work, housing, health care, and security. A nurturing society dispenses assistance in both good times and bad. A reassuring society offers identity, pride, loyalty, commitment, and stability. These societies possess the qualities of continuity and reliability. Change occurs, as it must, but in an orderly and nonthreatening way. Strong historical roots characterize functional societies—including a belief that the present can be meaningfully connected with a cherished past and a desirable future. All this depends on a context of healthy and abundant natural diversity. Effective societies recognize the essential links between the natural and social worlds.

Modern society, however, often fails to recognize our reliance on a rich and healthy natural environment for achieving lives of meaning and satisfaction. Frequently we encounter a vision of progress stressing large-scale development and the irrelevance of the natural world. Many act as if the social world of humans and the physical world of nature are two separate realms. Rarely do we encounter support for the notion that meaningful and satisfying places require healthy and accessible connections with the natural environment.

Studies conducted in the United States, Germany, and Japan reveal only limited support for maintaining environmental health and biological diversity.[39] Only a minority of citizens in these countries recognize the connections between human well-being and the natural environment. Positive values toward nature do emerge, but largely in the form of strong affection for a few selected species and landscapes possessing special historical significance or particular aesthetic appeal. Attitudes toward nature tend to be more sentimental than thoughtful. Support for conservation emphasizes human health issues or protecting a limited range of culturally relevant and historically familiar species. These perspectives occur especially in Japan and, to a far less extent, in Germany.

Yet promising trends also emerge. Young adults and the college-educated, especially in the United States and Germany, express far greater ecological awareness, ethical concern, and appreciation for nature and biological diversity than other groups. Among better-educated youth there is a growing realization of the importance of a healthy and productive natural environment for human material and psychological well-being. This concern often stems from increasing anxiety regarding the health effects of environmental pollution and contamination. But this shift in attitudes also reflects a rapidly expanding interest in outdoor recreation and a desire to restore aesthetically attractive landscapes.

Still, many remain unconvinced of the link between the quality of human life and the status of the natural environment. Most people in modern industrial society continue to ignore the critical influence of biological variability on our physical, emotional, and intellectual development. Too often our leaders fail to object with conviction and effectiveness to the current maelstrom of biological destruction and environmental degradation.

Ominous Trends

We have examined how a rich and diverse natural environment, a secure sense of place, and a reinforcing social and cultural milieu represent essential conditions for the healthy realization of the various expressions of biophilia. Unfortunately, certain trends in modern society have seriously compromised these prerequisites for satisfying affiliation with the natural world. We confront instead widespread symptoms of biological impoverishment, decaying places of residence and work, and prevailing norms of alienation from nature. Moreover, these ominous trends occur prominently in the world's most economically and politically advanced and powerful nations.

In recent years, however, a more encouraging recognition has developed among younger and better-educated persons of the importance of an abundant and healthy natural environment for human economic and psychological well-being. Perhaps this shift reflects a growing interest in nature when people have the opportunity, time, or ability to afford it. Yet it also suggests an expanding realization among important elements in modern society of an ancient wisdom of dependence on nature for achieving lives of meaning and satisfaction.

The book's final chapter will consider alternatives and incentives for arresting the contemporary drift toward biological decline and environmental degradation. We will examine ways of restoring the connections between healthy nature and healthy places of residence and work. We will consider how an expanded awareness of the relationship between natural functioning and human development can encourage a self-interested ethic of care and concern for nature and living diversity.

Chapter Twelve

The Pursuit of Self-Interest

Proclaiming the virtues of a rich and rewarding relationship with nature sometimes sounds like an invitation to nostalgia, a kind of idyllic calling for a return to a more bucolic, pastoral, and preindustrial past. Yet living in intimate relation and harmony with natural diversity can be compatible with modern, urban society. Achieving nurturing connections between people and nature represents a major challenge in the contemporary age, but it is far from impossible. Even in the modern metropolis, there exists more natural diversity and complexity than in the entire rest of the universe as we know it. A handful of soil in a city park, or a river passing through an urban center, can contain a profusion of natural wonder and, with care and consideration, healthy creation. As Edward O. Wilson reminds us, there exists in our modern lives, whether in the city or country, "more order and richness of structure, and particularity of history, than in the entire surfaces of all the other (lifeless) planets."[1]

But will we be concerned enough to maintain and enhance healthy connections between ourselves and natural diversity? Encouraging indications abound of a new renaissance of environmental awareness and understanding. Expanding outdoor recreational interest finds more Americans than ever participating in wildlife-related activities, visiting national parks, and engaging in nature tourism.[2] Unprecedented numbers of people are pursuing knowledge and experience of the natural world through film, books, magazines, photographs, television, posters, and assorted household products. We are visiting zoos, gardens, parks, and aquariums in extraordinary numbers, and some 10 percent of the American public reports membership in one or another environmental organization.[3] All this and more suggests a growing desire to incorporate nature into our contemporary lives.

Still, these interactions with the natural world remain largely peripheral, secondary, and vicarious. The direct experience of natural diversity as part of our everyday lives continues to elude us. Healthy and abundant nature has not yet achieved meaningful and sustained integration into most people's places of residence and work. Meanwhile the biological capital necessary for making these connections continues to disappear at a dizzying pace.

We need to establish, as basic goals of our society, both preserving the environment's health and incorporating the routine experience of nature into our everyday lives. Personal enrichment, a sound economy, and a socially secure future depend on achieving these ends. We need to recognize how much an ecologically abundant and healthy world continues to represent an essential condition for our material and psychological well-being—neither a luxurious indulgence nor a charitable concern.

Three strategies for restoring the rich experience of nature are stressed in this chapter. First, the importance of protecting and enhancing biological diversity—above all, restoring species of cultural and biological significance whose depleted status renders them a particular focus of concern are underscored. The importance of maintaining the ecological systems that make all this living diversity possible—particularly damaged landscapes and natural processes—and preserving pristine areas are especially stressed. We will also need to devise ways to utilize species of material significance in ways that are environmentally sustainable and ethically respectful.

Second, I want to emphasize the necessity of breaking the vicious cycle of disaffection and alienation from nature that persists in many of our communities, cities, and towns today. We need to promote places of residence and work where intimate connection and satisfying engagement with natural diversity can be achieved. We must devise strategies for integrating nature—healthy and abundant nature—into our rural, suburban, and urban lives. And we need to develop ways for linking the natural world with the human-built environment.

Finally, I want to stress the importance of education and ethics. We need to promote the intellectual, emotional, and ethical understanding of how healthy nature and living variety contribute to a life of material wealth, psychological satisfaction, and spiritual reward. We must emphasize how our moral and ethical self-interest relies, ultimately, on vibrant connections with a world of living abundance and natural integrity.

Arresting Biological Decline

The science of conserving biological diversity can be considered only narrowly here, ignoring the many difficulties and details of achieving this complex objective.[4] Three broad strategies for accomplishing this goal are stressed: protecting and restoring biologically rich and diverse natural systems; preventing irreversible loss through extinction; and creating incentives for utilizing wild living resources in an ecologically sustainable and ethically responsible way.

As we noted earlier, an estimated 5 to 100 million species exist. As emphasized, too, the combined forces of habitat destruction, exotic species introductions, and excessive exploitation have contributed to an estimated 15,000 to 30,000 extinctions each year. Moreover, significant reductions in the populations of many species are occurring short of their actual endangerment or elimination. Two aspects of the current biodiversity crisis should be evident by now: first, how little we know about the distribution and requirements of life on earth; and second, how inadequate is any species protection strategy that focuses only on the needs of a single creature. Preserving the world's rapidly declining biological heritage and the ecosystems that make all this existence possible demands a broader strategy of land and habitat protection. Yet, as we will see, protecting and restoring imperiled species is not only a biological but also an ethical necessity.

Above all we need to preserve natural habitats and ecosystems distinguished for their biological abundance and uniqueness, particularly areas threatened by large-scale human development.[5] Key areas include tropical forests, coral reefs, wetlands, and geographically isolated habitats. The ecologist Norman Myers has identified eighteen biological "hot spots" around the globe where conditions of species richness and uniqueness prevail—all facing considerable pressures due to human activity.[6] A sample includes Hawaii, parts of California, rain forests along the coasts of Colombia and Brazil, Madagascar, the eastern Himalayas, the Malaysian peninsula, northern Borneo, southwestern Australia, and others. In addition to these key threatened areas, any large wilderness warrants some degree of protection, given current pressures of human population growth, expanding international markets, and developing technologies.

Creating protected areas, such as national parks and biosphere reserves, is an especially important strategy for preserving biological diversity. Establishing effective parks and reserves, however, represents a daunting and complex undertaking. A particularly elusive goal is managing these protected lands in a way that minimizes conflict and even enhances the socioeconomic needs of people who live nearby, especially resource-dependent peoples in impoverished nations. Moreover, we have much to learn about the optimal size and shape of these reserves, as well as how to site and manage them in ways that relate ecologically to other regions of biological importance.[7]

Resolving these problems extends beyond the scope of this book, but one promising strategy combines the concepts of the biosphere reserve and community-based conservation.[8] The biosphere reserve represents a zoning strategy for managing protected areas.[9] In most cases, a relatively pristine core area of considerable biological variability is identified and then strictly protected. This core area is surrounded by zones of lesser biological importance—areas where past human disturbance has occurred and where compatible human activities continue to take place and are even promoted. The biosphere reserve approach contrasts with the traditional national parks strategy. In national parks, permanent human residence and resource extraction are usually precluded and the park is maintained for aesthetic and cultural reasons as well as for its ecological value.

Along with the biosphere reserve there is usually a community-based conservation effort, since human needs cannot be addressed without considerable involvement of local people.[10] Such a protected area strategy is consistent with this book's emphasis on the role of healthy nature in meeting our physical and psychological needs. Together the biosphere reserve and community-based conservation endeavor to connect the two goals of biodiversity protection and human development—a condition rarely achieved when people's intimate and ongoing contact with natural diversity is thwarted. Cases exist, of course, where the biological importance of a vulnerable area requires strict protection and minimal human use. But with careful planning and monitoring, we can protect biodiversity while encouraging people's contact with nature.

Another protection strategy is to conserve and restore species in jeopardy of extinction. The logic of spending so much energy and capital on the needs of a single creature has been questioned on political, economic, and biological grounds. Focusing on certain endangered species is indeed debatable when we consider the thousands of species lost each year due to habitat destruction and the impossibility of protecting each of these species on a case-by-case basis. Nonetheless, there are many compelling reasons for focusing on individual species of imperiled wildlife.[11] For one, practical benefits can result. All creatures represent unique and irreplaceable creations, their behavior, biology, and genetics reflecting untold aeons of evolutionary trial and error. Many of these adaptations can be pragmatically useful to human society. Even the chore of conserving a particular species increases the likelihood of discovering some attribute relevant and beneficial to human existence.[12]

Focusing on endangered wildlife can also produce important cultural, historical, and aesthetic benefits. These species often represent powerful emotional and ethical symbols. Their preservation signifies our striving for a new compatibility with nature, an effort to atone for a history of destructive excess. Protecting and restoring wolves, whales, grizzly bears, tigers, rhinoceroses, pandas, whooping cranes, bald eagles, crocodiles, sea turtles, and many other creatures can address a variety of human emotional, intellectual, and spiritual needs. These creatures render our lives more attractive, more wondrous, more worthwhile. Saving them constitutes a tangible act of redemption for having jeopardized so much of creation. In the process, we replace guilt with pride, futility with accomplishment, cynicism with hope.

The protection of species like grizzly bears and bald eagles can assist in the preservation of many other creatures and habitats.[13] Because these species are often at the apex of their food chains and have extensive territorial requirements, they cast a protective shadow for conserving many other creatures and landscapes. Protecting them also helps to educate people about the many material, cultural, historical, aesthetic, and ecological values of wild nature.

Protecting and recovering endangered wildlife often entails considerable difficulty, cost, and sometimes political risk. To accomplish this challenging objective, we must take into account various scientific, socioeconomic, organizational, and motivational factors.[14] A paramount consideration is to gain information about the feeding, reproductive, behavioral, physiological, and other biological characteristics of the endangered species. A creature's rarity can make this information difficult to obtain, our lack of knowledge having often contributed to the species' endangerment in the first place. Recovering imperiled wildlife further requires a thorough understanding of a creature's past and present interactions with people, especially the socioeconomic and political interests affected by a species' protection and recovery.

Restoring endangered wildlife also depends on effective and efficient government agencies and other political entities.[15] The U.S. Endangered Species Act represents one of the most ambitious environmental laws ever enacted.[16] Yet the act has been plagued by enormous administrative difficulties resulting in a record of limited effectiveness.[17] Indeed, government agencies have been accused of inefficiency and sometimes ineptitude: endangered species recovery is often a story of conflicting goals, inconsistent agendas, rigid decision-making procedures, inappropriate rewards, inadequate accountability, poor communications, and questionable leadership.[18] Protecting imperiled wildlife depends as much on resolving these organizational problems as on having enough scientific knowledge.

Finally, conserving endangered species demands public understanding and support. People's motivation and values cannot be ignored.[19] We need to expand the public's recognition of the many ways living diversity contributes to all aspects of our well-being. Rare and endangered species especially challenge this understanding. The willingness to modify our institutions and behavior to protect endangered wildlife depends on appreciating the many ways nature contributes to a life of richness and quality.

This educational challenge can sometimes be achieved by focusing on well-known and charismatic species. Consider the grizzly.[20] Through this animal we may better understand how nature confers beauty, mystery, and value. Hiking or visiting "grizzly country" produces excitement and pleasure just in knowing that the largest of all land carnivores exists. Fascination and respect are engendered by understanding the bear's many wondrous physical and behavioral qualities. How does the grizzly "sleep" for so many months? Why doesn't this inactivity result in muscle or bone loss or cardiovascular breakdown? Why does the bear become impregnated during the early summer but delay its implantation and birth until the colder months? How can this enormous creature sometimes subsist on a diet of moths? How does a solitary male find and secure a mate in the vastness of its mountain wilderness? The answers to such questions inform and captivate, leading us to ever more probing inquiries and an ever deeper appreciation of life and nature.

The answers can also produce practical benefits. Deciphering the puzzle of the grizzly's diet, physiology, and sleeping habits, for example, could create knowledge useful in treating human heart disease. Many other benefits derive from the grizzly's symbolic, aesthetic, and emotional qualities. Few creatures possess its intelligence and social significance. The bear often reminds us of ourselves—standing erect, looking forward, possessing a disklike face, even its eclectic diet and imperious attitude at the zenith of its world.[21] This animal figures prominently in our culture, remaining the most favored image of children's toys and one of our most cherished symbols of wilderness. For these and other reasons, the grizzly's extinction represents an irreplaceable loss. Its preservation offers more to the human spirit than just the saving of another facet of biological diversity. Its restoration offers us the chance to mend our tattered connections with the living and natural world.

Protecting biological diversity also means we must establish standards for exploiting commercially significant wildlife in ecologically sound and ethically respectful ways.[22] As we have seen, the endangerment and extinction of species has sometimes occurred for reasons of unrestrained, and unsustainable, levels of exploitation. Utilizing wildlife should take place with care and compassion, respecting the gift nature offers humanity. Exploiting other life constitutes a privilege, not an unlimited right.

Our material reliance on living species can, theoretically at least, occur in perpetuity and is neither inevitably harmful nor intrinsically wrongful. As we noted in Chapter 2, there are various arguments for and against harvesting wildlife. The case of the elephant was offered there as a powerful illustration of the many ecological, economic, and ethical difficulties of achieving acceptable standards of wildlife use. Species that suffered grievously in the past serve as a reminder of what we must do to achieve a more humane and sustainable future. These species instill in us a realization of the many benefits we obtain from wild creatures—benefits beyond the merely material, including a host of emotional, intellectual, and spiritual gains. Occasionally, these values may even recommend foregoing the killing and consumption of certain species.

We must utilize wildlife with caution and restraint, recognizing the limits of our knowledge and the many contributions these creatures make to other species and associated ecosystems. The goal of maximum exploitation should be replaced by a prudential buffer against human ignorance.[23] Exploiting wildlife, whether for material ends or recreational purposes, should embrace an attitude of deep ethical regard and respect for nature.

Ensuring Places of Vigor and Integrity

These strategies for protecting and restoring biological diversity have emphasized the importance of various scientific, governmental, and organizational activities. We will not achieve the goal of creating and maintaining conditions necessary for the healthy expression of human biophilia, however, if we fail to stress the role of individuals, local officials, and developers in making nature a part of our lives. To achieve this objective, we must conserve and restore environmentally sound and socially secure places of residence and work. We need to build communities offering everyday opportunities for connecting with natural health and diversity.

We must seek to restore attributes of aesthetic appeal, ecological connection, and intellectual richness to our rural landscapes. A vision of this rural way of life is offered by the Nobel Prize winner René Dubos in his characterization of the France he knew as a child: "Environmental diversity . . . provided nourishment for the senses and for the psyche. . . . The mosaics of cultivated fields, pastures, and woodlands, as well as the alteration of sunlit surfaces and shaded areas . . . increased awareness of the interdependence between human beings and their total environment."[24]

Today the reality of many rural areas is one of eroded natural health and loss of cultural identity. Areas once treasured for their enriching aesthetic and ecological attributes now appear afflicted with numbing monotony, unattractiveness, and polluted environments. We see in these rural landscapes accelerating cycles of biological damage: agricultural monocultures having eliminated natural predators, thus fostering pest irruptions, necessitating ever greater toxic applications; excessive irrigation and elimination of cover crops having generated soil erosion and water pollution, requiring increased reliance on fertilizers and biocides, thus exacerbating conditions of environmental contamination. Many agricultural towns and communities once widely acclaimed for their bucolic appeal have consequently been diminished aesthetically, ecologically, and materially. Loyalty and commitment, once a benchmark of rural life, has declined. Many young people view their future as residing elsewhere.

We need to question the lifestyle, health, and long-term commercial impact of destroying so much natural and cultural capital in the rural landscape. Fortunately, these impacts have encouraged major reform movements. We now encounter in organic farming, integrated pest management, agro-ecology, permaculture, holistic resource management, and other efforts—as well as in the eloquent writings of Wendell Berry, Wes Jackson, Allan Savory, and others—a yearning for positive change.[25] These approaches see healthy nature as a template for agricultural function and a plan for the restoration of the rural way of life. They aspire to new methodologies that cultivate human food more benignly and efficiently while protecting and restoring the integrity of natural systems. An expanding knowledge base suggests that high levels of food production can be achieved in a context of ecological health, attractive landscapes, and vigorous rural communities. These practices suggest, too, that biologically diverse environments can restore soil fertility, assure clean and abundant water supplies, control pests, pollinate plants, provide livestock forage, offer new economic opportunities, and meet our recreational, aesthetic, and spiritual needs. All these opportunities for human growth and economic development depend on maintaining natural health, reinvigorating regional economies, and recognizing the rural landscape as a place where people not only generate income, but live.

These efforts signify how maintaining viable connections between culture and ecology encourages more sustainable communities and lifestyles. Enhanced pride and a belief in a more rewarding future, especially among young people, also results. This shift embraces a view of agriculture and the rural way of life as a community first and commodity second. People exploit the land and its resources, as they must, but with a gentler hand and a stronger respect for nature as an ancient and proven economy essential to both our material and psychological well-being.

A similar logic linking biological health with more satisfying places and communities can be extended to urban and suburban communities. In many urban areas, a widespread fallacy prevails that we no longer require everyday contact with nature to experience lives of meaning and satisfaction.[26] In many cities open spaces have been managed with indifference, contempt, and callous disregard, their value measured largely in the currency of economic development and environmental disfigurement. Rarely is natural amenity a concern. Seldom are the environmental damages associated with industrial and housing development, building, and road construction taken into consideration. If they are considered at all, they are often treated as a trivial matter. Few developers or municipal leaders recognize the connections between a community's natural environment, quality of life, and long-term economic stability. Protecting nature and biological diversity are frequently perceived as noisome regulatory obstacles, receiving little attention in budgets, and often disappearing from sight in times of political and economic difficulty.

Ironically, the historic growth and prosperity of many great cities once depended on the health, abundance, and attractiveness of their natural amenities and resources.[27] These urban areas sprang up along coasts, lakes, estuaries, mountains, and other striking environmental features. Economic incentives, such as accessible transportation corridors and extractable resources, played a role in this siting and growth. But equally important, noneconomic factors spurred their development. These areas attracted people to sink deep and enduring roots because they overflowed with attributes of natural beauty, intellectual challenge, emotional connection, and spiritual inspiration. These places provided an abundance of environmental opportunities for personal growth and social relationship.

The link between healthy nature and vibrant urban cultures and economies still exists, but it often goes unrecognized. As noted in the previous chapter, the influx of young people into such American cities as Boise, Boston, San Francisco, and Seattle has occurred as much because of their natural amenities as their economic opportunities. Businesses and jobs have often followed these people, especially young educated families, as much as the reverse. The flight of so many people—from environmentally degraded cities to ecologically healthier and more attractive areas—reflects this phenomenon.

The long-term economic and cultural viability of city and suburb depends on maintaining connections between people and a healthy and biologically diverse natural environment. Urban areas should be aesthetically attractive, ecologically viable, and environmentally accessible. And they can be. The prevailing urban malaise of declining open space, extensive air and water pollution, biological simplification, litter and waste, sprawl and fragmentation must desist. We need to reject the assumption that environmental degradation is the price of urban progress.

We must also dispel the belief that everyday contact with nature is incompatible with areas of high population density and an extensively built environment. This perspective erroneously regards urbanity and nature as conflicting forces. It ignores the many opportunities for fulfilling contact between people and the natural world even in our most populated cities. Nearly every urban area has the potential for healthy and abundant natural diversity whether in parks or neighborhoods, urban forests or wetlands, harbors or reservoirs. As Aldo Leopold once noted: "The weeds in a city lot convey the same lesson as the redwoods."[28]

Conditions of natural grace and vitality can prevail in the modern city and suburb. This will depend, however, on the conscious strivings of community leaders, politicians, developers, architects, teachers, parents, and just plain citizens. Thoughtful planning and design can produce satisfying connections between urban residents and the natural world. Considerable economic and political reward awaits those leaders and entrepreneurs daring enough to capture the aesthetic and ecological virtues of the natural environment and weave them into the lives of the average urban citizen.

The current lack of meaningful contact with nature in the modern city and suburb reflects a deficiency of imagination rather than an intrinsic flaw of modern urban life. We need planners, developers, and architects willing and able to devote careful attention to the many ways nature's diversity can become an integral aspect of park management, housing development, shopping center and building construction. Environmentally sensitive design means more than just energy efficiency, contaminant removal, or effective waste disposal. It also means celebrating nature's capacity for enriching our lives. Urban communities and structures that foster pleasure and pride in their natural connections will inevitably enhance productivity, loyalty, and commitment.

We need to devote particular attention to our urban parks and open spaces. Too often the management of these areas focuses on organized recreation, sports, and a contrived aesthetic. These areas should also provide an oasis where people can experience intimate and spontaneous contact with the natural world. Urban parks offer the potential for natural discovery, adventure, and wonder, especially for young people. These open spaces provide critical opportunities for encountering the various woods, fields, wetlands, and other natural habitats to be found in any urban area. Parks and open spaces should also offer unstructured opportunities for encountering natural diversity. Whimsy, impulse, and freedom ought to be part of experiencing nature in a city as much as in a wilderness. As Robert Pyle remarks: "Nature reserves and formal greenways are not enough to ensure connection. Such places, important as they are, invite a measured, restricted kind of contact. . . . Young naturalists need the 'trophy,' hands-on stage . . . where [they] can wander off a trail, lift a stone, poke about, and merely wonder. . . . We would do well to maintain a modicum of open space with no rule but common courtesy, no sign besides animal tracks."[29]

Even the modern office building can incorporate the satisfying experience of nature and biological diversity. The value of such contact is suggested by the frequent tendency of office employees to try—through posters, pictures, and potted plants—to insert some aspect of natural diversity into their often lifeless and sterile work environments. Judith Heerwagen and Gordon Orians have found that "people in windowless offices use more nature posters and pots to decorate their work spaces than do people in windowed offices where views of nature are available."[30] Contact with natural diversity can improve a worker's satisfaction and productivity. Even in the modern office building, aesthetically pleasing and ecologically engaging encounters with nature can be pragmatically relevant.

To assume that our economically stressed cities can no longer afford the luxury of healthy, attractive, and diverse natural environments is a narrow and shortsighted calculus. Pride, satisfaction, and reward inevitably derive from more satisfying contacts with nature in the modern city. People crave nourishing affiliations with nature. A city without positive environmental attributes is ultimately less appealing.

Cities paralyzed by the short-term costs of environmental remediation impede their long-term recovery. The vitality of the modern city depends on ecologically healthy and accessible natural environments. Pollution and biological degradation strain our health, both physical and mental, and thwart our potential for personal growth and social development. These debilitating conditions must be replaced by environmental quality, grace, and integrity.

New Renaissance or Dark Age?

Abandoning modern urban life for a more bucolic existence represents for most people an impractical and unnecessary alternative. Humanity will remain dependent for the foreseeable future on contemporary technology and the city for meeting most of its physical and cultural needs. Barring some catastrophe, we are unlikely to stray far from urbanization, industrial production, and modern technology.

Yet contemporary life can become more environmentally sustaining and satisfying. We can indeed integrate nature and living diversity into our places of work, residence, and community. But we will need to alter our prevailing assumptions about what comprises a life of meaning and value. We will have to recognize how much our physical and mental well-being continues to depend on healthy and enriching affiliations with the natural world.

A new ethic for conserving nature must reflect an expanded understanding of personal and societal self-interest. When we impoverish the natural world, we inevitably reduce our potential for physical, material, emotional, intellectual, and spiritual growth and well-being. We diminish the possibilities for individual and collective development. A life of meaning and value depends on the richness of our connections with the natural fabric. We achieve our fullest humanity by celebrating our widest and deepest dependence on nature and life.

This environmental ethic embraces more than just preventing harm to our favorite creatures.[31] Of course we must seek to eliminate suffering among species whose experience we can readily empathize with, often the higher vertebrates. Yet an environmental ethic that excludes the bulk of life (the lower vertebrates, invertebrates, and plants), as well as the systems which render all this existence possible, represents too narrow a basis for valuing and protecting nature's diversity.

Nor is it enough to embrace a broad ethic that views nature as possessing intrinsic worth and warranting protection under any and all circumstances. This moral posture rarely offers much guidance when we are making tough decisions about competing interests—particularly choosing between the relative worth of human existence versus inflicting some environmental harm.[32] What do we do, for example, when confronted with the choice of killing some creature or providing a treatment for some human disease? How do we choose between eliminating a natural habitat or constructing needed housing, factories, and office buildings? What about impounding rivers and draining wetlands to produce electricity and agricultural irrigation?

We can conceive of many scenarios where critical human needs conflict with nature's well-being. How do we select one over the other if all creatures and habitats possess ethical rights equivalent to our own? If nature possesses moral worth independent of human beings, how can we ever opt for our own well-being if it results in significant environmental injury? A morality that rejects human interests in favor of nature's convinces few and invites decision-making paralysis in exactly those situations where an ethic is most needed.

Perhaps we might advocate an environmental ethic based on human material interests viewed over the long run.[33] This perspective encourages protecting nature in cases where human knowledge and technology can produce medical, industrial, agricultural, or other tangible benefits. Such an ethic does not rely on people's empathy for a restricted range of creatures. Nor does it assert that all nature possesses equivalent moral value under all circumstances. Instead, it allows us to make ethical choices by encouraging the defense of those aspects of nature that contribute to society's long-term material and economic interests.

While perhaps more practical and appealing, this ethic too seems narrow and, in many ways, self-defeating. Most creatures and habitats will never result in tangible benefits to people and society. Moreover, entering into this material calculus encourages us to eradicate nature whenever our economic interests unequivocally favor this exploitation.[34] The seeds of destruction are sown in any ethic that extends practical value to only a portion of the natural world and declares, by implication, the rest expendable. Such an ethic might also be foolish. Is it wise to place confidence in a materialistic ethic that contributed so much to our environmental crisis in the first place?

The ethic advocated throughout this book expands the concept of self-interest beyond the narrow limits of material and economic benefit. All the expressions of biophilia outlined here reflect practical and utilitarian gains provided by the natural world to people and society—whether these be aesthetic inspiration, creative capacity, empirical understanding, emotional solace, or bodily comfort. Each aspect of biophilia reveals how humanity reaps physical and mental reward from the matrix of our connections with the diversity of life. We have expanded the myriad ways nature renders our existence emotionally, intellectually, spiritually, and materially richer and more fulfilling.

We have examined how human life depends on a complex of subtle and profound ecological functions and processes. These connections assure the cycling of energy and nutrients, the production of oxygen and water, the reproduction of plants and animals, and the decomposition of wastes and organic material, as well as a variety of other life-support systems and processes. Our knowledge of these crucial ecological links, however, remains meager. Reducing the amount and distribution of life on earth irreversibly damage these ecological connections and inevitably risk our well-being, perhaps even our survival.

We have explored our various material relations to the world's vast storehouse of actual and potential genetic wealth. All species represent the product of unimaginable evolutionary effort and travail. Their adaptations enhance our own well-being as we unlock the mystery of their functioning. To eliminate this potential would be particularly ironic as we stand on the threshold of revolutionary changes in genetics, molecular biology, and bioengineering, changes that portend a dramatic increase in our ability to exploit nature to serve various human needs. Species represent an incredible bequest of irreplaceable wealth. Could we be so ignorant and so arrogant as to destroy this future just to satisfy cravings for immediate gratification? It would be equivalent to burning the world's books just to keep warm for a few winter days.

Nature and living diversity also offer immense opportunities for emotional growth and intellectual development. Our world would be immeasurably lonelier if we no longer shared it with whales, wolves, elephants, tigers, pandas, cranes, eagles, and other creatures. Living diversity offers us inspiration, a source of language, story, and myth, a bedrock of understanding of beauty and significance. Nature instructs us mentally and enriches us psychologically. Other life forms the basis of our culture and humanity. To eliminate natural diversity is to replace a community of interest with a burden of sadness and guilt. Isolation displaces kinship, alienation supplants connection, ugliness pushes aside beauty, homogeneity substitutes for variety, an enfeebled intellect succeeds a rich and varied communication.

Natural diversity provides a wellspring of exploration and discovery. The trout in the mountain stream, the bear in the wilderness haunt, the elephant in the grassy savanna, the crane in the wetlands marsh, all feed our craving for challenge, adventure, accomplishment. The instructive experience of these and so many other creatures and habitats would be lost if they were to become irrelevant or their environments ruined. Human ingenuity and technology can never replace the challenge of a life in the wild. Nature in the zoo, or on the television set, or in the fantasy world of virtual reality will remain a vicarious fraud—a vain striving after the authentic by the contrived.[35]

Nature and living diversity ultimately offer us spiritual solace, comfort, and salvation. We find in them the possibility for harmony, meaning, and a nurturing relation to the rest of creation.

An ethic of self-interest recognizes how the richness of human existence depends on various ties with the diversity of life. The more we probe the depths of our dependence on nature, the more we recognize its unrivaled capacity to nourish the human body, mind, and spirit. All the diverse expressions of biophilia emerged because they enhance our potential for growth and development. They reflect how we will always rely on the fullness of our connections with the nonhuman world. They suggest how natural diversity is still the anvil on which our fitness and fulfillment are forged.

Human society pauses between two environmental futures as we move toward the next millennium—a dark age versus a new renaissance. This morality play reflects our profound uncertainty and uneasiness regarding the road we will travel. The path of environmental destruction leads us to an eroded and depauperate world. Apocalyptic alarms can be suggested. The most likely outcome is a greatly diminished physical, emotional, and intellectual humanity. We can survive dirty air, polluted water, contaminated soil, and the decimation of species. But we will certainly not thrive materially or prosper spiritually under such conditions. Moreover future generations will view this legacy as the bequest of a twentieth century of overwhelming shortsightedness, ignorance, and irresponsibility. They will regard us with the same moral disdain we now project on a previous dark age of decline and destruction following the Fall of Rome.

A more enlightened future also looms possible. This depends on our recognizing the essential connections between a healthy and abundant natural world and a rich and rewarding human existence. This renaissance of life-affirming engagement will demand no less than our realization that much of our sanity and salvation depend on a self-interested ethic of respect for all creation.

As elsewhere in the book, let us draw to a close with a story.

The Hernandez family rocked precariously between dysfunction and disintegration. Rico and Sue's relationship had become sullen and uncommunicative. Rico returned home most nights exhausted and drained from another day's effort at being a successful Wall Street investment banker. Lately, he possessed neither the patience nor energy for dealing with Sue's depression and her complaints. He tried living with her unhappiness. Perhaps it would disappear or at least be displaced by all her cultural and philanthropic activities, luncheons, dinner parties, friends, and clubs. But it didn't. Eventually Rico's weariness and impatience gave way to indifference and an increasing reluctance to participate in various social events and refusing to explain why.

Sue realized her deep depression and demands had driven a wedge between her and Rico. Yet she felt powerless to stop. She could only grasp for distractions that might dispel the pervasive gloom which seemed to surround her. She constantly reminded herself, like some repeated mantra, of their incredible good fortune—money, status, security, a beautiful apartment overlooking Central Park, possessions beyond her dreams, their boy at one of New York's finest schools—as if all this might drive away the ubiquitous despair.

Rico earned a king's ransom compared to what their fathers had made—Rico's father as a small rancher in New Mexico, her's as a hardware salesman in Missouri. She smiled at the memory of their penniless status as graduate students at the University of Michigan and their dream of one day earning an adequate income as public servants. Rico did spend one year in a thankless bureaucratic position following graduate school. Then he accepted the Wall Street job. Perhaps they had offered him the opportunity because he was Hispanic. But he was so successful and soon earned so much money that, before long, Sue was able to quit her boring job as an accountant and devote herself to being the mother of their son, Tad, and doing various good works. She made many new friends, joined clubs, became active in an assortment of charitable organizations.

Despite all their good fortune, Sue felt hollow at the core. She felt somehow unconnected with her inner self, thwarted, frustrated, and unfulfilled. She even longed for those graduate school days when their life possessed an intimacy and vitality far more satisfying than their present wealthy existence. She recalled their many walks along the river in Ann Arbor, strolls in the city parks and nearby forests, watching sunsets along the lakeshore, searching for driftwood and signs of the distant past.

Their troubles had finally spilled out onto their nine-year-old son, Tad. Sue tried hiding her discontent in a show of conviviality and attentiveness, yet the boy sensed his mother's deep unhappiness, his parents' tension and recriminations, and began revealing symptoms of a widening despondency. The boy's teachers complained he had become uncommunicative and aggressive, sometimes fighting with other children. The school counselor reported Tad fluctuating wildly between feverish activity and gloomy withdrawal. Meanwhile the boy's grades declined. Meetings between Sue, Rico, and various school officials produced mostly anger and mutual blame.

Their son's rapid deterioration forced Sue and Rico to confront how their life together was poised on the brink of dissolving. They decided to take a long vacation—go somewhere as a family and try to resolve their problems before it was too late. The decision to leave was especially difficult for Rico, for he was in the middle of a major deal. At first his partners pressured him to remain, but once they realized the seriousness of the situation, they wished him all the best. One of his colleagues even offered the use of a vacation house on an island off Nova Scotia. After some discussion, Rico and Sue decided to accept.

One early June morning—anxious, uncertain, irritable—the Hernandez family boarded a two-engine plane for their journey to Brier Island.[36] *The one-and-a-half-hour flight initially took them to the small city of Yarmouth. There they rented a car, drove fifty miles to the town of Digby, drove another twenty miles out a narrow peninsula, and boarded a ferry to a twelve-mile-long-island. At the end of it they boarded yet another ferry for Brier Island.*

About 350 people live on the 2,200-acre island, mostly fishermen and their families, along with countless birds, shellfish, and finfish in its rich surrounding waters, even a large congregation of seals and whales. Dangling off the southwestern tip of Nova Scotia, Brier Island is buffeted by strong ocean currents where the Atlantic Ocean meets the Bay of Fundy. The bay is renowned for its tides, the most dramatic in the world—the northern end regularly experiencing forty- to fifty-foot fluctuations. Near Brier Island, the tide causes treacherous currents, leading these waters to be known as the "Graveyard of the Fundy," a place where the wrecks of many ships litter its shores and surrounding seas.

They stared at the swirling pools spinning rapidly past the hull as the small ferry was forced to angle steeply down the passage separating the islands in order to land on the opposite side. As the ferry approached their destination, Sue and Rico experienced an odd combination of hope and despair. An assortment of colorful yet weather-beaten houses strung out along the shore made up the small village of Westport, Brier

Island's only town. Sue sensed their time on the island would either force them to come to terms with their marriage or witness its final dissolution.

People glanced curiously at them as they disembarked from the ferry, not unfriendly but not especially welcoming either. After making some wrong turns, asking instructions, and masking their anxiety in petty quarreling, they finally found the driveway leading to the house.

They proceeded down a steep, winding, potholed road, finally spying the house and sea beyond. From the car the modest-sized house looked like it had grown out of its granite base at the foot of a long rocky peninsula extending another quarter of a mile out into the ocean. White surf crashed along its sides, a picture of rugged beauty, combining strength with a roughly hewn harmony. The foundation and first floor of the house consisted of field stone; the second floor was wooden logs; the steep pitched roof covered with slate. A stone chimney anchored one end, large windows facing the sea, a deck and porch surrounding the perimeter. Firs, spruce, and rhododendrons ran along the sides and behind the house, many of the trees stunted and twisted into odd shapes by the prevailing winds.

As they exited the car, the absence of machine sounds startled them. The background clamor of nonstop travel, and their New York existence, made such sounds almost a constant in their lives. Yet this place was far from silent: they confronted a continuous roar of crashing surf, wind through the trees, the cries of squawking ravens and gulls.

Entering the house, a great stone fireplace dominated the living room, a smaller version in an upstairs bedroom. The walls of yellow pine glowed, giving the house a soft warmth despite the large windows offering various vantage points of the sea and rocky peninsula.

Sue felt strangely relaxed and excited—like meeting an old relative she had lost touch with. She reminded herself that this was the way she used to be, not dispirited and petulant. Immediately she began thinking about planting flowers and vegetables in the garden plot she had seen alongside the house. One thing seemed certain—there would be no dining out on Brier Island as they often did in New York. She speculated about buying fish off the boats, even gathering mussels and other shellfish from the nearby waters.

Absorbed and distracted by the house, Sue and Rico had lost track of time but suddenly realized that Tad had disappeared. Then, calling out for the boy, a mounting panic took hold of them. To their relief, they soon heard Tad's returning cry from down the peninsula. Quickly they ran to him—only to find the boy sitting joyfully in the middle of a tide pool in the rocks, examining various creatures trapped after the waters had receded. Their initial anger quickly dissolved at the sight of Tad's smile and beaming eyes. He was absorbed in a way they had rarely observed of late.

The Hernandez family soon settled into an established but far from uneventful routine. They explored the island's many coves, bogs, forests, fields, and other habitats. They delighted in seeing its abundant marine life—crabs, mussels, lobsters, snails, cormorants, gulls, puffins, murres, seals, the shadow of schooling fish, and more. Rico revived his old interest in birdwatching. Tad became absorbed in a world of adventure and exploration. The boy especially enjoyed finding pieces of plank and mementos from the shipwrecks along the shore.

They particularly treasured the times they went out on fishing boats, partaking in the harvest of abundant sea life in the exhilarating but occasionally rough and scary seas. They loved seeing whales and dolphins, especially the fast finbacks—the "greyhound of the seas"—and the humpbacks that sometimes breached clear of the water in spectacular displays of strength and agility. Twice they encountered North Atlantic right whales, the rarest and most endangered of the great whales, covered with barnacles in distinctive patterns that allowed them to single out individuals.[37] *The whales and dolphins seemed to exude gentleness, intelligence, and mystery, conveying the feeling of a humanlike mind in the waters.*

Sue devoted a good part of her day to gardening. Having purchased flower and vegetable seedlings at the local market, she especially enjoyed harvesting the peas and squash, which she mixed with various shellfish and finfish. She experimented with new dishes, mixing pasta with mussels, clams, lobsters, and crabs collected along the peninsula or on forays to nearby coves and ponds. Sometimes they met fishing boats at the docks, buying some of the catch, before it was mostly shipped off to the New England markets. She enjoyed conversing with the fishermen and their wives about their families, their histories, their hopes for the future. These people seemed to possess a self-confidence and love of their island home that greatly impressed her. Their incomes were limited, but they seemed to have all they needed.

Tad made new friends, particularly two boys and a girl who lived nearby. Although they ranged in age from eight to fourteen, they soon established a close bond and set off nearly every day for some cove, forest, shipwreck, or secret hideaway. At first Sue and Rico worried about Tad's safety, showering the boy with warnings and the need to be careful and home by a specified hour. Following repeated assurances from other parents that "kids pretty much run the island and everyone looks out for them," they ceased to pester him unduly. In fact, Tad suffered little more than a few minor scratches. They took special pleasure in seeing his look of contentment where once there had been a scowl. They delighted when he returned home with an armful of treasures and tales to tell. They were impressed by his new interest in marine life and the collection he organized using books and guides obtained from the library.

A new calm and intimacy sprang up among them. Sue's depression lifted like morning fog. Rico felt more alive than he had in years. Tad's alertness and curiosity returned. Meals became times when they indulged in the pleasure of one another's company, each recalling some incident or other from the day, dredging up its many details. Some days seemed endless. Yet, at the end of a week, Sue and Rico would shake their heads in bewilderment, astounded at how quickly it had gone by. Sue sometimes lay in bed at night, trying to recall the minutia of the day, before slipping off into a deep and luxuriant sleep—far preferable to the insomnia she had suffered over the past two years.

As the time approached for their return to New York, a palpable dread began to weigh on them. But a feeling of confidence was soon to displace their anxiety. They departed Brier Island with sadness and regret, but there was also a new enthusiasm for home, family, friends, work, school, and community. They took comfort in knowing they would return for many years to come. They had already found a piece of property to purchase.

As the plane approached New York's intimidating skyline, Rico worried their newly discovered delight in the natural world would be buried by the great metropolis's artificiality and concrete. A few months later, he was reassured. They were able, he found, to maintain their interests even within the huge city. They located unexpected pockets of natural beauty and abundance in New York's various forests, wetlands, rivers, parks, and other open spaces.

As the year progressed, their destination would vary according to the season. In the fall, they especially sought out migrating waterfowl and shorebirds along the city's bays and estuaries. In winter, they particularly looked for stately and ancient trees within its parks and forests. In spring, they enjoyed angling for anadromous fish along the Hudson. In summer, they focused on collecting butterflies and beetles within New York's wide diversity of habitats. Each foray created another thread of familiarity, knowledge, and relation binding them to this remarkable urban landscape they had barely noticed before. They took sustenance from the many connections increasingly linking them to the city's vast and varied matrix of life. Despite its pollution and environmental degradation, New York became more and more their place and their home.

Their commitment to one another and to the surrounding landscape sometimes created problems, of course. Rico would occasionally leave work early or take vacation days to explore certain areas with Tad and Sue. His partners, however, soon accepted his eccentricity—they knew how much more productive and contented he had become. Sue would sometimes neglect social and community obligations, but her renewed energy and optimism more than compensated for these moments away. Tad's teachers would occasionally balk at his absences, but his academic ranking near the top of his class and reputation for cooperation and leadership made these lapses tolerable.

Life was far from idyllic. Rico sometimes worked himself to exhaustion, returned home late, was sometimes away for days on business trips. Sue still experienced moments of deep depression. Their marriage occasionally lapsed into struggle and uncertainty. Tad despised the many restrictions and dangers of the city. Yet they all endured and found beauty amidst the squalor, permanence in the face of transience, commitment despite the anonymity of the metropolis. They discovered intimacy and connection within the city's natural fabric. Whatever the many obstacles and pitfalls of their life, they now knew their existence rested on a bedrock of enduring value.

[30 Years Later]

Tad Hernandez had looked forward to the day when he could escape the ugliness, restrictions, and pollution of New York City. He had been raised in the Big Apple during the 1990s, but his natural appetites had been nourished by summer vacations in Nova Scotia and wilderness programs in the United States and overseas. Exploring pockets of the natural world in and around New York had helped, but it hardly compensated for the city's ubiquitous grime and degradation.

He never dreamed he would one day choose to return and raise a family in this huge metropolis. Yet he willingly became a resident of New York, not just for its economic rewards, but because he believed, as did so many others, that the city offered an environmentally wholesome and satisfying place for his wife, two girls, and himself. The world had certainly changed. They had all benefited from a new era of reconciliation with nature—a time when places like New York emerged at the forefront of a new environmental covenant.

The girls' favorite haunt was the "biopark" established along an abandoned industrial shoreline in the South Bronx.[38] *They especially relished the immersion exhibits, where they became enmeshed in a sim-*

ulated world of other creatures and habitats from around the globe. They would snake along various terrains filled with unusual plants and landscapes, and intimately experience the lives of diverse and wondrous creatures. In the invertebrarium, the children encountered insects, worms, mollusks, and other spineless animals found in the backyards, parks, and open spaces of the city. The Magic Well exhibit took them through a never-ending search of a single creature's biology, behavior, and evolution.[39]

Tad and his wife, Ellen, took special satisfaction from participating in their building's roof garden co-op. They applied new methods for growing and harvesting fresh, organic vegetables and took pride in knowing that these innovative techniques produced invaluable by-products: clean air, fresh water, and open space. The solar greenhouse provided almost half of the building's heating and electricity needs, generating not only considerable savings but also a strong sense of self-reliance and self-sufficiency.

Tad also served on his office building's environmental committee. The skyscraper's solar collectors met most of its energy demands, and an aquarium, arboretum, and simulated wetlands could be found in the entryway, cafeteria, and rooftop. Studies had revealed that the improved aesthetics and opportunities for relaxation boosted employee morale and productivity.

Ellen's primary focus was the wilderness preserve connecting various greenways, parks, and other open spaces in and around the city and its suburbs. Her degree in ecology enabled her to assist with various species and habitat restoration projects, as well as the ambitious environmental education program. The wilderness preserve system now approached the conditions that prevailed in New York at the time of the European settlement. The only large animals missing were wolves and mountain lions, and some extremist environmental groups had even started advocating their reintroduction.

Fondly Tad and his family recalled the time they won the lottery, allowing them to camp in the preserve for three days. In their opinion, the experience was just as exciting as their eco-adventures in many pristine areas of the country and around the globe. Having now surpassed the Caribbean resorts as America's favorite vacation, ecotourism increasingly meant congested wilderness areas and national parks.

They enjoyed New York's many natural as well as cultural amenities—especially when much of the world still faced daunting environmental problems. Human population growth had stabilized, but the demands of 9 billion people continued to exceed the carrying capacity of many areas of the globe. Some countries still used highly polluting biocides and fertilizers. Toxic wastes were still being dumped in ineffectual and illegal ways. New and inadequately tested chemicals were still introduced into the environment. Huge amounts of energy consumption had altered the earth's atmospheric chemistry with uncertain long-term consequences. The cumulative effects of these various activities, along with the continuing destruction of natural habitat, continued to result in the extinction of some eight thousand species each year. The planet had already lost a half million species during the preceding twenty-five-year period.

Even so, considerable environmental progress had occurred. Every index of pollution and environmental damage showed signs of improvement, especially during the past decade. Although technological and scientific advances had spurred this change, reversing the tide owed as much to new attitudes of environmental respect and appreciation among much of the world's citizenry. Most people now firmly believed the human body, mind, and spirit depended on the richness of its connections with a healthy and abundant natural world. Some called it a new religion. Tad and Ellen merely viewed it as common sense.

Notes

PROLOGUE

1. Relevant information can be found in T. Martin and D. Finch, eds., *Ecology and Management of Neotropical Migratory Birds* (New York: Oxford University Press, 1995); R. DeGraaf and J. Rappole, *Neotropical Migratory Birds: Natural History, Distribution, and Population Change* (Ithaca: Cornell University Press, 1996); E. O. Wilson, *The Diversity of Life* (Cambridge: Harvard University Press, 1992).
2. See R. Carson, *Silent Spring* (Boston: Houghton Mifflin, 1962); P. Brooks, *The House of Life: Rachel Carson at Work* (Boston: Houghton Mifflin, 1972); A. Leopold, *A Sand County Almanac* (New York: Oxford University Press, 1966); S. Flader, *Thinking Like a Mountain: Aldo Leopold and the Evolution of an Ecological Attitude Toward Deer, Wolves, and Forests* (Columbia: University of Missouri Press, 1974).
3. B. Elkin, *The Wisest Man in the World: A Legend of Ancient Israel* (New York: Parents Magazine Press, 1976).

CHAPTER I: THE NOTION OF BIOPHILIA

1. E. O. Wilson, *Biophilia: The Human Bond with Other Species* (Cambridge: Harvard University Press, 1984).
2. Ibid., p. 114.
3. E. Fromm, *The Anatomy of Human Destructiveness* (New York: Holt, Rinehart & Winston, 1973), p. 366.

4. Ibid, p. 365.
5. This perspective is emphasized in my book: S. Kellert, *The Value of Life: Biological Diversity and Human Society* (Washington, D.C.: Island Press, 1996).
6. The notion of biocultural evolution is explained in C. Lumsden and E. O. Wilson, *Genes, Mind, and Culture* (Cambridge: Harvard University Press, 1981); "The Relation Between Biological and Cultural Evolution," *Journal of Biological Structure* 8(1983):343–359.
7. Useful statistics on global trends in species extinction and endangerment can be found in E. O. Wilson, *The Diversity of Life* (Cambridge: Harvard University Press, 1992); B. Groombridge, ed., *Global Biodiversity: Status of the Earth's Living Resources* (London: Chapman & Hall, 1992); N. Myers, "Questions of Mass Extinction," *Biodiversity and Conservation* 2(1994): 2–17; V. Heywood, ed., *Global Biodiversity Assessment* (Cambridge: United Nations Environment Programme/Cambridge University Press, 1995); W. Reid and K. Miller, *Keeping Options Alive: The Scientific Basis for Conserving Biodiversity* (Washington, D.C.: World Resources Institute, 1989); J. Savage, "Systematics and the Biodiversity Crisis," *BioScience* 45(1995):673–679.
8. The notion of nature and wildlife as a "magic well" is derived from Karl Von Frisch as discussed by S. McVay, "Prologue," in S. Kellert and E. O. Wilson, eds., *The Biophilia Hypothesis* (Washington, D.C.: Island Press, 1993).

CHAPTER 2: THE MATERIAL BASIS

1. United Nations, *World Economic Survey* (New York: United Nations, 1995).
2. See, for example, L. White, "The Historic Roots of Our Ecologic Crisis," *Science* 176(1967):1203–1207; K. Thomas, *Man and the Natural World* (New York: Pantheon, 1983); M. Oelschlaeger, *The Idea of Wilderness* (New Haven: Yale University Press, 1991); J. Passmore, *Man's Responsibility for Nature: Ecological Problems and Western Traditions* (New York: Scribner's, 1974).
3. White, "Historic Roots."
4. Ibid., p. 1205.
5. Thomas, *Man and the Natural World*, p. 237.

6. Ibid., p. 223.
7. A useful summary of the kinds of products people derive from wild living resources can be found in N. Myers, *The Sinking Ark: A New Look at the Problem of Disappearing Species* (Oxford: Pergamon, 1979), and *A Wealth of Wild Species: Storehouse for Human Welfare* (Boulder: Westview, 1983); M. Oldfield, *The Value of Conserving Genetic Resources* (Sunderland: Sinauer, 1989); C. Prescott-Allen and R. Prescott-Allen, *The First Resource* (New Haven: Yale University Press, 1986); B. Groombridge, ed., *Global Biodiversity: Status of the Earth's Living Resources* (London: Chapman & Hall, 1992); D. Pimentel et al., "Environmental and Economic Benefits of Biodiversity" (Cornell University, College of Agriculture and Life Sciences, 1996); D. Pearce and D. Moran, *The Economic Value of Biodiversity* (London: Earthscan, 1994); W. Reid and K. Miller, *Keeping Options Alive: The Scientific Basis for Conserving Biodiversity* (Washington, D.C.: World Resources Institute, 1989); R. DeGroot, *Functions of Nature* (Groningen: Wolteers-Noorhoff, 1992).
8. Groombridge, *Global Biodiversity,* p. 365.
9. Pimentel et al., "Benefits of Biodiversity."
10. Groombridge, *Global Biodiversity.*
11. J. Callicott and R. Ames, eds., *Nature in Asian Traditions of Thought* (Albany: State University of New York, 1989); S. Fitzgerald, *International Wildlife Trade: Whose Business Is It?* (Washington, D.C.: World Wildlife Fund, 1989); G. Hemley, ed., *International Wildlife Trade: A CITES Handbook* (Washington, D.C.: Island Press, 1994); A. Leung, *Chinese Herbal Remedies* (New York: Universe Books, 1994); H. Beinfield, *Between Heaven and Earth: A Guide to Chinese Medicine* (New York: Ballantine, 1991).
12. S. Kellert, "Japanese Perceptions of Wildlife," *Conservation Biology* 5(1991):297–308.
13. See, for example, J. LaSalle and I. Bould, eds., *Hymenoptera and Biodiversity* (Oxford: CAB International, 1993); Groombridge, *Global Biodiversity;* S. Kellert, "Values and Perceptions of Invertebrates," *Conservation Biology* 7(1993):845–855; C. Lindberg, "The Economic Value of Insects," *Traffic Bulletin* 10(1993):32–36; D. Pimentel, *Insects, Science, and Society* (New York: Academic Press, 1975).
14. Kellert, "Values and Perceptions of Invertebrates."

15. Pimentel et al., "Benefits of Biodiversity."
16. M. Duda, *Factors Related to Hunting and Fishing Participation in the United States* (Harrisonburg, Va.: Responsive Management, 1993); J. Swan, *In Defense of Hunting* (San Francisco: Harper, 1995); R. Hudson et al., eds., *Wildlife Production Systems: Economic Utilisation of Wild Ungulates* (Cambridge: Cambridge University Press, 1989).
17. U.S. Department of Interior, *National Survey of Fishing, Hunting, and Wildlife-Associated Recreation* (Washington, D.C.: Fish and Wildlife Service, 1995).
18. P. Shepard, "A Theory of the Value of Hunting," *Transactions of the North American Wildlife and Natural Resources Conference* 24(1959):504–512.
19. Groombridge, *Global Biodiversity,* p. 350.
20. See, for example, I. Palos, *The Chinese Art of Healing* (New York: Herder & Herder, 1971); M. Howson, *Chinese Medicine* (New York: Holt, 1990); Beinfeld, *Between Heaven and Earth;* H. Wallnofer, *Chinese Folk Medicine* (New York: Crown, 1965).
21. See Groombridge, *Global Biodiversity;* E. O. Wilson and F. Peters, eds., *Biodiversity* (Washington, D.C.: National Academy Press, 1988); O. Akerlele et al., *The Conservation of Medicinal Plants* (New York: Cambridge University Press, 1991).
22. Groombridge, *Global Biodiversity.*
23. Pimentel et al., "Benefits of Biodiversity."
24. E. O. Wilson, *The Diversity of Life* (Cambridge: Harvard University Press, 1992).
25. Myers, *A Wealth of Wild Species;* Groombridge, *Global Biodiversity.*
26. Groombridge, *Global Biodiversity;* Pimentel et al., "Benefits of Biodiversity."
27. See IUCN *Red Data Books* for world listings of varying taxa of endangered species. For a more historical perspective see P. Matthiessen, *Wildlife in America* (New York: Viking Press, 1989); V. Ziswiller, *Extinct and Vanishing Animals* (London: English University Press, 1967); C. Guggisberg, *Man and Wildlife* (New York: Arco, 1970).
28. V. Scheffer, *The Year of the Whale* (New York: Scribner's, 1969); Matthiessen, *Wildlife in America;* J. Scharff, "The International Management of Whales, Dolphins, and Porpoises," *Ecology Law Quarterly* 6(1977):243–352; S. Harmer, "History of Whaling," *Proceedings of the*

Linnaean Society 140(1928):51–95; R. Ellis, *Men and Whales* (New York: Knopf, 1991).

29. K. Norris, "Marine Mammals and Man," in H. Brokaw, ed., *Wildlife and America* (Washington, D.C.: Council on Environmental Quality, 1978), p. 320.
30. S. Kellert and V. Scheffer, "The Changing Place of Marine Mammals in American Thought," in J. Twiss and R. Reeves, eds., *Marine Mammals* (Washington, D.C.: Smithsonian Press, 1997).
31. See, for example, I. Douglas-Hamilton and O. Douglas-Hamilton, *Battle for the Elephants* (New York: Viking Press, 1992); J. Hanks, *The Struggle for Survival* (New York: Mayflower Books, 1993); D. Chadwick, *The Fate of the Elephant* (San Francisco: Sierra Club Books, 1992).
32. I. Douglas-Hamilton, "African Elephants: Population Trends and Their Causes," *Oryx* 21(1987):11–24.
33. See, for example, J. Thomsen and R. Luxmore, "Sustainable Utilization of Wildlife for Trade," and S. Foster, "Some Legal and Institutional Aspects of the Economic Utilisation of Wildlife" (two papers for Workshop 7, "Sustainable Utilisation of Wildlife," 18th IUCN General Assembly, Gland, Switzerland, 1990); V. Geist, "How Markets in Wildlife Meat and Parts, and the Sale of Hunting Privileges, Jeopardize Wildlife Conservation," *Conservation Biology* 2(1988):15–26; T. Swanson and E. Barbier, *Economics for the Wilds* (Washington, D.C.: Island Press, 1992); M. Freeman and U. Kreutzer, eds., *Elephants and Whales: Resources for Whom?* (London: Gordon & Breach, 1994).
34. Kellert, *The Value of Life;* M. Mangel et al., "Principles for the Conservation of Wild Living Resources," *Ecological Applications* 6(1996): 337–372.
35. Prescott-Allen and Prescott-Allen, *The First Resource;* Wilson, *The Diversity of Life;* Groombridge, *Global Biodiversity;* WRI/IUCN/UNEP, *Global Biodiversity Strategy* (Washington, D.C.: World Resources Institute, 1992); Pearce and Moran, *The Economic Value of Biodiversity;* Heywood, *Global Biodiversity Assessment.*
36. Pimentel et al., "Benefits of Biodiversity"; Groombridge, *Global Biodiversity.*
37. Pimentel et al., "Benefits of Biodiversity."
38. Groombridge, *Global Biodiversity,* p. 432.

39. Ibid.
40. Pimentel et al., "Benefits of Biodiversity."
41. Groombridge, *Global Biodiversity*, p. 350.
42. Pimentel et al., "Benefits of Biodiversity."
43. R. Mendelsohn et al., "Untapped Pharmaceuticals in Tropical Forests," *Economic Botany* 49(1996):223–228.
44. Groombridge, *Global Biodiversity.*
45. Kellert, "Values and Perceptions of Invertebrates"; C. Krebs, *Ecology* (New York: Harper & Row, 1978).
46. Pimentel, *Insects, Science, and Society.*
47. Pimentel et al., "Benefits of Biodiversity."
48. P. Ehrlich and A. Ehrlich, *Extinction: The Causes and Consequences of the Disappearance of Species* (New York: Random House, 1981).
49. Pimentel et al., "Benefits of Biodiversity."
50. Pimentel, *Insects, Science, and Society.*
51. Pimentel et al., "Benefits of Biodiversity."
52. Kellert, "Values and Perceptions of Invertebrates."
53. See, for example, O. Solbrig and D. Solbrig, *So Shall You Reap: Farming and Crops in Human Affairs* (Washington, D.C.: Island Press, 1994).
54. Kellert, "Values and Perceptions of Invertebrates."
55. See, for example, R. Rood, *Wetlands* (New York: HarperCollins, 1994); W. Mitsch, *Wetlands* (New York: Van Nostrand, 1986); *Wetlands: Characteristics and Boundaries* (Washington, D.C.: National Academy Press, 1995).
56. See, for example, T. Duffy, *The Vanishing Wetlands* (New York: F. Watts, 1994); A. McCormick, *Vanishing Wetlands* (San Diego: Lucent, 1995); F. Staub, *America's Wetlands* (Minneapolis: Carolrhoda Books, 1995).
57. A. Leopold, *A Sand County Almanac* (New York: Oxford University Press, 1966), p. 6.
58. Prescott-Allen and Prescott-Allen, *The First Resource.*
59. Pimentel et al., "Benefits of Biodiversity."

CHAPTER 3: THE AESTHETIC APPEAL

1. See, for example, E. O. Wilson, *Biophilia* (Cambridge: Harvard University Press, 1984); D. Berlyne, *Aesthetics and Psychobiology* (New York: Ballantine, 1971); S. Kaplan and R. Kaplan, *The Experience of Nature* (New

York: Cambridge University Press, 1989); Y. Tuan, *Passing Strange and Wonderful: Aesthetics, Nature, and Culture* (Washington, D.C.: Island Press, 1993); J. Appleton, *The Experience of Landscape* (London and New York: Wiley, 1975).

2. R. Ulrich, "Aesthetic and Affective Response to Natural Environment," in I. Altman and J. Wohlwill, eds., *Behavior and the Natural Environment* (New York: Plenum, 1983), p. 109.
3. B. Chokor and S. Mene, "An Assessment of Preference for Landscapes in the Developing World: Case Study of Warri, Nigeria, and Environs," *Journal of Environmental Management* 34(1992):237–256. See also R. Hull and G. Revell, "Cross-Cultural Comparison of Landscape Scenic Beauty Evaluations," *Journal of Environmental Psychology* 9(1989):177–191; R. Ulrich, "Biophilia, Biophobia, and Natural Landscapes," in S. Kellert and E. O. Wilson, eds., *The Biophilia Hypothesis* (Washington, D.C.: Island Press, 1993).
4. H. Rolston, "Beauty and the Beast: Aesthetic Experience of Wildlife," in D. Decker and G. Goff, eds., *Valuing Wildlife: Economic and Social Perspectives* (Boulder: Westview, 1987).
5. This issue is usefully discussed in J. Gleick, *Chaos: Making a New Science* (New York: Viking, 1987).
6. W. Stevens, *Collected Poems* (New York: Knopf, 1955).
7. A. Leopold, *A Sand County Almanac* (New York: Oxford University Press, 1966), pp. 129–130.
8. G. Schaller, *Stones of Silence* (New York: Viking, 1982).
9. See, for example, Ulrich, "Biophilia, Biophobia, and Natural Landscapes"; J. Heerwagen and G. Orians, "Humans, Habitats, and Aesthetics," in S. Kellert and E. O. Wilson, eds., *The Biophilia Hypothesis* (Washington, D.C.: Island Press, 1993); J. Wohlwill, "Environmental Aesthetics: The Environment As a Source of Affect," in I. Altman and J. Wohlwill, eds., *Human Behavior and the Natural Environment* (New York: Plenum, 1976).
10. H. Peitgen cited in Gleick, *Chaos,* p. 229.
11. G. Eilenberger cited in Gleick, *Chaos,* p. 117.
12. This issue is insightfully discussed in Heerwagen and Orians, "Humans, Habitats, and Aesthetics"; Ulrich, "Biophilia, Biophobia, and Natural Landscapes"; G. Orians, "An Ecological and Evolutionary Approach to Landscape Aesthetics," in E. C. Penning-Roswell and D. Lowenthal, eds.,

Landscape Meaning and Values (London: Allen & Unwin, 1986); G. Orians and J. Heerwagen, "Evolved Responses to Landscapes," in J. Barlow et al., *The Adapted Mind: Evolutionary Psychology and the Generation of Culture* (New York: Oxford University Press, 1992).

13. Ulrich, "Biophilia, Biophobia, and Natural Landscapes."
14. Y. Saito, *The Aesthetic Appreciation of Nature: Western and Japanese Perspectives and Their Ethical Implications* (Ann Arbor: University Microfilms, 1983).
15. Heerwagen and Orians, "Humans, Habitats, and Aesthetics."
16. C. Rush, "Toward a Testable Model of Biophilia and Aesthetics" (New Haven, Yale University School of Forestry and Environmental Studies, 1994).
17. Ibid., p. 13.
18. K. Caffrey, *The Mayflower* (New York: Stein & Day, 1974).
19. Ibid., p. 111.
20. E. O. Wilson, "Biophilia and the Conservation Ethic," in Kellert and Wilson, *The Biophilia Hypothesis,* p. 39.
21. See, for example, Ulrich, "Biophilia, Biophobia, and Natural Landscapes"; Kaplan and Kaplan, *The Experience of Nature;* T. Hartig et al., "Restorative Effects of the Natural Environment," *Environment and Behavior* 23(1991):3–26; T. Hartig, "Nature Experience in Transactional Perspective," *Landscape and Urban Planning* 25(1993):17–36; T. Herzog and P. Bosley, "Tranquility and Preference As Affective Qualities of Natural Environments," *Journal of Environmental Psychology* 12(1992):115–127; D. Relf, ed., *The Role of Horticulture in Human Well-Being and Social Development* (Portland: Timber Press, 1992); R. Ulrich and O. Lunden, "Effects of Nature and Abstract Pictures on Patients Recovering from Open Heart Surgery," paper presented at International Congress of Behavioral Medicine, Uppsala, Sweden, 1990.
22. Ulrich, "Biophilia, Biophobia, and Natural Landscapes," p. 107.
23. See, for example, Ulrich, ibid.; R. Morris and D. Morris, *Men and Snakes* (London: Hutchinson, 1965); S. Minelka et al., "Observational Conditioning of Snake Fear in Rhesus Monkeys," *Journal of Abnormal Psychology* 93(1984):355–372; A. Ohman, "Face the Beast and Fear the Face: Animal and Social Fears As Prototypes for Evolutionary Analyses of Emotion,"

Psychophysiology 23(1986):123–145; E. Murray and F. Foote, "The Origin of Fear of Snakes," *Behavioral Research and Therapy* 17(1979):489–493.

24. See, for example, B. Lopez, *Of Wolves and Men* (New York: Scribner's, 1978); E. Zimen, *The Wolf* (New York: Delacorte Press, 1981); J. Nee, ed., *Wolf!* (Ashland: Northwood Press, 1988); R. Dunlap, *Saving America's Wildlife* (Princeton: Princeton University Press, 1988); S. Kellert, *The Value of Life: Biological Diversity and Human Society* (Washington, D.C.: Island Press, 1996).
25. S. Kellert et al., "Human Culture and Large Carnivore Conservation in North America," *Conservation Biology* 10(1996):977–990.
26. S. Young, *The Wolf in American History* (Caldwell: Caxton, 1946), p. 46.
27. Kellert, *Value of Life.*
28. E. Hoyt, "Whalewatching Around the World: A Report on Its Value, Extent, and Prospects," *Journal of the Whale Conservation Society* 7(1994): 1–35.
29. See, for example, Saito, *Aesthetic Appreciation of Nature;* M. Anesaki, *Art, Life, and Nature in Japan* (Rutland: Tuttle, 1932); H. Watanabe, "The Conception of Nature in Japanese Culture," *Science,* 183(1973):279–282; Kellert, "Japanese Perceptions of Wildlife."
30. Kellert, *Value of Life,* p. 139.
31. Ibid., p. 140.
32. A. Graphard, "Nature and Culture in Japan," in M. Tobias, ed., *Deep Ecology* (San Diego: Avant Books, 1985), p. 243.
33. Saito, *Aesthetic Appreciation of Nature,* p. 192.

CHAPTER 4: THE MEASURE OF EMPIRICAL KNOWLEDGE

1. E. O. Wilson, *The Diversity of Life* (Cambridge: Harvard University Press, 1993).
2. J. Robinson and K. Redford, eds., *Neotropical Wildlife Use and Conservation* (Chicago: University of Chicago Press, 1991); G. Barney, ed., *Global 2000 Report to the President: Entering the 21st Century* (Washington, D.C.: Council on Environmental Quality, 1980).
3. I heard a somewhat related account from Dr. Robert Stephenson of the Alaska Department of Fish and Game when he studied wolves among Native American groups in Alaska.
4. J. Diamond, "New Guineans and Their Natural World," in S. Kellert and E. O. Wilson, eds., *The Biophilia Hypothesis* (Washington, D.C.: Island Press, 1993), pp. 255–256.

5. R. Nelson, "Searching for the Lost Arrow: Physical and Spiritual Ecology in the Hunter's World," in Kellert and Wilson, *The Biophilia Hypothesis,* p. 206.
6. E. O. Wilson, *Biophilia* (Cambridge: Harvard University Press, 1984), p. 22.
7. S. Kellert, *The Value of Life* (Washington, D.C.: Island Press, 1996); T. Kuhn, *The Structure of Scientific Revolutions* (Chicago: University of Chicago Press, 1970); K. Thomas, *Man and the Natural World* (New York: Pantheon Books, 1983).
8. See, for example, F. Bormann and G. Likens, *Patterns and Process in a Forested Ecosystem* (New York: Springer-Verlag, 1979); L. Margulis and J. Lovelock, "Gaia and Geognosy," in M. Rambler et al., eds., *Global Ecology: Towards a Science of the Biosphere* (Boston: Academic Press/Harcourt Brace Jovanovich, 1989).
9. See, for example, B. Bloom, ed., *Taxonomy of Educational Objectives, Handbook 1: Cognitive Domain* (New York: David McKay, 1956); C. Maker, *Teaching Models in Education* (Austin: Pro-Ed, 1982), chap. 2; J. Braus and D. Wood, *Environmental Education in the Schools* (Washington, D.C.: North American Association of Environmental Education, 1993).
10. J. Diamond, "New Guineans and Their Natural World," in Kellert and Wilson, *The Biophilia Hypothesis.*
11. S. Kellert, "Values and Perceptions of Invertebrates," *Conservation Biology* 7(1993):845–855.
12. Wilson, *Diversity of Life.*
13. D. Pimentel, *Insects, Science, and Society* (New York: Academic Press, 1975).
14. E. Southwick, "Estimating the Economic Value of Honey Bees (Hymenoptera: Apidae) As Agricultural Pollinators in the United States," *Journal of Economic Entomology* 85(1992):621–633; D. Pimentel, "Environmental and Economic Benefits of Sustainable Agriculture," in M. Paoletti et al., *Socio-Economic and Policy Issues for Sustainable Farming Systems* (Padua: Cooperativa Amicizia SRI, 1993); R. Gill, "The Value of Honeybee Pollination to Society, *Acta Horticulturae* 288(1991):62–68.
15. Wilson, *Biophilia.*
16. A. Leopold, *A Sand County Almanac* (New York: Oxford University Press, 1966).

17. S. McVay, "Introduction to Conference on Informal Learning at the Zoo," *Philadelphia Zoo Review* 3(1987):4.
18. H. Beston, *The Outermost House* (New York: Ballantine Books, 1971), p. 174.

CHAPTER 5: NATURE AS METAPHOR

1. See, for example, P. Shepard, *Thinking Animals: Animals and the Development of Human Intelligence* (New York: Viking Press, 1978); P. Shepard, *The Others: How Animals Made Us Human* (Washington, D.C.: Island Press, 1996); E. Lawrence, "The Sacred Bee, the Filthy Pig, and the Bat Out of Hell: Animal Symbolism As Cognitive Biophilia," in S. Kellert and E. O. Wilson, eds., *The Biophilia Hypothesis* (Washington, D.C.: Island Press, 1993); D. Abram, *The Spell of the Sensuous: Perception and Language in a More-Than-Human World* (New York: Pantheon, 1996).
2. K. Morton, "The Story-Telling Animal," *New York Times Book Review*, December 23, 1984, p. 1.
3. Lawrence, "Sacred Bee."
4. C. Lévi-Strauss, *Totemism* (Boston: Beacon Press, 1963), p. 89.
5. Shepard, *Thinking Animals.*
6. Ibid., p. 249.
7. R. Nelson, "Searching for the Lost Arrow," in Kellert and Wilson, *The Biophilia Hypothesis.*
8. W. Whitman, *Leaves of Grass (and Other Works)* (London: Putnam, 1897).
9. Shepard, *The Others.*
10. Lawrence, "Sacred Bee," pp. 336–337.
11. Shepard, *Thinking Animals* and *The Others.*
12. Shepard, *Thinking Animals,* p. 247.
13. Lawrence, "Sacred Bee," p. 302.
14. E. Leach, "Anthropological Aspects of Language: Animal Categories and Verbal Abuse," in E. H. Lenneberg, ed., *New Directions in the Study of Language* (Cambridge: MIT Press, 1975).
15. Shepard, *The Others,* p. 60.
16. Shepard, *Thinking Animals;* M. Allen, *Animals in American Literature* (Urbana: University of Illinois Press, 1983); Lawrence, "Sacred Bee."
17. R. Lukens, *A Critical Handbook of Children's Literature* (Glenview: Scott, Foresman, 1986).

18. Shepard, *The Others;* B. Bettelheim, *The Uses of Enchantment* (New York: Vintage Books, 1977).
19. Shepard, *Thinking Animals.*
20. See, for example, N. Chomsky, *Knowledge of Language: Its Nature, Origin, and Uses* (New York: Pantheon, 1986), and *Reflections on Language* (New York: Pantheon, 1975); D. Mandelbaum, ed., *Selected Writings of Edward Sapir in Language, Culture, and Personality* (Berkeley: University of California Press, 1949).
21. S. Kellert, *The Value of Life* (Washington, D.C.: Island Press, 1996).
22. C. Lévi-Strauss, *The Savage Mind* (Chicago: University of Chicago Press, 1966).
23. Shepard, *The Others,* p. 58.
24. See, for example, C. Jung, *Man and His Symbols* (Garden City: Doubleday, 1964); *The Archetype and the Collective Unconscious* (New York: Pantheon, 1959); *Memories, Dreams, Reflections* (New York: Pantheon, 1963); *Basic Writings* (New York: Modern Library, 1959). See also Bettelheim, *Uses of Enchantment;* J. Campbell, *Myths to Live By* (New York: Bantam, 1984), *The Power of Myth* (New York: Doubleday, 1968), *The Way of the Animal Powers* (New York: A. van der Marck, 1983), and *The Hero with a Thousand Faces* (Princeton: Princeton University Press, 1972); C. Lévi-Strauss, *The Savage Mind* (Chicago: University of Chicago Press, 1968) and*The Raw and the Cooked* (New York: Harper & Row, 1970).
25. Jung, *Man and His Symbols,* p. 70.
26. Lévi-Strauss, *Savage Mind.*
27. Bettelheim, *Uses of Enchantment.*
28. Shepard, *The Others,* p. 76.
29. Lawrence, "Sacred Bee"; Kellert, *Value of Life;* Bettelheim, *Uses of Enchantment.*
30. Shepard, *The Others,* p. 281.
31. S. Elliot, "Super Bowl Was Animal Lovers Paradise," *New York Times,* February 30, 1996, pp. D1, 20.
32. T. Johnson, ed., *Poems of Emily Dickinson* (Cambridge: Harvard University Press, Belknap Press, 1958).
33. M. Oelschlaeger, *The Idea of Wilderness* (New Haven: Yale University Press, 1991), p. 377.

34. R. Nash, *The Rights of Nature: A History of Environmental Ethics* (Madison: University of Wisconsin Press, 1989), pp. 39–40.
35. Whitman, *Leaves of Grass.*
36. Wilson, "Biophilia and the Conservation Ethic," in Kellert and Wilson, "The Biophilia Hypothesis," p. 32.
37. Lawrence, "Sacred Bee," pp. 336–337.

CHAPTER 6: THE QUEST FOR EXPLORATION AND DISCOVERY

1. H. Beston, *The Outermost House* (New York: Ballantine, 1971), p. 17.
2. See, for example, S. Kellert, *The Value of Life* (Washington, D.C.: Island Press, 1996); E. O. Wilson, *Biophilia* (Cambridge: Harvard University Press, 1984); S. Kaplan and R. Kaplan, *The Experience of Nature* (New York: Cambridge University Press, 1989); R. Pyle, *The Thunder Tree: Lessons from an Urban Wildland* (Boston: Houghton Mifflin, 1993).
3. See, for example, Kellert, *Value of Life;* M. Duda and K. Young, *Americans and Wildlife Diversity* (Harrisonburg, Va.: Responsive Management, 1994); W. Shaw and W. Mangun, "Nonconsumptive Use of Wildlife in the United States," U.S. Fish and Wildlife Service, Resource Publication 154, 1986; A. Nelson, "Going Wild," *American Demographics* 50(1990):34–37. See also the statistics in U.S. Department of Interior, *National Survey of Hunting, Fishing, and Wildlife-Related Recreation and Visitation to National Parks* (Washington, D.C.: Fish and Wildlife Service and National Park Service, 1985, 1990); recreational statistics of the U.S. Forest Service, Department of Agriculture; W. Whelan, *Nature Tourism* (Washington, D.C.: Island Press, 1991); and T. Swanson and E. Barbier, eds., *Economics for the Wilds* (Washington, D.C.: Island Press, 1992).
4. See, for example, A. Ewert, *Outdoor Adventure Pursuits: Foundations, Models and Theories* (Scottsdale: Publishing Horizons, 1989); Kaplan and Kaplan, *Experience of Nature;* B. Driver et al., "Wilderness Benefits: A State-of-the-Knowledge Review," in R. C. Lucas, ed., *Proceedings of the National Wilderness Research Conference,* General Technical Report INT-220 (Ft. Collins: USDA Forest Service, 1987).
5. J. Ortega y Gasset, *Meditations on Hunting* (New York: Macmillan, 1986).
6. See, for example, Wilson, *Biophilia;* R. Ulrich, "Biophilia, Biophobia, and Natural Landscapes," in S. Kellert and E. O. Wilson, eds., *The Biophilia*

Hypothesis (Washington, D.C.: Island Press, 1993); Kaplan and Kaplan, *Experience of Nature;* Ewert, *Outdoor Adventure Pursuits.*

7. See, for example, Pyle, *Thunder Tree;* G. Nabhan and S. Trimble, *The Geography of Childhood: Why Children Need Wild Places* (Boston: Beacon Press, 1994).
8. G. Seilstad, *At the Heart of the Web* (Orlando: Harcourt Brace Jovanovich, 1989), p. 285.
9. Wilson, *Biophilia,* pp. 10, 76.
10. Nabhan and Trimble, *Geography of Childhood,* pp. 36–37.
11. R. Lee and I. DeVore, eds., *Man the Hunter* (Chicago: Aldine, 1968); S. Washburn, ed., *The Social Life of Early Man* (Chicago: Aldine, 1961); P. Shepard, *The Tender Carnivore and the Sacred Game* (New York: Scribner's, 1973).
12. See, for example, R. Ardrey, *The Hunting Hypothesis* (New York: Atheneum, 1976); Ewert, *Outdoor Adventure Pursuits;* A. Easley et al., eds., *The Use of Wilderness for Personal Growth, Therapy, and Education,* General Technical Report RM-193 (Ft. Collins: USDA Forest Service, 1990).
13. R. Schreyer et al., "Episodic versus Continued Wilderness Participation—Implications for Self Concept Enhancement," in Easley et al., *Use of Wilderness.*
14. Ewert, *Outdoor Adventure Pursuits.*
15. Kaplan and Kaplan, *Experience of Nature.*
16. S. Kaplan and J. Talbot, "Psychological Benefits of a Wilderness Experience," in I. Altman and J. Wohlwill, eds., *Behavior and the Natural Environment* (New York: Plenum, 1983).
17. See, for example, B. Driver and L. Johnson, "A Pilot Study of the Perceived Benefits of the Youth Conservation Corps," *Journal of Environmental Education* 15(1983):3–11; P. Kahn Jr. and B. Friedman, "Environmental Views and Values of Children in an Inner-City Black Community," *Child Development* 66(1995):1403–1417. See also the publications of the Baltimore Project, Urban Resources Institute, Yale University School of Forestry and Environmental Studies.
18. R. Ulrich, "Aesthetic and Affective Response to Natural Environment," in Altman and Wohlwill, eds., *Behavior and the Natural Environment,* p. 109.
19. Lee and DeVore, *Man the Hunter;* Shepard, *Tender Carnivore;* Ortega y Gasset, *Meditations on Hunting.*

20. M. Duda, *Factors Related to Hunting and Fishing Participation in the United States* (Harrisonburg, Va.: Responsive Management, 1993).
21. Kellert, *Value of Life.*
22. Ortega y Gasset, *Meditations on Hunting,* pp. 110–111.
23. J. Madson and E. Kozicky, "The Hunting Ethic," *Rod and Gun* 66(1964): 12.
24. Ortega y Gasset, *Meditations on Hunting,* p. 142.
25. Kellert, *Value of Life.*
26. E. Hoyt, "Whalewatching Around the World," *Journal of the Whale Conservation Society* 7(1994):1–35.
27. S. Kellert and V. Scheffer, "The Changing Place of Marine Mammals in American Thought," in J. Twiss and R. Reeves, eds., *Marine Mammals* (Washington, D.C.: Smithsonian Press, 1997); K. Lewis, "Report on Attitudes of Whalewatchers in New England" (Yale University School of Forestry and Environmental Studies, 1988); W. Tilt, "Report on Attitudes of Whalewatchers in California" (Yale University School of Forestry and Environmental Studies, 1986).
28. Kellert, *Value of Life;* J. Dunlap and S. Kellert, "Zoos and Zoological Parks," in W. Reich, ed., *Encyclopedia of Bioethics* (New York: Macmillan, 1994).
29. S. Bitgood and A. Benefield, *Visitor Behavior: A Comparison Across Zoos,* Technical Report 86–20 (Jacksonville: Jacksonville State University, 1987); C. Hill, "An Analysis of the Zoo Visitor," *Education* 11(1971): 158–165; D. Marcellini and T. Jensen, "Visitor Behavior in the National Zoo's Reptile House," *Philadelphia Zoo Review* 3(1987):35–42; S. Swensen, *Comparative Study of Zoo Visitors at Different Types of Facilities* (New Haven: Yale University School of Forestry and Environmental Studies, 1982); S. Kellert and J. Dunlap, *Informal Learning at the Zoo* (New Haven: Yale University School of Forestry and Environmental Studies, 1989).
30. B. Birney, *A Comparative Study of Children's Perceptions and Knowledge of Wildlife as They Relate to Field Trip Experiences at the Los Angeles County Museum of Natural History and the Los Angeles Zoo* (Ann Arbor: University Microfilms, 1986).
31. Kellert, *Value of Life.*
32. S. Kellert et al., "Wildlife and Film: A Relationship in Search of Understanding," *BKTS Journal* 10(1986):38–63; R. Fortner, "Influence of an

Environmental Documentary on Knowledge and Attitudes" (Ohio State University, School of Natural Resources, 1986); Kellert, *Value of Life.*

33. Kellert, *Value of Life;* Fortner, "Knowledge and Attitudes"; C. Parsons, *True to Nature* (Cambridge: Patrick Stephens, 1982). See also various studies and reports of Dr. Jeffrey Boswall, BBC Natural History Unit, Bristol, England.
34. Pyle, *Thunder Tree.*
35. Ibid., p. 66.
36. Nabhan and Trimble, *Geography of Childhood,* pp. 7, 107.

CHAPTER 7: YEARNING FOR KINSHIP AND AFFECTION

1. See, for example, J. Serpell, *In the Company of Animals* (Oxford: Basil Blackwell, 1986); A. Katcher and A. Beck, eds., *New Perspectives on Our Lives with Companion Animals* (Philadelphia: University of Pennsylvania Press, 1983); R. Anderson et al., *The Pet Connection* (Minneapolis: University of Minnesota Press, 1984); B. Fogle, *Interrelations Between People and Pets* (Springfield: Thomas, 1981); B. Levinson, *Pets and Human Development* (Springfield: Thomas, 1972).
2. K. Thomas, *Man and the Natural World* (New York: Pantheon, 1983).
3. See, for example, publications and reports in the journal *Anthrozoos* and data from the Humane Society of the United States.
4. See, for example, B. Levinson, *Pet Oriented Child Psychotherapy* (Springfield: Thomas, 1969); S. Corson and E. Corson, "The Socializing Role of Pet Animals in Nursing Homes," in L. Levi, ed., *Society, Stress, and Disease* (London: Oxford University Press, 1977); S. Corson et al., "Pet Dogs As Nonverbal Links in Hospital Psychiatry," *Comprehensive Psychiatry* 18(1976):61–72; Katcher and Beck, *New Perspectives;* Serpell, *In the Company of Animals.* See also publications in the journal *Anthrozoos* and those of the Delta Society.
5. Serpell, *In the Company of Animals,* p. 66.
6. See, for example, Katcher and Beck, *New Perspectives;* Serpell, *In the Company of Animals;* J. Siegel, "Stressful Life Events and Use of Physician Services Among the Elderly: The Moderating Role of Pet Ownership," *Journal of Personality and Social Psychology* 58(1990):1081–1086.
7. Serpell, *In the Company of Animals,* p. 77. See also Levinson, *Pet Oriented Child Psychotherapy,* and various publications of the journal *Anthrozoos* and the Delta Society.

8. B. Lopez, *Of Men and Wolves* (New York: Scribner's, 1978), p. 282.
9. See, for example, Katcher and Beck, *New Perspectives.*
10. Ibid., p. 159.
11. A. Katcher and G. Wilkins, "Dialogue with Animals: Its Nature and Culture," in S. Kellert and E. O. Wilson, eds., *The Biophilia Hypothesis* (Washington, D.C.: Island Press, 1993), p. 180.
12. R. Ulrich, "Biophilia, Biophobia, and Natural Landscapes," in Kellert and Wilson, *Biophilia Hypothesis;* A. Katcher et al., "Comparison of Contemplation and Hypnosis for the Reduction of Anxiety and Discomfort During Dental Surgery," *American Journal of Clinical Hypnosis* 27(1984): 14–21; T. Hartig et al., "Restorative Effects of Natural Environment Experiences," *Environment and Behavior* 23(1991):3–26; R. Ulrich et al., "Stress Recovery During Exposure to Natural and Urban Environments, *Journal of Environmental Psychology* 11(1991):201–230.
13. Ulrich, "Biophilia, Biophobia, and Natural Landscapes," p. 106.

CHAPTER 8: THE URGE TO MASTER

1. See, for example, A. Ewert, *Outdoor Adventure Pursuits* (Scottsdale: Publishing Horizons, 1989); A. Easley et al., eds., *The Use of Wilderness for Personal Growth, Therapy, and Education,* General Technical Report RM-193 (Ft. Collins: USDA Forest Service, 1990); M. Iida, "Adventure-Oriented Programs—a Review of Research," in B. van der Smissen, ed., *Research Camping and Environmental Education,* HPER Series, no. 11 (University Park: Pennsylvania State University, 1976); S. Kaplan and R. Kaplan, *The Experience of Nature* (New York: Cambridge University Press, 1989); J. Miles, "Wilderness As a Learning Place," *Journal of Environmental Education* 18(1986):33–41; N. Scott, "Toward a Psychology of Wilderness Experience," *Natural Resources Journal* 14(1974):231–237; R. Schreyer et al., *The Role of Wilderness in Human Development,* General Technical Report SE-51 (Washington, D.C.: U.S. Forest Service, 1988); R. Young and R. Crandall, "Wilderness Use and Self-Actualization," *Journal of Leisure Research* 16(1984):149–160; J. Hendee et al., *Wilderness Management* (Washington, D.C.: U.S. Forest Service, 1978). See also various publications of Outward Bound (Greenwich, Conn.), the National Outdoor Leadership School (Lander, Wyo.), and the Association of Experiential Education (Boulder, Colo.).
2. Ewert, *Outdoor Adventure Pursuits.*

3. R. Ulrich, "Biophilia, Biophobia, and Natural Landscapes," in S. Kellert and E. O. Wilson, *The Biophilia Hypothesis* (Washington, D.C.: Island Press, 1993).
4. S. Herrero, "Man and the Grizzly Bear, *BioScience* 20(1970):1148–1153; S. Kellert, "Public Attitudes Toward Bears and Their Conservation," in J. J. Clear et al., eds., *Proceedings of the 9th International Bear Conference* (Missoula: U.S. Forest Service, 1994); K. Jope and T. Shelby, "Hiker Behavior and the Outcome of Interactions with Grizzly Bears," *Leisure Sciences* 6(1984):257–270.
5. S. Bacon, "The Evolution of the Outward Bound Process," in Easley et al., *Use of Wilderness.*
6. R. Godfrey, "A Review of Research and Evaluation Literature on Outward Bound and Related Educational Programs," an informal paper presented at the Conference on Experiential Education, Estes Park, Colo., October 8–11, 1974.
7. C. Pierce, *Glamour,* May 1978, p. 126.
8. J. Rhodes, *Review,* December 1977, p. 14.
9. See, for example, Ewert, *Outdoor Adventure Pursuits;* Kaplan and Kaplan, *Experience of Nature;* Easley et al., *Use of Wilderness.*
10. A. Rice, *Psychology Today,* December 1979, p. 81.
11. See, for example, S. Kellert, *The Value of Life* (Washington, D.C.: Island Press, 1996); J. Swan, *In Defense of Hunting* (New York: HarperCollins, 1995); J. Dizard, *Going Wild: Hunting, Animals Rights, and the Contested Meaning of Nature* (Amherst: University of Massachusetts, 1994); C. Clarke, "Autumn Thoughts of a Hunter," *Journal of Wildlife Management* 22(1958):420–426.
12. V. Bourjaily, *The Unnatural Enemy* (New York: Dial Press, 1963); J. Ortega y Gasset, *Meditations on Hunting* (New York: Macmillan, 1986); P. Shepard, *The Tender Carnivore and the Sacred Game* (New York: Scribner's, 1973).
13. See, for example, G. Carson, *Men, Beasts and Gods* (New York: Scribner's, 1972); T. Regan, *All That Dwell Therein: Animal Rights and Environmental Ethics* (Berkeley: University of California Press, 1982); P. Singer, *Animal Liberation: A New Ethics for Our Treatment of Animals* (New York: New York Review, 1975); E. Hargrove, ed., *The Animal Rights/Environmental*

Ethics Debate (New York: State University of New York Press, 1992); Dizard, *Going Wild.*

14. H. Rolston, *Philosophy Gone Wild* (Buffalo: Prometheus Books, 1986), p. 88.
15. Ortega y Gasset, *Meditations on Hunting,* p. 109.
16. Ewert, *Outdoor Adventure Pursuits;* Kaplan and Kaplan, *Experience of Nature.*
17. Kaplan and Kaplan, *Experience of Nature.*
18. See F. Nietzsche, *Beyond Good and Evil* (Chicago: Regnery, 1972) and *The Philosophy of Nietzsche* (New York: Modern Library, 1954); W. Kaufman, *Nietzsche* (Princeton: Princeton University Press, 1974).
19. Ibid.
20. K. Fischer, *Nazi Germany: A New History* (New York: Continuum, 1995).
21. B. Lopez, *Of Wolves and Men* (New York: Scribner's, 1978), pp. 141, 165.

CHAPTER 9: SEEKING MEANING AND TRANSCENDENCE

1. E. O. Wilson, *The Diversity of Life* (Cambridge: Harvard University Press, 1993).
2. P. Ehrlich and A. Ehrlich, *Extinction* (New York: Ballantine, 1981).
3. E. O. Wilson, "Biophilia and the Conservation Ethic," in S. Kellert and E. O. Wilson, *The Biophilia Hypothesis* (Washington, D.C.: Island Press, 1993).
4. Ibid., p. 39.
5. A. Huxley, *The Perennial Philosophy* (Freeport: Books for Libraries Press, 1972).
6. L. Eisley, *The Immense Journey* (New York: Random House, 1946), pp. 209–210.
7. See, for example, J. Callicott, "Traditional European and American Indian Attitudes Toward Nature: An Overview," *Environmental Ethics* 4(1982):293–318; R. Nelson, *The Island Within* (Chicago: University of Chicago Press, 1991); J. Hughes, *American Indian Ecology* (El Paso: Texas Western Press, 1983); A. Booth et al., "Ties That Bind: Native American Beliefs As a Foundation for Environmental Consciousness," *Environmental Ethics* 12(1990):27–43.
8. R. Nelson, "Searching for the Lost Arrow," in Kellert and Wilson, *Biophilia Hypothesis,* p. 218.

9. Luther Standing Bear, *Land of the Spotted Eagle* (Lincoln: University of Nebraska Press, 1933), p. 45.
10. See, for example, J. Callicott and R. Ames, eds., *Nature in Asian Traditions of Thought* (Albany: State University of New York, 1989); N. Nash, ed., *Tree of Life: Buddhism and Protection of Nature* (Hong Kong: Buddhism Protection of Nature Project, 1987); R. Nash, *The Rights of Nature: A History of Environmental Ethics* (Madison: University of Wisconsin Press, 1989).
11. From Nash, *Rights of Nature,* p. 113.
12. See, for example, L. White, "The Historic Roots of Our Ecologic Crisis," *Science* 176(1967):1203–1207; M. Oelschlaeger, *The Idea of Wilderness* (New Haven: Yale University Press, 1991); W. Leiss, *The Domination of Nature* (New York: Braziller, 1972); H. Watanabe, "The Conception of Nature in Japanese Culture," *Science* 183(1974):279–282; S. Kellert, *The Value of Life* (Washington, D.C.: Island Press, 1996); M. Soulé and G. Lease, eds., *Reinventing Nature? Responses to Post-Modern Deconstruction* (Washington, D.C.: Island Press, 1994).
13. J. Passmore, *Man's Responsibility for Nature: Ecological Problems and Western Traditions* (New York: Scribner's, 1974), p. 12.
14. Nash, *Rights of Nature,* p. 60.
15. Ibid., pp. 61–62.
16. J. Steinbeck, *Log from the Sea of Cortez* (Mamaroneck: Appel, 1941), p. 93.
17. W. Whitman, *Leaves of Grass (and Other Works)* (London: Putnam, 1897).
18. K. Thomas, *Man and the Natural World* (New York: Pantheon, 1983).
19. Wilson, "Conservation Ethic."
20. A. Leopold, *A Sand County Almanac* (New York: Oxford University Press, 1966).
21. D. Sagan and L. Margulis, "God, Gaia, and Biophilia," in Kellert and Wilson, *Biophilia Hypothesis,* p. 352.
22. H. Rolston, *Philosophy Gone Wild* (Buffalo: Prometheus Books, 1986), p. 18.
23. See, for example, Rolston, *Philosophy Gone Wild;* P. Wenz, *Environmental Justice* (Albany: State University of New York, 1988); J. Callicott, *In Defense of the Land Ethic: Essays in Environmental Philosophy* (Albany: State University of New York, 1988); M. Sagoff, "Zuckerman's Dilemma: A Plea for Environmental Ethics," *Hastings Center Report* 21(1991):32–41;

P. Taylor, *Respect for Nature: A Theory of Environmental Ethics* (Princeton: Princeton University Press, 1986).

24. Nash, *Rights of Nature.*
25. Leopold, *A Sand County Almanac.*
26. T. Regan, *The Case for Animal Rights* (Berkeley: University of California Press, 1983); P. Singer, *Animal Liberation* (New York: New York Review, 1975).
27. See, for example, T. Regan and P. Singer, eds., *Animal Rights and Human Obligations* (Englewood Cliffs: Prentice-Hall, 1976); C. Amory, *Man Kind?* (New York: Harper & Row, 1974).
28. J. Krutch, "The Sportsman or the Predator: A Damnable Pleasure," *Saturday Review,* August 19, 1957, p. 9.
29. S. Kellert, *The Value of Life* (Washington, D.C.: Island Press, 1996); E. O. Wilson, *Sociobiology: The New Synthesis* (Cambridge: Harvard University Press, 1975).
30. Rolston, *Philosophy Gone Wild,* p. 25.
31. G. R. Dodge Foundation Poetry Festival, Morristown, N.J., 1992.
32. M. Oelschlaeger, *The Idea of Wilderness* (New Haven: Yale University Press, 1991).
33. D. Feeny et al., "The Tragedy of the Commons: Twenty-Two Years Later," *Human Ecology* 18(1990):1–19; F. Berkes, "Fishermen and the Tragedy of the Commons," *Environmental Conservation* 12(1985):199–206.
34. C. Martin, *Keepers of the Game: Indian-Animal Relationships and the Fur Trade* (Berkeley: University of California Press, 1978).
35. M. Gadgil, "India's Deforestation: Patterns and Processes," *Society and Natural Resources* 3(1992):131–143.
36. J. Ryan, "Life Support: Conserving Biological Diversity," *Worldwatch Report* 108(1992):1–24.
37. M. Freeman and S. Kellert, "International Attitudes to Whales, Whaling, and Whale Products," in M. Freeman and U. Kreuter, eds., *Elephants and Whales: Resources for Whom?* (London: Gordon & Breach, 1994).

CHAPTER 10: OF FEAR AND LOATHING

1. S. Kellert, *The Value of Life* (Washington, D.C.: Island Press, 1996); R. Ulrich, "Biophilia, Biophobia, and Natural Landscapes," and E. O. Wilson, "Biophilia and the Conservation Ethic," both in S. Kellert and

E. O. Wilson, eds., *The Biophilia Hypothesis* (Washington, D.C.: Island Press, 1993).

2. Ulrich, "Biophilia, Biophobia, and Natural Landscapes"; A. Öhman, "Face the Beast and Fear the Face: Animal and Social Fears As Prototypes for Evolutionary Analyses of Emotion," *Psychophysiology* 23(1986): 123–145.
3. An analogous North Atlantic storm is depicted by J. Rousmaniere in *Fastnet, Force 10* (New York: Norton, 1979).
4. A similar incident described in the Fall 1994 issue of *Cruising World* concerns a South Pacific storm occurring between the Bay of Islands and Fiji in the spring of 1994.
5. Öhman, "Face the Beast and Fear the Face"; A. Öhman and U. Dimberg, "An Evolutionary Perspective on Human Social Behavior," in W. M. Waid, ed., *Sociophysiology* (New York: Springer-Verlag, 1984); A. Öhman et al., "Animal and Social Phobias: Biological Constraints on Learned Fear Responses," in S. Reiss and R. Bootzin, eds., *Theoretical Issues in Behavior* (New York: Academic Press, 1985); A. Öhman and J. Soares, "On the Automatic Nature of Phobic Fear: Conditioned Electrodermal Responses to Masked Fear-Relevant Stimuli," *Journal of Abnormal Psychology* 84(1993): 41–45.
6. Ulrich, "Biophilia, Biophobia, and Natural Landscapes."
7. T. Schneirla, *Principles of Animal Psychology* (Englewood Cliffs: Prentice-Hall, 1965); T. Hardy, "Entomophobia: The Case for Miss Muffett," *Entomology Society of America Bulletin* 34(1988):64–69; J. Hillman, *Going Bugs* (Gracie Station: Spring Audio, 1991); S. Mineka et al., "Observational Conditioning of Snake Fear in Rhesus Monkeys," *Journal of Abnormal Psychology* 93(1984):355–372; A. Bowd, "Fears and Understanding of Animals in Middle Childhood," *Journal of Genetic Psychology* 145(1984):143–144; I. Marks, *Fears and Phobias* (New York: Academic Press, 1969); E. Murray and F. Foote, "The Origin of Fear of Snakes, *Behavioral Research* 17(1979):489–493; M. Seligman, "Phobias and Preparedness," *Behavior Therapy* 2(1971):307–320.
8. Ulrich, "Biophilia, Biophobia, and Natural Landscapes"; Öhman, "Face the Beast and Fear the Face"; Marks, *Fears and Phobias.*
9. S. Kellert et al., "Human Culture and Large Carnivore Conservation in North America," *Conservation Biology* 10(1996):977–990.
10. B. Lopez, *Of Wolves and Men* (New York: Scribner's, 1978), pp. 136–137.

11. Öhman, "Face the Beast and Fear the Face," p. 128.
12. P. Singer, *Animal Liberation* (New York: New York Review, 1975).
13. Lopez, *Of Wolves and Men,* p. 163.
14. S. Kellert, "Values and Perceptions of Invertebrates," *Conservation Biology* 7(1993):845–855.
15. Kellert, *Value of Life.*
16. D. Pimentel, *Insects, Science and Society* (New York: Academic Press, 1975); J. Cloudsley, *Insects and History* (New York: St. Martin's Press, 1976); T. Southwood, "Entomology and Mankind," *American Science* 65(1992): 30–39; Kellert, "Values and Perceptions of Invertebrates."
17. Hardy, "Entomophobia"; Hillman, *Going Bugs;* T. Moore and J. Hillman, eds., *A Blue Fire: Selected Writings of James Hillman* (New York: Harper & Row, 1989); Kellert, "Values and Perceptions of Invertebrates"; Marks, *Fears and Phobias.*
18. Hillman, *Going Bugs.*
19. Ibid.
20. Ibid.
21. Ulrich, "Biophilia, Biophobia, and Natural Landscapes."
22. J. Adams, ed., *Insect Potpourri: Adventures in Entomology* (Gainesville: Sandhill Crane Press, 1992).
23. J. Dobie, *Rattlesnakes* (Boston: Little, Brown, 1965); R. McNally, "Preparedness and Phobias: A Review," *Psychological Bulletin* 101(1987): 283–303; R. Morris and D. Morris, *Men and Snakes* (London: Hutchinson, 1965); J. Campbell, *Myths to Live By* (New York: Viking Press, 1973), *The Hero with a Thousand Faces* (Princeton: Princeton University Press, 1972), and *The Way of Animal Powers* (New York: Van der Marck, 1983).
24. Murray and Foote, "Origin of Fear of Snakes"; S. Mineka et al., "Fear of Snakes in Wild- and Laboratory-Reared Rhesus Monkeys," *Animal Learning and Behavior* 8(1980):653–663.
25. E. O. Wilson, "Biophilia and the Conservation Ethic," p. 34.
26. J. Ortega y Gasset, *Meditations on Hunting* (New York: Macmillan, 1986).
27. A. Gussow, *A Sense of Place: The Artist and the Land* (San Francisco: Friends of the Earth and Seabury Publishing, 1972); J. Flexner, *First Flowers of Our Wilderness: American Painting* (Boston: Houghton Mifflin, 1969); M. Norelli, *American Wildlife Painting* (New York: Watson-Guptill, 1975); J. Pearce, *American Painting, 1560–1913* (New York:

McGraw-Hill, 1964); R. Nash, *Wilderness and the American Mind* (New Haven: Yale University Press, 1976).

28. R. Nelson, "Searching for the Lost Arrow," in Kellert and Wilson, *Biophilia Hypothesis.*

CHAPTER II: DIMINISHING NATURE, SELF, AND SOCIETY

1. S. Kellert, *The Value of Life* (Washington, D.C.: Island Press, 1996); E. O. Wilson, *Biophilia* (Cambridge: Harvard University Press, 1984); S. Kellert and E. O. Wilson, eds., *The Biophilia Hypothesis* (Washington, D.C.: Island Press, 1993).
2. Kellert, *Value of Life.*
3. Ibid.
4. Ibid.
5. Ibid.
6. Wilson, *Biophilia,* p. 114.
7. E. O. Wilson, *The Diversity of Life* (Cambridge: Harvard University Press, 1993).
8. See, for example, Wilson, *Diversity of Life;* B. Groombridge, ed., *Global Biodiversity* (London: Chapman & Hall, 1992); G. Barney, ed., *Global 2000 Report* (Washington, D.C.: Council on Environmental Quality, 1980); N. Myers, "Global Biodiversity II: Losses," in G. Meffe and C. Carroll, eds., *Principles of Conservation Biology* (Sunderland: Sinauer, 1994); L. Kaufman and K. Mallory, eds., *The Last Extinction* (Cambridge: MIT Press, 1993); Kellert, *Value of Life;* J. Savage, "Systematics and the Biodiversity Crisis," *BioScience* 45(1995):673–679; V. Heywood, ed., *Global Biodiversity Assessment* (Cambridge: United Nations Environment Programme/Cambridge University Press, 1995).
9. Statistics on listed species are published regularly in U.S. Fish and Wildlife Service, *Endangered Species Technical Bulletin* (Washington, D.C.: U.S. Department of Interior).
10. Wilson, *Diversity of Life.*
11. Ibid.
12. Savage, "Systematics and the Biodiversity Crisis."
13. Kellert, *Value of Life;* C. Guggisberg, *Man and Wildlife* (New York: Arco, 1970); V. Ziswiller, *Extinct and Vanishing Species* (London: English University Press, 1967).

14. P. Vitousek et al., "Human Appropriation of the Products of Photosynthesis," *BioScience* 36(1991):368–373.
15. See, for example, R. Noss and A. Cooperrider, *Saving Nature's Legacy* (Washington, D.C.: Island Press, 1994).
16. Wilson, *Diversity of Life.*
17. See, for example, W. Minckley and J. Deacon, eds., *Battle Against Extinction: Native Fish Management in the American West* (Tucson: University of Arizona Press, 1991).
18. Ibid.
19. W. Courtenay, "Exotic Species," in H. Brokaw, ed., *Wildlife and America* (Washington, D.C.: Council on Environmental Quality, 1978).
20. Kellert, *Value of Life.*
21. P. Matthiessen, *Wildlife in America* (New York: Viking, 1989); R. Dunlap, *Saving America's Wildlife* (Princeton: Princeton University Press, 1988).
22. See, for example, A. Berger, *Hawaiian Birdlife* (Honolulu: University of Hawaii Press, 1981); J. Scott et al., "Forest Bird Communities of the Hawaiian Islands: Their Dynamics, Ecology, and Conservation," *Studies in Avian Biology* 9(1986):518–527.
23. Berger, *Hawaiian Birdlife;* C. Van Riper et al., "Distribution and Abundance Patterns of the Palila on Mauna Kea, Hawaii," *Auk* 95(1978):518–527.
24. M. Bean, *The Evolution of National Wildlife Law* (New York: Praeger, 1983); D. Rohlf, *The Endangered Species Act: A Guide to Its Protection and Implementation* (Stanford: Stanford Environmental Law Society, 1990).
25. See, for example, Matthiessen, *Wildlife in America;* A. Schroger, *The Passenger Pigeon* (Madison: University of Wisconsin Press, 1955).
26. Matthiessen, *Wildlife in America.*
27. Ibid., p. 192.
28. Ibid., p. 187.
29. A. Leopold, *Sand County Almanac* (New York: Oxford University Press, 1966).
30. See, for example, E. Relpf, *Place and Placelessness* (London: Pion, 1976); J. Jackson, *A Sense of Place, a Sense of Time* (New Haven: Yale University Press, 1994).
31. M. Sagoff, "Settling America or the Concept of Place in Environmental Ethics," *Journal of Energy, Natural Resources, and Environmental Law* 12(1992):351–418.

32. S. Weil, *The Need for Roots* (New York: Harper Colophon, 1971), p. 38.
33. R. Pyle, *The Thunder Tree* (Boston: Houghton Mifflin, 1993), p. 66; G. Nabhan and S. St. Antoine, "The Loss of Floral and Faunal Story: The Extinction of Experience," in S. Kellert and E. O. Wilson, eds., *The Biophilia Hypothesis* (Washington, D.C.: Island Press, 1993).
34. Sagoff, "Settling America," pp. 352–353, 358.
35. See, for example, D. Orr, *Earth in Mind: On Education, Environment, and the Human Prospect* (Washington, D.C.: Island Press, 1994); A. Gussow, *A Sense of Place: The Artist and the Land* (San Francisco: Friends of the Earth and Seabury Publishing, 1972).
36. The link between culture, nature, and the concept of place has been thoroughly examined by K. Spencer of the Yale University School of Forestry and Environmental Studies.
37. See, for example, Noss and Cooperrider, *Saving Nature's Legacy;* G. Burger, "Agriculture and Wildlife," in H. Brokaw, ed., *Wildlife and America* (Washington, D.C.: Council on Environmental Quality, 1978).
38. Relph, *Place and Placelessness,* p. 6.
39. Kellert, *Value of Life.*

CHAPTER 12: THE PURSUIT OF SELF-INTEREST

1. E. O. Wilson, *Biophilia* (Cambridge: Harvard University Press, 1984), pp. 13–14.
2. W. Hammit and D. Cole, *Wildland Recreation: Ecology and Management* (New York: Wiley, 1987); R. Knight and K. Gutzwiller, eds., *Wildlife and Recreationists: Coexistence Through Management and Research* (Washington, D.C.: Island Press, 1995); K. Lindberg and D. Hawkins, eds., *Ecotourism: A Guide for Planners and Managers* (North Bennington: Ecotourism Society, 1993); T. Whelan, *Nature Tourism* (Washington, D.C.: Island Press, 1991).
3. S. Kellert, *The Value of Life* (Washington, D.C.: Island Press, 1996).
4. See, for example, R. Noss and A. Cooperrider, *Saving Nature's Legacy* (Washington, D.C.: Island Press, 1995); M. Hunter, *Wildlife, Forests, Forestry* (Englewood Cliffs: Prentice-Hall, 1989); W. Reid and K. Miller, *Keeping Options Alive: The Scientific Basis for Conserving Biodiversity* (Washington, D.C.: World Resources Institute, 1989); M. Mangel et al., "Principles for the Conservation of Wild Living Resources," *Ecological Ap-*

plications 6(1996):337–372; WRI/IUCN/UNEP, *Global Biodiversity Strategy* (Washington, D.C.: World Resources Institute, 1992); E. Norse, *Global Marine Biological Diversity* (Washington, D.C.: Island Press, 1993); T. Clark et al., eds., *Endangered Species Recovery: Finding the Lessons, Improving the Process* (Washington, D.C.: Island Press, 1994).

5. Noss and Cooperrider, *Saving Nature's Legacy.*
6. N. Myers cited in E. O. Wilson, *The Diversity of Life* (Cambridge: Harvard University Press, 1993).
7. See, for example, G. Meffe and C. Carroll, eds., *Principles of Conservation Biology* (Sunderland: Sinauer, 1994); R. Grumbine, *Ghost Bears: Exploring the Biodiversity Crisis* (Washington, D.C.: Island Press, 1992); M. Soulé, "Conservation: Tactics for a Constant Crisis," *Science* 253(1991):744–750.
8. See, for example, D. Western et al., eds., *Natural Connections: Perspectives in Community-Based Conservation* (Washington, D.C.: Island Press, 1994).
9. M. Batisse, "Biosphere Reserve: An Overview," *Nature and Conservation* 29(1993):3–5; Kellert, *Value of Life.*
10. Western et al., *Natural Connections;* C. Gibson and S. Marks, "Transforming Rural Hunters into Conservationists: An Assessment of Community-Based Wildlife Management Programs in Africa," *World Development* 23(1995):941–957.
11. Kellert, *Value of Life;* K. Kohm, ed., *Balancing on the Brink of Extinction: The Endangered Species Act and Lessons for the Future* (Washington, D.C.: Island Press, 1991).
12. Wilson, *Diversity of Life.*
13. R. Noss, "From Endangered Species to Biodiversity," in Kohm, *Balancing on the Brink.*
14. S. Kellert and T. Clark, "The Theory and Application of a Wildlife Policy Framework," in W. Mangun and S. Nagel, eds., *Public Policy and Wildlife Conservation* (New York: Greenwood, 1991); Kellert, *Value of Life.*
15. Clark et al., *Endangered Species Recovery;* O. Houck, "The Endangered Species Act and Its Implementation by the U.S. Departments of Interior and Commerce," *University of Colorado Law Review* 64(1993):278–369; T. Clarke and D. McCool, *Staking Out the Terrain: Power Differentials Among Natural Resource Agencies* (Albany: State University of New York Press, 1985).

16. M. Bean, *The Evolution of National Wildlife Law* (New York: Praeger, 1983); D. Rohlf, *The Endangered Species Act* (Stanford: Stanford Environmental Law Society, 1990).
17. S. Yaffee, *Prohibitive Policy: Implementing the Federal Endangered Species Act* (Cambridge: MIT Press, 1982); Clark et al., *Endangered Species Recovery.*
18. T. Clark et al., "Designing and Managing Successful Endangered Species Recovery Programs," *Environmental Management* 13(1989):159–170; S. Yaffee, *The Wisdom of the Spotted Owl: Policy Lessons for a New Century* (Washington, D.C.: Island Press, 1994).
19. Kellert, *Value of Life.*
20. P. Shepard and B. Sanders, *The Sacred Paw: The Bear in Nature, Myth, and Literature* (New York: Viking Penguin, 1985); T. McNamee, *The Grizzly Bear* (New York: Knopf, 1984); S. Kellert et al., "Human Culture and Large Carnivore Conservation in North America," *Conservation Biology* 10(1996):977–990; S. Herrero, "People and the Grizzly Bear," in C. Kirkpatrick, ed., *Wildlife and People* (West Lafayette: University of Indiana, 1978).
21. Shepard and Sanders, *Sacred Paw.*
22. Kellert, *Value of Life; M.* Mangel et al., "Principles for the Conservation of Wild Living Resources," *Ecological Applications* 6(1996):338–362.
23. Mangel et al., "Principles."
24. R. Dubos, *Ecology and Religion in History* (New York: Oxford University Press, 1969), p. 129.
25. See, for example, A. Savory, *Holistic Resource Management* (Washington, D.C.: Island Press, 1988); W. Berry, *What Are People For?* (San Francisco: North Point, 1990), *Unsettling of America* (San Francisco: Sierra Club Books, 1977), and *The Gift of Good Land* (San Francisco: North Point, 1981); B. Mollison, *Introduction to Permaculture* (Califon, N.J.: Permaculture Resources, 1995); K. Ausubel, *Seeds of Change* (Sante Fe: Seeds of Change, 1994); W. Jackson, *Man and the Environment* (Dubuque: Brown, 1971).
26. Kellert, *Value of Life.*
27. S. Kellert, "Environmental Values, the Coastal Context, and a Sense of Place," in M. Sagoff, ed., *Place, Locality and Community in Enclosed Coastal Seas* (Princeton: Princeton University Press, 1997).

28. A. Leopold, *A Sand County Almanac* (New York: Oxford University Press, 1966), p. 266.
29. R. Pyle, *The Thunder Tree* (Boston: Houghton Mifflin, 1993), p. 149.
30. J. Heerwagen and G. Orians, "Humans, Habitats, and Aesthetics," in S. Kellert and E. O. Wilson, eds., *The Biophilia Hypothesis* (Washington, D.C.: Island Press, 1993), p. 166.
31. See, for example, P. Singer, *Animal Liberation* (New York: New York Review, 1975); T. Regan, *All That Dwell Therein* (Berkeley: University of California Press, 1982) and *The Case for Animal Rights* (Berkeley: University of California Press, 1983).
32. See, for example, P. Wenz, *Environmental Justice* (Albany: State University of New York, 1988); P. Taylor, *Respect for Nature* (Princeton: Princeton University Press, 1986); E. Hargrove, ed., *The Animal Rights/Environmental Ethics Debate* (New York: State University of New York, 1992); B. Norton, *Why Preserve Natural Variety?* (Princeton: Princeton University Press, 1987).
33. See, for example, E. O. Wilson, "Biophilia and the Conservation Ethic," in Kellert and Wilson, *Biophilia Hypothesis;* D. Pearce and D. Moran, *The Economic Value of Biodiversity* (London: Earthscan, 1994); W. Reid and K. Miller, *Keeping Options Alive* (Washington, D.C.: World Resources Institute, 1989).
34. Kellert, *Value of Life.*
35. See, for example, the essay by A. Borgmann, "The Nature of Reality and the Reality of Nature," in M. Soulé and G. Lease, eds., *Reinventing Nature?* (Washington, D.C.: Island Press, 1995).
36. A book on Brier Island: C. Norwood, *Life on Brier Island, Nova Scotia* (Westport, N.S.: Northwood, 1993).
37. D. Beach and M. Weinrich, "Watching the Whales," *Oceanus* 32(1989): 84–88; J. Gibbs, *Whales Off New England* (Newberry: Gibbs & Gibbs, 1982); R. Barstow, *Meet the Great Whales* (West Hartford: American Cetacean Society, 1987); R. Ellis, *The Book of Whales* (New York: Knopf, 1980).
38. M. Robinson, "Zoos Today and Tomorrow," *Anthrozoos* 2(1989):10–14.
39. S. McVay, "Prologue," in Kellert and Wilson, *Biophilia Hypothesis.*

Index

Abstract art, 39, 40
Adaptation and survival, 27
- aesthetic response to nature, 35–46
- fearing/rejecting nature, 156–61
- genetic tendencies encoded in human animal, 163–64
- immersion in nature, 87–94
- kinship and affection for natural world, 108–19
- mastering/contesting nature, 127–32
- scientific/ecological outlook on nature, 62–68
- symbolizing nature, 74–81
- unity in nature, underlying, 142–45

Adolescence, 167
Adventure programs, outdoor, 123–25
Advertising and symbolizing nature, 80
Aesthetic response to nature:
- benefits of beauty, 49
- consistency in, 33–35
- harmony/balance and symmetry, 36
- healing and mental restoration, physical, 45–46
- mystery and discovery, 44–45
- order and organization, 37–40
- safety/sustenance and security, 40–44
- variation and change, 46–49

Africa, wildlife excursions in, 165–66
Agriculture:
- ecological processes benefiting, 28–29
- invertebrates, antipathy towards, 154
- wild species improving production, 25–28

Amazon River, 149–51
Analysis and intellectual growth, 64
Anecdote of the Jar (Stevens), 37
Animals:
- advertising, 80
- aesthetic response to nature, 38
- children's books, 75
- classifying, 75–76
- companion, 106–7
- degradation, environmental, 173–83
- diversity and variability, 133–34
- intelligence bound to presence of, 70
- lower creatures, 65–66
- *see also* Kinship and affection for natural world; Predators; *various subject headings;* Wild resources/nature

Anthropomorphism, 74, 79, 108
Anthrozoos, 109
Application of knowledge, 63–64
Aquariums, 98–100
Arresting biological decline, 193–99
Art and order, 39, 40

Asian nations:
medicines, traditional, 19
wild resources/nature, 15
Attention deficit disorders, 116
Audubon, John J., 179
Authoritarianism, 131
Aversive tendencies, 151
Avoidance and defense, 158–59
Awe and respect, 159–60

Balance, sense of, 36
Bears, 197–98
Beck, Alan, 115
Bees, 15, 28, 65
Beston, Henry, iv, 67, 85
Bettelheim, Bruno, 78
Bible, The, 81, 137
Biocultural evolution, 4, 6
Biophilia:
biocultural evolution, 4
competitive aspect of, 122
defining, 1
in degraded environments, 7
disconnection from nature, 7–8
Fromm's interpretation, 2
intrinsic worth of expressions of, 160–61
self-interest expressed in preserving, 9, 206–9
wide-ranging expressions of, 4–6
worth and importance imputed to natural world, 3
see also Functional development of biophilia; *various subject headings*
Biophilia Hypothesis, The (Kellert & Wilson), 3
Bioremediation, 29
Biosphere reserves, 194–95
Birds:
birding, 97–98
extinctions and endangered species, 175–78
immersion in nature, 91
insect damage, 29
warblers, spring migration of, xii–xvi
Bloom, Benjamin, 63
Bonding and companionship, 106, 108
see also Kinship and affection for natural world
Bright colors in nature, 41
Buddhist-Hindu perspective, 136

Caffrey, Kate, 43
Campbell, Joseph, 77
Cancer and wild resources/nature, 27–28
Captive wildlife, 98–100
Celebrating connections with nature, 4
Character-building effects of outdoor experiences, 91–93
Charismatic species, 197–98
Childhood development, 6, 166–71
Classifying nature, 75–76
Cognitive biophilia, 70, 83
Colorado Plateau, changing perceptions about, 42–43
Communication/thought and symbolizing nature, 80–81
Community-based conservation, 194–95
Companion animals, 106–7
see also Kinship and affection for natural world
Competitive aspect of biophilia, 122
see also Mastering/contesting nature
Comprehension, 63
Confidence and security, personal, 143
Conserving and protecting nature, 143–45
see also Restoring biological diversity
Constable, John, 42
Contesting nature, *see* Mastering/contesting nature
Contextual learning, 164–65
Controlled production of wild resources/nature, 11
Convention on International Trade in Endangered Species of Flora and Fauna, 23
Cooperation, 111, 142–43
Coral reefs, 30, 65
Corn, wild, 26
Corson, Elizabeth, 109
Courage and contesting nature, 131–32
Cultural milieu, a supportive, 170–71, 188–89

Curiosity and immersion in nature, 89–90

Decomposition of organic wastes, 29, 65–66
Defending against danger, 158–59
Deference and respect for nature, 159–60
Deforestation, 28, 30
Degradation, environmental, *see* Exploiting nature
Delta Society, 109
Developing countries:
 medicines, traditional, 19
 wild resources/nature, 14
Diamond, Jared, 57–58
Dickinson, Emily, 81
Disconnection from nature, 7–8
Disease:
 invertebrates and, 154
 resistance of domesticated crops/animals, 26
Diversity of the natural world, 133–34
 see also Restoring biological diversity
Douglas-Hamilton, Ian, 23
Dreams, symbolic use of, 78–79
Duality distinguishing people from nature, 137
Dubos, René, 199

Ecological processes:
 benefiting from, 28–32
 scientific focus on, 61–62
Economics:
 agricultural production increased by wild resources/nature, 25, 26
 birds and insect damage, 29
 elephant trade, 23–24
 fishing and hunting, recreational, 16
 wildlife utilization, 24, 32, 176
Ehrlich, Anne, 29
Ehrlich, Paul, 29
Eilenberger, Gert, 39–40
Eisley, Loren, 135
Elephant Protection Bill, 23
Elephants, 22–24
Emotional connections to nature, 105, 109–11
 see also Kinship and affection for natural world
Empirical and objective knowledge, 60–62, 64–66
Endangered species:
 corn, Mexican, 26
 deforestation, 28
 elephants, 23
 environment, healthy and diverse, 173–83
 protection strategies, 195–98
 whales, 22
 wildlife trade, 21
 see also Exploiting nature
Endangered Species Act, 196–97
Environment, healthy and diverse, 170
 physical/emotional/intellectual health dependent on, 171–73
 scale of decline, 173–78
 significance of declining diversity, 178–83
Ethics, modern, 140–42, 204–9
Evaluation and intellectual growth, 64
Ewert, Alan, 92
Exploiting nature:
 deforestation, 28, 30
 diminished appreciation for role of natural diversity, 7
 extracting sustenance from land/animals, 16–17
 habitat destruction, 174–75
 Hawaii's bird life, 176–78
 meaningful lives balanced against, 178–79
 nonnative species, introduction of, 175
 pigeons, passenger, 179–82
 see also Endangered species
Exploration and discovery, 27, 130
 see also Immersion in nature
Extinction of experience, 102, 184
Extinctions and endangered species, *see* Endangered species

Fairy tales, 73–74, 78–79
Fantasy play, 168–70
Fearing/rejecting nature, 147
 avoidance and defense, 158–59

Fearing/rejecting nature (*continued*)
  awe and respect, 159–60
  balance or distortion, 160–61
  invertebrates, 153–56
  personal growth and connection to nature, 149–51
  predators, 152
  research studies, 151
  safety and survival, 156–58
  storms, 148–49
Film and immersion in nature, 100–101
Firewood, cutting, 30–31
Fish:
  coral reefs, 30
  economics, 16
  ethical debates over fishing, 141
  extinctions and endangered species, 173
  global production, 14, 15
  immersion in nature, 95
  last harvest of free-roaming animals, 14
  mastering/contesting nature, 125–26
  nonnative organisms and disease, 175
  personal growth and connection to nature, 17–18
Food production and wild resources/nature, 14, 15–16
Frisch, Karl Von, 67
Fromm, Erich, 2
Functional development of biophilia:
  childhood development, 166–71
  contextual learning, 164–65
  cultural milieu, a supportive, 170–71, 188–89
  environment, healthy and diverse, 171–83
  ominous trends, 189–90
  residence and work, satisfying places for, 170–71, 183–88
  wildlife excursions, 165–66

Gadgil, Madhav, 144
Gaia hypothesis, 139
Genetics:
  crop breeding programs, diversity in, 25–26
  tendencies encoded in human animal, 163–64
  unity in nature, underlying, 134
Graphard, Alan, 48–49
Greco-Roman beliefs, 12
Grizzly bears, 197–98
Group loyalty, 142–43

Habitat destruction, 174–75, 194
Hahn, Kurt, 123
Harmony, sense of, 36
Hawaii's bird life, 176–78
Healing and mental restoration, physical, 45–46, 115–19
Heerwagen, Judith, 41, 204
Heroism and contesting nature, 131–32
Herons, 91
Hillman, James, 155
Hines, Jamie, 51–60
Historic Roots of Our Ecologic Crisis, The (White), 12
Honey, 15
Honeycreepers, Hawaiian, 177
Hornaday, William, 152
Human development and affiliation with natural diversity, 5–6
Hunting:
  ethical debates over, 141
  immersion in nature, 95–96
  mastering/contesting nature, 125–26
  meat, obtaining, 16
Huxley, Aldous, 134

Imagination and immersion in nature, 90
Immersion in nature, 85–86
  captive wildlife, 98–100
  curiosity and imagination, 89–91
  film and TV, 100–101
  fishing/hunting and observation, 95–98
  peace of mind, 93–94
  physical fitness and vitality, 88–89
  self-confidence and self-esteem, 91–93
  spontaneity diminished, 101–4
Independence and contesting nature, 129–30
India, land conservation in, 144
Indigenous people:
  conserving and protecting nature, 144
  ethical debate over hunting, 141–42

knowledge about nature, 51–60
religion and mysticism, 136
Industrialized countries and wild resources/nature, 14
Industrial products from wild resources/nature, 20–21
Insects:
agricultural production, 29
fearing/rejecting nature, 153–56
scientific/ecological outlook on nature, 65–66
variability among, 134
Intellectual growth and scientific/ecological outlook on nature, 63–64
Intelligence bound to presence of animals, 70
Invertebrates, 65–66
fearing/rejecting nature, 153–56
Ivory, 23

Japan:
aesthetic response to nature, 48–49
wild resources/nature, 15
Judeo-Christian perspective, 12, 136–37
Jung, Carl, 77

Kaplan, Rachel, 92
Kaplan, Stephen, 92, 93
Katcher, Aaron, 109, 115
Kinship and affection for natural world:
emotional sustenance and security, 109–11
healing and mental restoration, physical, 115–19
nature of the bond, 105–8
self-esteem and self-respect, 113–15
sociability and affiliation, 111–12
Kozicky, Ed, 96
Krutch, Joseph W., 141

Land ethic, 140–41
Landscape painters, 160
Landscapes, natural, 34
Language acquisition and symbolizing nature, 74–76
Latex, 20
Lawrence, Elizabeth, 70, 72, 83
Leach, Edmund, 73
Learning, contextual, 164–65
Learning about and developing expressions of biophilia, 4, 6
Leaves of Grass (Whitman), 71, 138
Leopold, Aldo, 38–39, 140, 181–82
Levinson, Boris, 109
Lévi-Strauss, Claude, 70, 77, 78
Lopez, Barry, 113, 132, 153
Lubricants, 20

Madson, John, 96
Margulis, Lynn, 139
Mastering/contesting nature, 121–22
courage and heroism, 131–32
exploration and adventure, 130
fishing and hunting, 125–26
outdoor adventure, 123–25
physical strength and mental prowess, 128–29
questioning relevance of, 126–27
self-reliance and independence, 129–30
Matthiessen, Peter, 180
McVay, Scott, 67
Medical benefits from wild resources/nature, 19–21
Mental prowess and contesting nature, 128–29
Middle school years, 167
Molecular structure and underlying unity in nature, 134
Mollusk species, 173
Moral discourse and symbolizing nature, 81
Morton, Kathryn, 70
Muir, John, 81
Mushrooms, 18–19
Myers, Norman, 194
Mystery, sense of, 44–45
Mysticism and religion, 136–38
Myths, 73–74, 78

Nabhan, Gary, 90, 103
Nash, Roderick, 137
National Cancer Institute, 27
Nature/natural diversity, *see* Biophilia
Nelson, Richard, 58–59, 136, 161

Nietzsche, Friedrich, 131
Nonliving nature's healing impact, 116–17
Nonnative organisms and disease, 175
Norris, Kenneth, 22
Nursing homes and kinship/affection for natural world, 110–11

Observation, organized, 97–98
Ohman, Arne, 151
Organization and structure, perceptions of, 37–40
Orians, Gordon, 41, 204
Ortega y Gasset, José, 95–96
Outdoor adventure programs, 92–93, 123–25
Outermost House: A Year of Life on the Great Beach of Cape Cod (Beston), iv
Outward Bound, 123–25

Palila vs. *the Hawaii Department of Land and Natural Resources* (species protection), 177–78
Parasitology, 154
Parks, urban, 203–4
Passmore, John, 137
Peace of mind and immersion in nature, 93–94
Perennial philosophy, 134
Periwinkle, rosy, 28
Permian age, 134
Personal growth and connection to nature, 16
  commitment to interacting with nature, 209–18
  fearing/rejecting nature, 149–51
  firewood, cutting, 30–31
  fishing, 17–18
  indigenous peoples' knowledge about nature, 51–60
  kinship and affection for natural world, 110–11, 112, 114–15, 117–19
  mushrooms, 18–19
  see also Immersion in nature
Pests, agricultural, 29, 65
Pet-facilitated psychotherapy, 113
Pets, 106–7
  see also Kinship and affection for natural world
Pharmaceutical manufacturing, 20
Physical fitness/strength/vitality, experiencing nature and, 88–89, 128–29
Pigeons, passenger, 179–82
Pilgrims and aesthetic response to nature, 43–44
Pimentel, David, 15, 25, 29, 32
Plants:
  deforestation, 28
  emotional connection to nature, 110
  extinctions and endangered species, 174
  see also Wild resources/nature
Political campaigns and symbolizing nature, 72–73
Pollinating activities of wild species, 28, 65
Pollutants and ecological processes, 29
Predators:
  extinctions and endangered species, 173
  fearing/rejecting nature, 152
  mastering/contesting nature, 122–23
Preschool period, 166
Prescott-Allen, Christine, 32
Prescott-Allen, Robert, 32
Profanity and symbolizing nature, 73
Psychosocial development and symbolizing nature, 76–79
Public support for saving endangered species, 197
Purpose, motivating sense of, 135
Pyle, Robert, 102, 184, 203

Rain forests, tropical, 28
  indigenous peoples' knowledge about, 51–60
Recreational contact with natural world:
  captive wildlife, 98–100
  ethical debates, 141
  evolutionary history, 16
  film and TV, 100–101
  hunting, 95–96
  mastering/contesting nature, 125–26
  observation, organized, 97–98
  statistics on, 87
Religion and mysticism, 136–38

Relph, Edward, 187
Reserves, biosphere, 194–95
Residence and work, satisfying places for, 170–71
  environment, healthy and diverse, 183–88
  restoring biological diversity, 199–204
Resources, ethics and overexploiting, 144
  see also Wild resources/nature
Respect for nature, 66–68, 159–60
Restoring biological diversity, 192
  arresting biological decline, 193–99
  ethics and education, importance of, 204–9
  personal commitment to interacting with nature, 209–18
  residence and work, integrating nature into, 199–204
Rice, hybrid, 25
Rolston, Holmes, 36, 140, 142
Roosevelt, Theodore, 152
Roots, people sinking, 183–84
Rubber, 20
Rush, Colleen, 42

Safety/sustenance and security, 40–44, 156–58
Sagan, Dorion, 139
Sagoff, Mark, 184
Saito, Yuriko, 49
Savage, Jay, 174
Schaller, George, 39
School-aged children, 166–67
Schreyer, Richard, 92
Schweitzer, Albert, 137
Scientific/ecological outlook on nature:
  ecosystem concept, 61–62
  empirical and objective knowledge, 60–62, 64–66
  indigenous peoples' knowledge about nature, 51–60
  intellectual growth, 63–64
  restraint and respect for nature, 66–68
  unity in nature, underlying, 139
  Western assumptions about wild resources/nature, 13
Self-confidence and connection to nature, 16–17, 91–93, 113–15
Self-interest expressed in preserving biophilia, 9, 206–9
Self-reliance and contesting nature, 129–30
Serpell, James, 109, 113
Shellfish, 15
Shepard, Paul, 70, 76, 79
Silent Spring (Carson), xv
Singer, Peter, 153
Snakes, 157–58
Social bonding and affiliation, 111–12
Soil fertility, 29–30
Specicide, 153
Sperm whale oil, 20
Sperm whales, 21
Spiders, 153–56
Spiritual connection to nature, *see* Personal growth and connection to nature
Standing, Luther, 136
Steinbeck, John, 137–38
Storms, 148–49
Stress mitigation, 93–94
Sustainable wildlife, 24–25
Symbolizing nature, 69–70
  communication and thought, 80–81
  continuing reliance on, 82–83
  fairy tales and myths, 73–74
  language acquisition, 74–76
  Leaves of Grass, 71
  political campaigns, 72–73
  psychosocial development, 76–79
  snakes, 157–58
Symmetry and association, 36, 135
Synthesis and intellectual growth, 64

Talbot, Janet, 93
Technology, *see* Scientific/ecological outlook on nature
Television and immersion in nature, 100–101
Therapy, nature used in, 115–19
Theriophobia, 153
Thinking Like a Mountain (Leopold), xv
Thinking skills, critical, 63

Tidal wetlands, 30
Timber products, 14–15
Totemic creatures, 78
Trees:
deforestation, 28, 30
firewood, cutting, 30–31
rain forests, tropical, 28, 51–60
timber products, 14–15
Tribal societies, 141–42

Ulrich, Roger:
fearing/rejecting nature, 151, 156
health and attractive natural settings, 45
natural *vs.* built views, 34
stress mitigation, 93
Underdeveloped countries and wild resources/nature, 12
Unity in nature, underlying:
confidence and security, 143
conserving and protecting nature, 143–45
ethics, 140–42
group loyalty and cooperation, 142–43
religion and mysticism, 136–38
science, 139
symmetry and association, 135
Urban landscapes, 34, 152, 201–4
Utilizing wild resources, 14–19, 176, 198–99

Values, crisis of, 187
Variability/intricacy of human response to nature, 5, 46–49
Vitality and immersion in nature, 89

Warblers, spring migration of, xii–xvi
Wastes, decomposition of organic, 29, 65–66
Water and aesthetic response to nature, 42
Water quantity and quality, 30
Western assumptions about wild resources/nature, 12–13, 15
Wetlands, 30
Whales:
aesthetic response to nature, 47–48
exploitation of, 21–22
oil, sperm wale, 20
recreational contact with natural world, 98
Whitman, Walt, 71, 138
Wildlife excursions, 165–66
Wildlife trade, complexities of, 21–25
Wild resources/nature:
benefiting from ecological processes, 28–32
controlled production of, 11
domestic production improved using, 25–28
medical and industrial benefits, 19–21
modern society's dependence on, 13–14
utilizing, 14–19
Western assumptions about, 12–13
wildlife trade, complexities of, 21–25
Wilkins, Gregory, 115
Wilson, Alexander, 179
Wilson, Edward O.:
biophilia, coining the term, 1
environment, healthy and diverse, 172
extinctions and endangered species, 174
fearing/rejecting nature, 158
imagination and inquiry, 90
order and richness of structure, 191
unity in nature, underlying, 134, 139
Wolves:
aesthetic response to nature, 46–47
fearing/rejecting nature, 152
mastering/contesting nature, 132
Wonder, sense of, 44–45, 90
Work, *see* Residence and work, satisfying places for
World Conservation Monitoring Centre, 14, 19, 25–26
Worth and importance imputed to natural world, 3

Yellowstone National Park, 152
Yew, Pacific, 28
Young, Stanley, 47

Zoos, 98–100